The Gift and Task
of Lutheran Higher Education

The Gift and Task
of Lutheran Higher Education

TOM CHRISTENSON

AUGSBURG FORTRESS / MINNEAPOLIS

THE GIFT AND TASK OF LUTHERAN HIGHER EDUCATION

Published under the auspices of the Division for Higher Education and Schools, Evangelical Lutheran Church in America, in memory of Dr. Conrad Bergendoff and in honor of Dr. W. Robert Sorensen.

Text editing and design: Sylvia Ruud
Cover Design: Michelle Cook
Cover photos: Getty Images

The cataloging-in-publication data is on file with the Library of Congress.

ISBN 0-8066-5023-0

The paper used in this publication meets the minimum requirements of American National Standard for Information Sciences—Permanence of Paper in Printed Library Materials, ANSI Z329.48-1984.

Manufactured in the U.S.A.
08   07   06   05   04   1   2   3   4   5

CONTENTS

ACKNOWLEDGMENTS

I want to thank several institutions and people for their help and support to me in this project. First of all my thanks go to Capital University for the sabbatical necessary to work on this manuscript. In particular, I want to thank our provost, Cheryl Ney, and the chair of my department, David Belcastro, for their continuing encouragement to pursue this project. Second, my thanks to Arne Selbyg, the Director for Colleges and Universities of the ELCA Division for Higher Education and Schools, for pressing me to write about these things. Third, my thanks to to my co-inquirers in the first Lutheran Academy of Scholars, where many of these thoughts first sprouted. Fourth, to all the people who read and commented on drafts of chapters: Joy Schroeder, Kurt Keljo, Walt Bouman, Darrell Jodock, Bruce Reichenbach, Mark Schwehn, and William Kiblinger. Finally to the faculty and staff members of Thiel, Augsburg, Gustavus Adolphus, and St. Olaf Colleges, and Valparaiso, California Lutheran, and Capital Universities who invited me to discuss chapters in gatherings at each institution. To these people and institutions I am grateful. Because of these discussions many things got changed, a chapter was added, and the questions that make up the final chapter were generated.

I want to dedicate my efforts in writing this book to all those teachers I have known as a student and as a colleague who helped inform me about the gift and task of Lutheran higher education. They are too many for me to name, too many even for me to remember. But I do want to name a few: Martha Brennun, Oscar Anderson, Eric Fietz, Reidar Thomte, Olin Storvick, Carl Bailey, Cyrus Running, Barbara Glasrud, Albert Anderson, Clair Haugen, Les Meyer, Don Luck, Gregg Muilenburg, and Carl Skrade.

Introduction

Faith, academe, and fearfulness

Many academics are fearful of any sort of talk about faith-related higher education. Given the historical reality of religious inquisitions, persecutions, religious wars, and intolerances of all sorts it is not all that difficult to understand such fears.

The assumption of many of the fearful is that faith-related communities are not really interested in the truth, but in promoting and preserving a particular set of beliefs or practices dear to them. As a consequence, the assumption continues, faith-related higher education is closed, parochial, dogmatic, antirational, and bent on making converts of all students and faculty who wander into its web. If faith communities and the schools they sponsor are like this, then what self-respecting academic would want to work there?

It would be a big mistake to suppose that this never happens—but it is also a big mistake to suppose that it always happens, or even that it frequently happens. My experience has led me to believe that such fears expressed by faculty (and much less frequently by students) at Lutheran colleges and universities are based on several misunderstandings. It is part of my purpose in writing this book to make such fears, their assumptions, and the misunderstandings they contain explicit, and to make a case for an understanding of education shaped by the Lutheran tradition that is neither closed, parochial, nor antirational, but open, free, fearless, respectful of other views and faiths, and thoroughly devoted to the whole truth.

There are also some academics who, making many of the same assumptions as the fearful noted above, suppose that because Lutheran institutions of higher learning are not closed, dogmatic, indoctrinating, and parochial that they are not Lutheran in any important sense. The argument is sometimes heard that such institutions shouldn't be considered Lutheran at all. Perhaps they at one time were, but not any more. It is my purpose to argue that they, too, are mistaken.

My office is located in the same building as the religion faculty, the chapel, and the campus pastor's office. As a consequence I often overhear student tour guides addressing the question of the religious orientation of the university as prospective students and their parents walk through the building. I commonly hear comments like these: "This is a Lutheran university *but* they treat people of other faiths really well. Lots of the students who go here are Catholic and they're never hassled about it." "This is a Lutheran university and some courses in religion are required. *But* they're really open-minded. They're some of the most critical and liberating courses on the campus." "This is a Lutheran university and they have chapel services, *but* no one will pressure you to go. It's completely up to you." As I listen I have all I can do to keep myself from running out into the hall and shouting, "Take the 'but' out of that sentence and you'd be telling the truth."

It isn't that we do these things *in spite of* being a Lutheran university, though that's what the tour guides' speech implies. I believe we do these things *because* we are a Lutheran university. So we also, I would argue, avoid parochialism, avoid being indoctrinating, treat other views in a respectful and welcoming way, pursue truth thoroughly and fearlessly, precisely *because* we have the faith tradition we have. That possibility surprises and confounds many, I know, but that is not a reason to suppose it is not true.

I am not so naive as to suppose that pointing out things like this will make everyone's fears go away. Fears are not often removed by argument. But maybe I am misguided in my desire. Maybe these fears should not go away. Maybe we should not want to be rid of them nor of those who express them. Maybe they play an important role in the life of our institutions, insofar as we are called to think them through and address them, just as they play an important role in the dialectic of this book.

What does knowing have to do with faith?

Put slightly differently, what does the university or college have to do with church or religious community? Or, as it has sometimes been phrased, what has Athens to do with Jerusalem?

Frequently in the history of ideas knowing and faith have been set off against each other as a kind of absolute either/or. Sometimes knowing has been defined over against faith or belief as essentially opposed to it or understood as an alternative to it. That has occurred several times in the history of my own subject, philosophy. Socrates and Plato attempted it, trying to replace communally held beliefs, traditions, stories, and practices with lives and institutions firmly based in genuine knowledge. As some have put it, they tried to replace *mythos* with *logos*. Descartes attempted it as well, trying to replace his beliefs with a method of knowing that would ground his thinking in absolute certitude. Enlightenment thinkers tried to replace the fervor of (often very combative) faiths with a universal brotherhood of experience and reason.

Our own thinking and the institutions of university and college have certainly been shaped by all three of these attempts. It should not, therefore, be surprising that there are many of us in the academic circle who are skeptical of attempts to combine faith and knowing, and are puzzled or troubled at the suggestion of having a faith tradition sponsor and undertake efforts at knowing. So we ask, "Why can't these faith people go away and just let us knowledge people get on with our knowing?"

If Socrates and Plato had succeeded in replacing belief, community practice, and story with a grounding in knowledge, if they had been able to create or discover, as they attempted to do, a *logos* that could completely replace *mythos*, then the academy could (and should?) have become completely divorced from faith traditions. But this did not happen. Philosophical schools, in many cases, themselves became and still become indistinguishable from faith communities, with their own myths, rituals, high priests, and sacred scriptures. They have established themselves as rival schools, rival faiths, demanding as much loyalty from their followers as any religion ever did. In other cases philosophical schools wedded themselves to faith traditions that thrived and continue to thrive to the present day.

If Descartes had succeeded in reestablishing knowing on a foundation beyond all doubt, if he had been able to generate a way of knowing that was completely impersonal and value free, if reason and experience had been able to settle all questions and create a known world large enough to live in, then the university (the knowing community) would (and should?) have nothing much to do with communities of faith.

But Socrates and Plato, Descartes, and the Enlightenment thinkers did not succeed in this undertaking. This is not, of course, to say that they did not succeed at anything. They surely did. But at the beginning of the twenty-first century we realize from a careful reading of human intellectual history that knowing is always dependent on a practicing community, it always makes assumptions and commitments, it always operates with deep values, it answers questions existentially and historically that it cannot answer intellectually, and it relies on a *mythos* that it only sometimes bothers to make explicit. We have learned from the history of human ideas that knowing and faith (of some kind, in some thing) are inextricably connected even where we have been most confident that they were not. So the question that needs to be asked is not whether faith and knowing are related, but how? What kind of faith does an explicit dialogue with knowing create? What kind of knowing is created in dialogue with faith? How does this dialogue shape those who engage it and are engaged by it? These are the big questions this book attempts to answer.

The question put another way

Many people claim not to believe in God. They say, "I don't believe in the old judge in the sky," or something like that. To which I usually respond, "Neither do I."

Luther wrote, "Anything on which your heart relies and depends . . . that is really your God."[1] What answers for each of us the questions, "Who am I? What gives life meaning? What, if I lost it, would leave me and my life empty, directionless, without a horizon? What is the end that I arrange everything else in my life to serve? What do I most fear; what do I most fervently hope? On what do I depend when everything else begins to fall apart?" I would submit that these are the god-revealing questions for us.

We "sophisticated" Westerners are not so tempted to worship at the shrines of those old gods with foreign-sounding names: Zeus, Hera, Aphrodite, Apollo, Dionysos, or even Yahweh, Jesus, or Allah, for that matter. The gods we are more likely to worship have very familiar cultural names: Ego, Success, Prestige, Comfort, Wealth, Amusement, Power, Sex, Violence, Patriotism, Oblivion. This is the pantheon in whose processions most of us dance, whose temples we build, whose stories we ritually repeat in our life-informing myths. The worshipers of these divinities have constructed and maintain colleges and universities, and we know pretty much what they look like. There are lots of them.

So, what god or gods do Christians worship? In one sense it is the god without a name, a god who responds, when asked for a name, "I am there whoever I am there," who frustrates every effort to be named.[2] In another sense it is a god with three names: Creator, Redeemer, Spirit-that-lives-in-us. In another sense it is the god with only one name, Love—Love that embraces the world in a way that takes the shape of a cross, a love that, in turn, transforms everything and can be shared by each of us by embracing our world and those in it.

That's the story at the heart of the Lutheran telling of the Christian vision, which is itself a telling of an old Hebrew story of a loving God. That's the story about which we ask, "How does this story inform knowing, learning, teaching, and human becoming in the contemporary world? What kind of college or university should be built and maintained by those who tell such a story? What kind of work is there for us to do in such a place?" It is the asking and answering of these questions that I am attempting here.

An invitation to think outside of the box

Lutheran colleges and universities in North America represent an amazing diversity. They are diverse in age, in size, in educational focus, in endowment, in location, and in self-understanding. Some are very proud to have preserved the ethnic identity of their founders. Some assume that because they have preserved the ethnic identity of their founders they have preserved a Lutheran identity as well. Some assume that since they have preserved a high degree of religiousness and piety they have preserved their Lutheran identity. Some assume they are Lutheran because there are so many Lutherans there. I want to challenge all of these assumptions. But in particular I want to challenge those who assume that they no longer have a Lutheran identity worth talking about. Many assume that (intentionally or unintentionally) they have left their Lutheran-ness behind. They suppose that "Lutheran" is part of their history, but not really part of their present nor their future. This book is for people at all of these kinds of institutions and for those somewhere in the middle of the mix as well, those rather confused about the whole business. This book is intended to help all of us at all of these institutions rethink what this Lutheran connection is all about, where it is located, and how it is manifest in the life of our institutions.

For those in the latter group of institutions, those who think that maybe they are not Lutheran anymore, let me relate the following story: Prof. Martha Alcock, a colleague of mine at Capital University in the department of education, was talking to a class of students who were, the next day, about to begin their student-teaching internships. All of them were excited, and more than a few were quite nervous about what was going to happen as they put their learning to its practical test. In order to encourage them, Prof. Alcock asked them to think about going into the classroom with someone precious and important to them standing with them, supporting them at their shoulder. "Who would that be for you?" she asked each student in the group. Many mentioned a parent or grandparent, some a previous teacher, someone who had been a support and encouragement to them in their process of becoming a teacher. But one young man, brilliant and outspoken throughout his course work leading to this experience, said, "Nobody! I don't want anybody with me. I'm completely independent; I want to do it completely on my own." He then paused and stood silently for a moment, reflecting. Then he added, "And I get this radical independence from my mom."

What's the point of the story? The point is that very often this spirit of independence in the life of a person or an institution has a source deep in its traditional roots. There is perhaps something deeply and authentically Lutheran in the suspiciousness and rebelliousness of institutions thinking themselves not so Lutheran anymore. What I want to do is to get the faculty, students, and administrators of such institutions to reflect that, perhaps, what they have rejected is not so essentially Lutheran as what, by rejecting, they may have endorsed and preserved. I hope, in other words, to get faculty to look for the Lutheran connection in some places other than those in which we typically have supposed it to reside.

So much of our thinking is shaped by the categories we have brought along and the assumptions that these categories bring with them. We very often miss seeing something for what it is because we are so inclined to place it in one of the categorical boxes we have available. The most significant learning, therefore, occurs when we can reexamine how we have boxed things, when we can deconstruct the rigid categories that shape our thought. On the last day of one course I taught a student came up and thanked me for what she had learned. She said, "I know I haven't been the best student in your class, but what I learned here has been very important for me. I used to think of myself as a very bad Catholic. But, thanks to you, I now think I might actually be a pretty good Lutheran. But don't tell my mom I said that."

I'm hoping that, in the process of this book, many people might come to recognize themselves as "pretty good" Lutheran educators who never would have thought of themselves in that way before. I am also hoping that at least some who read this book will be excited by the vision of higher education that is sketched here, whether or not they are excited about its being Lutheran. It is a vision, I believe, that flows out of a cluster of important Lutheran theological ideas and that has the power to serve our society and our age in a transforming way. But, failing my well-fabled ability to win converts, I hope that what I have written here provokes a significant discussion and aids others in the articulation of some clarified thinking about the vocation of being Lutheran colleges and universities.

The focal argument

We live in a world still shaped, largely, by Enlightenment conceptions of knowledge and knowing. These conceptions offer us a narrowed vision of knowledge and consequently a narrowed understanding of truth, the world we live in, and education as well. As a consequence our institutions of higher learning, with few exceptions, know and teach a world too small and too one-dimensional for us to live in.

This book is a Christian critique of that Enlightenment ideal, its epistemology and ontology. It is also an imaginative reconstruction of what education of whole persons for full humanity in an enlarged reality might look like. That is, I believe, what education shaped by the Lutheran tradition has the gift and task to be.

The intended audience

Every writer learns to ask the question, "Who is my intended audience?" When I posed to myself this question I was surprised at the length of the answer. This book is written for:

— the fearful, those I mentioned at the outset of this introduction

— faculty and administration at Lutheran colleges and universities who have long been employed in Lutheran higher education without ever being able to give an explicit account of what was Lutheran about it

— Lutheran pastors who haven't known how to respond to young people who ask, "What's so special about a Lutheran college and why should I go there?"

— students at such colleges who are left having to explain the same thing to others and to themselves

— people in the culture who make rather narrow assumptions about what faith-related education is, and what Lutheran higher education might be

— new and prospective faculty and students trying to understand what kind of thing a Lutheran college or university is

— presidents and boards of trustees of Lutheran colleges and universities who have difficulty translating their concern for faith-related higher education into programs and policies

— people engaged in faith-related higher education from other traditions, who, I have found, are often curious and eager to learn what it is that Lutherans are doing

My hope is that all of these people will find this book provocative and enabling. It is designed to provoke discussion, not end it, and enable discussion, not befuddle it.

This book approaches this task in eight chapters: The first, "How Is a College or University Lutheran?" discusses how "Lutheran" ought to be related to "college" or "university," and how we frequently misdirect the question about what makes a college or university Lutheran. The second chapter, "Luther, Lutheran Theology, and Eight Focal Theological Themes," provides background, historical and theological, for the discussions that follow. Chapter three, "Whole Humans—Toward a Lutheran

Anthropology," works through a contemporary but tradition-informed answer to the questions, "What does it mean to be human? Who are we trying to educate? Toward what? And by whom is this to be done?" Chapter four critically considers a variety of voices addressing the question, "What is responsible knowing?" Chapter five argues toward a Lutheran way of understanding knowing, i.e., it tries to uncover a Lutheran epistemology. Those two chapters then become the foundation for the discussion of chapter six, "Implications—Curriculum and Pedagogy," which works toward a Lutheran "theology of education." Chapter seven addresses the question, "What kind of community is necessary to pursue knowing and teaching in these ways?" The final chapter attempts to answer directly some of the hard questions that are raised by the preceding discussions. Chapters one, three, four, five, and seven are the heart of the argument of the book. Chapter two is intended mainly for people not already conversant with the Lutheran tradition who wish some explanatory background for the concepts employed in the rest of the text. The final chapter responds to many of the questions posed by people who read drafts of the text or who heard parts of it presented when I took it "on tour" before writing the final draft.

I realize that a book of such design will be somewhat repetitive. Several ideas will arise over again at various points. The idea of vocation, for example, is introduced in the first chapter, explained in the second, and employed several times to explain other ideas in later chapters. Reencountering the same idea can be tiresome, but sometimes it can also be illuminating. We can often catch the meaning of an idea better when we see it used than if we merely hear it explained.

I.

How Is a College or University Lutheran?

More than half the work is done when we
have put the question right.

—Sig Royspern

On Nouns and Adjectives

First, a brief word about the noun, i.e., the notion of college or university. Universities can be a collection of quite a variety of functions; one only has to look at the phone book of a major university to see what a complex thing it is. But not all of those capacities and functions are equally important and not all are essential. At the heart of the idea of university are some things that have been there from the very beginning: (1) A university is a place to pursue and preserve knowledge, understanding, perhaps even wisdom; it is a place of knowing and learning. This is why universities have, from the beginning, had libraries, museums, galleries, laboratories, etc. (2) A university is a *collegium*, i.e., a critical community of learners and sharers of learning. That is why they are and have been places of argument, debate, deep discussion, disputation, public lecture, and publication. (3) Very soon after the first universities were founded in Europe to pursue those first two purposes, they also came to serve a third. They came to be places for the preparation and maturation of young adults, i.e., they became places of human becoming, places to grow, develop, and mature. People came to find that these *collegia* were good places for people to train for professions, learn about the wider world and one's place in it, and develop as thoughtful and useful persons in community. So, when in the process of this book we pursue the question, "What is a Lutheran college or university?" we are asking about these *three essential functions*. What resources could Lutherans bring to establishing or maintaining a university? In what ways might the tasks of knowing and understanding, learning and teaching, and facilitating human growth be informed by the Lutheran out-look and the community it gives shape to?

Not all adjectives do their work in the same way. We can avoid some confusion, perhaps, by examining how the word "Lutheran" works when it is applied to the nouns "college" and "university." Some adjectives name characteristics that are very externally related to the noun described. If I say about my philosophy colleague that she is "a well-tanned philoso-pher," I may have told you something significant about her, but I've told you nothing about her *as a philosopher*. Sometimes adjectives that desig-nate religions or religious groups work in this non-essentially related way. If, on the other hand, I tell you my colleague is "a feminist philosopher" I have related a good deal about her as a philosopher. The adjective tells us how she does what the noun identifies her as doing, philosophy. It tells significant things about how her work is focused, what her priorities are, whom she is likely to study, what kinds of things are of concern to her, etc. This is the model I want to suggest that we follow in speaking of "a Lu-theran college" or "a Lutheran university." The word "Lutheran" here should not just tell us something incidentally true of the university, e.g., that long ago it was founded by Lutherans, but it should tell us something about *the way in which the place is a university and the way it does those things essential to its being a university*. Sometimes people pose the ques-tion, "How can a college or university become Lutheran?" This posing of the question in this form reveals the assumption that the college/univer-sity is there already and then we add something to it to make it Lutheran. I propose that "Lutheran-ness" cannot be added in that way without com-pletely misunderstanding it. It is not something added to essential func-tions already present, but it is the way those functions are themselves understood and pursued. The Lutheran character of an institution is not added like frosting to a generic cake. It is more like the sour in sauerkraut. It is not an ingredient you can add at the last minute and expect it to work.

"Lutheran" is not a univocal adjective. It has a range of meanings that vary, partly depending on the noun they modify. We should not expect that "Lutheran" will mean the same thing when applied to a church, a seminary, a retirement community, or a university. Yet sometimes we fall into the pattern of expecting that. Consider this variety of meanings: (1) "Lutheran" might be supposed to mean "related to the Lutheran church." In that case it would designate an external relation between institutions. Some people writing a history of Lutheran higher education have begun with that assumption. (2) "Lutheran" also might be taken to mean "by and for Lutherans." In that case the term becomes less applicable the smaller the number of Lutherans served and/or serving in it. (3) "Lutheran" might be taken to designate the presence of a worshiping Lutheran community. It is the faith community that is Lutheran; anything else is only through association or loose conjunction with it. If a college or university were the thing designated as Lutheran in each of the above cases, the adjective would basically be naming a relationship—to the church, to the Lutherans present, to the worshiping community. But in none of the above cases would "Lutheran" tell us anything essential about the knowing, learning, or human becoming pursued there. A corollary of the above meanings is that the task of realizing or maintaining "Lutheran-ness" then falls to a particular person or office within the university—in the first case the office of church relations, in the second case the offices of those who recruit students and faculty, in the third case the office of the campus pastor.

My claim is that none of these are the essential meaning of "Lutheran" in "Lutheran college/university." My argument is that a Lutheran college/university is one that pursues the essential tasks of a university in a way informed by Lutheran theology, particularly as it shapes an understanding of what it means to be human (a Lutheran anthropology), the enterprise of knowing and learning (a Lutheran epistemology), and our understanding of community. If this latter meaning is followed, then *the task of maintaining the Lutheran identity of a college/university is the work of all those engaged in knowing and enabling mutual human becoming*, virtually everyone—students, staff, and all faculty—who find themselves at such a place.

Some people at Lutheran colleges and universities have not understood this very well. As a consequence they have thought of "Lutheran" as not saying anything essential about them as colleges or universities but as giving some kinds of superfluous information, such as "once there were a lot of Lutheran faculty and students here," or "sometimes Lutherans worship in one of our buildings," or "we have a Lutheran bishop who serves on our board of trustees." It is because they have seen "Lutheran" as such an incidental adjective that they have sometimes replaced it with "church-related," or some other innocent and quite empty phrase.[1]

In the process of this book I want to argue that *"Lutheran" ought to say something particular and significant about how we are colleges and universities*. It ought to say something about how we engage in inquiry; how we conceive learning; how we pursue teaching; how we understand the community we create to facilitate these things; how we understand ourselves, our students, and the world about which, in which, and into which we educate. "Lutheran" is, by my way of thinking, an important and exciting word. If I did not think so I would not have wasted my time writing this book, nor should you waste your time reading it.

Posing the Question

In thirty some years of teaching at Lutheran colleges and universities, I cannot count the number of times I have heard someone ask, "What is it that makes a college/university Lutheran?" The widespread view is that this question is asked so frequently because it is so hard to answer or because Lutherans do not really know what they are doing. I don't believe that either of these responses is correct. I believe the question is asked so frequently because the question itself is misunderstood or out of focus and the query is misaimed and consequently ends up being fruitless, or worse, downright misleading. In Zen Buddhist practice the Zen master sometimes responds to a student's question by bellowing, "Mooo!" This response indicates that the master has no intention of answering the student's question because there is something wrong with the question. Learning will take place not by answering it but by leading the student to understand what it is about the question (or the questioner) that aims in the wrong direction.

So I think it's important to spend a little time talking about the question, talking about how it gets misaimed, talking about what prejudices we bring to thinking about it before I proceed to try and answer it. As my friend Sig Royspern has said, "More than half the work is done when we have put the question right."

Misaiming the Question

The question about the Lutheran character of a college or university may be misaimed insofar as it really poses a different question with a different agenda. We often cannot tell that the Lutheran identity question is a surrogate until we see the kinds of things people start to point to as relevant to answering it. I want to suggest four different questions, counterfeit questions, that hide therein; all of them are very likely to lead us in the wrong direction.

"How religious are we?" or "Can we still be really Lutheran if the college is not as religious as it used to be?" These questions assume that the index of Lutheran-ness is the quantity and quality of identifiably religious activity that takes place on campus. How often do we have chapel? Is it mandatory? What percentage of students, faculty, and staff participate? Do we begin our meetings with prayer and hymns? Do we begin and end and mark our year and its turnings with worship? If so, how many attend? Do we have a choir that sings Lutheran music? Is there a cross on campus and how big is it? These questions are fairly easy to answer, and that is one reason why they are a tempting surrogate for the Lutheran identity ques-

tion. Now I do not want to demean these questions nor the features to which they point. They may be important questions to ask.[2] That will depend on the context. Some of them may be essential questions to ask about a church, which is fundamentally a worshiping community. They may be vital questions to ask about a seminary, where we understand that the adjective "Lutheran" says something different than it does when applied to "university."

Part of our confusion comes from the fact that "Lutheran" is not univocal. Its meaning may change as the noun it is modifying changes. A Lutheran seminary, for instance, trains people for the Lutheran ministry. It is an enterprise primarily by Lutherans for Lutherans. As such it is proper that its teachings be based in the Lutheran confessions, and that its focus be on teaching Lutheran theology to its students. A Lutheran university, by contrast, educates people for full responsible humanness and service to the world. Its focus is not inimical to the seminary, but it is very different. Its Lutheran-ness lies in how it understands and does its task. "Lutheran" applied to "seminary" implies many things that it does not imply when applied to "university." The same model does not work for both.

I do not think that evidences of religiousness address the heart of what it means for a college or university to be Lutheran. They may be very important, but I do not believe they are essential. Most of the Lutheran colleges and universities in the United States are less religious than they used to be. That, by itself, is not a sign that they are less Lutheran. In some cases it may even be a sign that they are more so.

"How many Lutherans are there?" This is a question that is sometimes posed about students, sometimes about faculty, sometimes about key administrators. What it assumes is that higher education is Lutheran in proportion to how much it is *for* Lutherans or *by* Lutherans. But it has been my experience that some of the most essential people in maintaining the Lutheran character of an academic community may not be the Lutherans who are there. Counting Lutherans also relies on the assumption that people who call themselves Lutheran are, in every important sense, alike. My experience is that this is not the case at all. There may be a wider variance between nominal Lutherans than between a Lutheran and a Buddhist, or a Lutheran and an Evangelical, or a Lutheran and a Catholic.

Many are the times I have heard an argument for a "critical mass" of Lutherans on any given campus. In one way that is a proposition that is true by definition. That is, "How many Lutherans are necessary?" can always be answered, "Enough to make it work." But frequently the critical-mass metaphor is introduced as an argument for a particular percentage of faculty or students that the institution is trying to reach. That seems to me to be a misapplication of the idea. I would ask instead, "How many engaged, articulate people in what key positions are required to keep the Lutheran dialogue alive?" Critical mass is reached with nuclear material when fission begins to occur, i.e., when energy is generated. Similarly, in an institution we may ask: "Is energy being generated?" "Has the pile started to cook?" "Is the Lutheran spirit alive here shaping the life of the institution?" This contribution to liveliness is not identical with being Lutheran in the denominational membership sense. One can easily imagine twenty Lutherans on a faculty who contribute little or nothing to the Lutheran life of the institution. One can imagine twenty who, because they fight so fiercely with each other, give neither inspiration nor leadership to the rest of the community. I do not have to imagine non-Lutherans who do make great contributions because I know a whole host of them personally. Non-Lutherans can (and often do) carry the Lutheran yeast into the dough. In many institutions they are key persons because of the things they assert, the questions they ask, the concerns they bring. Baird Tipson, president of Wittenberg University, has suggested, "Rather than counting the number of Lutherans on our faculties, we might well try to increase the number of those whose reflections have led them to pursue their vocation more self-consciously out of their commitments."[3] Out of the presence of such faculty vital energy may be generated.

I would suggest that the question of Lutheran character is a question of quality rather than one of quantities.[4] Certainly the latter may affect the former, but they are not to be confused. *What is essential is the quality of the dialogue that takes place and the way the dialogue informs the institution.* I have seen excellent dialogues have no effect at an institution because of lack of leadership, so excellence of the dialogue is a necessary but not a sufficient condition for institutional vitality. In either case, a quota of Lutherans is neither sufficient nor necessary.

"Are we ethnically Lutheran?" Very often what people think about when they think about the Lutheran identity of a place is the maintenance of its ethnic identity. It is fairly easy for institutions to maintain an ethnic identity if they are located in an area where the descendants of its original founders still live. As long as there are lots of Scandinavians living in Minnesota it is fairly easy for St. Olaf and Concordia and Gustavus Adolphus to maintain ethnic connection, ethnic traditions and identity. But what happens when the founding community of Swedes that founded Upsala College in New Jersey has moved west? What happens if the resident community is now African American, Italian, and Hispanic? Can the college no longer be considered Lutheran? If ethnic and Lutheran identity are the same or if they are essentially linked, then the Lutheran-ness of the place

went west with the Swedes. But I do not think they are essentially connected. I think it is very possible, and I have it on good authority, that Upsala College was a Lutheran college up to the very day it closed its doors. This claim causes us to question our assumptions. This is an important realization for many Lutheran institutions, not just eastern ones. We don't know what migration patterns people will follow in the next century. The communities around Texas Lutheran and California Lutheran may become more and more Hispanic. The communities around Augsburg College and Capital University may become more Hispanic, African American, and Indigenous American. Pacific Lutheran might find itself in a neighborhood of Asian Americans. We, as reminiscent alums, may then lament, "Well, the place just isn't what it used to be." But that does not imply that it has become one bit less Lutheran. The new situation may, in fact, be the opportunity for the institution to become clear as it never was before about its mission and identity and the ways these empower the learning and teaching done there.

"How are we unique?" Frequently the question about Lutheran identity is posed as a question about what makes us different from others. Confusing these questions is a serious mistake. The problem is not with being different. Being authentically Lutheran will surely make us different from some, but it may also make us similar to others. The problem is not with difference but with making difference the defining characteristic. That is what happens when marketing becomes management. We should do what is right for us. If it is something others want to pursue as well, all the better—if, that is, it also fits what they are about. If we begin with the question, "How can we be different?" we will end up in the wrong place just as much as if we started out with the question, "How can we be like everyone else?" As an insightful person in a discussion some time ago so beautifully put it, "We should be concerned to be *authentically Lutheran*, not *distinctively Lutheran*." I believe that if the "authentic" part is taken care of, the "distinctive" part will look after itself. It is not a question of either/or, but a question of priority. I once heard Willem de Kooning say to an audience of aspiring young painters, "Be true to your self, your vision and your paint—and eventually out of that dialogue your own style will emerge. The artist who sets out in search of a distinctive style ends up being a phony."

I am not suggesting that concern about uniqueness or market niche is bad. It is good to raise such questions and for some persons to be concerned with doing that. I was, myself, hired to be concerned with such things at one point in my career. But we should not mistake those questions, the marketer's questions, with the question about institutional identity and institutional calling.

Lutherans talk a good deal about vocation, about being called to use our particular gifts in service to the needs of those around us. A young person may discover that her gifts suit her particularly well to be a high school math teacher, or nurse, or administrator of a company. If there is also a need for such work, one of these may be her vocation. Should she, at that point, lament that her vocation is not unique? I do not believe so. What may be unique is the way she does the job for those particular others she is called to serve. A person who teaches math or serves in health care professions or administration *in order to be unique* is focused on the wrong thing, namely, on something beyond the vocation. We should no more be preoccupied with being unique than we should with being the same as someone else.

Prejudices We Bring to Answering the Question

Perhaps we have all have heard the story of the man down on his hands and knees searching for his car keys. A policeman sees him and joins him in the search. After a while the policeman asks in frustration, "Where exactly did you drop them?" The man replies, "Oh, way over there on the other side of the parking lot." The policeman irately asks, "Then why are we searching on this side?" The man responds, "Because the light is better over here!"

The Fallacy of Exclusive Disjunction

In the above misdirections of our question we have already seen many assumptions at work. But these are not the only ones that shape our thinking and our discussions. We are frequently tempted to think of things in terms of polar opposites. Something is either X or the opposite of X, we suppose. This pattern of thinking is so common that it has even been designated a fallacy, the black and white fallacy or, as it is sometimes called, the fallacy of exclusive disjunction. When the topic of higher education and religion comes up many people assume there are only two possibilities: either an institution is a secular college or university or it is a rigidly moralist/fundamentalist school. Since we do not want to be the latter, their reasoning runs, we obviously want to be the former.

Some Lutheran colleges, believing these were their only choices, have moved toward embracing the secular alternative. This is quite consistent with elements in their Lutheran identity, for Lutherans can embrace the secular in ways that many religious traditions cannot. So, if these were the only alternatives, the secular one might be the better choice for Lutherans. But *these are not the only alternatives.*

This assumption about the nature of faith-relatedness, that there really are only two choices, also reinforces "slippery slope" thinking—"If you give those religious folks an inch they will soon have us swearing loyalty oaths and teaching Genesis 1 and 2 as science." It is hard to convince such people that many who are interested in promoting religiously related higher education do not want to follow that model at all and, in fact, are vigorously opposed to it. The assumption is, "If you are promoting faith-related education you must want us to become like Oral Roberts University."

Sometimes people can expand to thinking in terms of three possibilities. In such cases the third possibility is usually Catholic higher education. I have heard faculty explicitly say, "These are the three models available. You've agreed that you don't want us to become a fundamentalist college and you don't want us to follow the model of a Catholic school and make everyone major in St. Thomas Aquinas. So you must agree with me that we should drop all talk of being religiously related and become a secular university." But why are those the only options? Why should thinking amount to sorting things into only two or three boxes? Because those are the only ones we know about? If so, we need to wake up and look around, because faith-related education takes a great many forms, not just one or two. What I want to argue here is that Lutheran higher education *very deliberately* does not want to follow the moralist/fundamentalist model and it does not want to follow the old Catholic Thomist model either. What we want to do (and have done in many cases) is to create a model appropriate to a Lutheran understanding of the world and what it means to be a human in it. So, what I am inviting readers to do is to enter this inquiry with an open mind and more numerous, more elastic, and less caricatured categories. But, to quote my friend Sig Royspern again, "By far the hardest part of learning is unlearning."

The Lure of the Secular Model

There are at least two hurdles that need to be cleared away before one can think seriously and open-mindedly about what education shaped by the Lutheran tradition might look like. The first hurdle is the one we have just talked about, the way the fundamentalist/moralist paradigm pervades our thinking. The second hurdle is the assumption that higher education, at its best, is embodied by the purely secular university. This outlook is rooted deep in our culture and depends on a whole host of assumptions about the secular ideal that became part of our thinking as a legacy of the Enlightenment. I want to make them explicit here so they may be questioned and so that we can see more clearly, later on, how the Lutheran vision differs.

Assumption 1: The paradigm of knowledge is objective, commitment free, pure (i.e., non-applied), value free, and politically, socially, and morally disengaged.

I have colleagues who assert that their disciplines are value free, i.e., that they make no value commitments. If one were to convince them that this is not true—that, in fact, they both assume and serve a very clear value agenda—they would be crushed. Somewhere along the line, probably in graduate school, they learned that value commitments were a bad thing, a thing to be avoided, and that their discipline properly pursued should avoid them. If one begins with that assumption it is very hard to make sense of faith-related learning and teaching. It will seem like a failure. If, on the other hand, one believes that it is impossible to pursue any inquiry without assuming or serving some set of values, without making some kinds of commitments, then faith-related learning and teaching is very understandable. The question for debate in this latter case is which values, which assumptions, which basic commitments one is going to make. In many cases the attempt to be value free has left the disciplines absolutely defenseless against being used by those most powerful in the culture. Science has served the military and economic agenda, very often without so much as questioning it and often by pledging quiet allegiance to it. When scientists have raised ethical questions about what they are doing they, like Robert Oppenheimer for example, become suspect and lose their ticket to the big game. Oppenheimer had the audacity to bring moral scruples into the making of scientific decisions. How much better off he would have been if he had only behaved as a onetime physicist colleague of mine did. When an ethical question came up in discussion he said, "I can't address such questions because they are not my specialty." My response to him on that occasion is one I still believe in: "We do not make ethical inquiries because they are our specialty, we make them because we are human. We avoid such issues only by sacrificing a good bit of our humanity." Is it possible that as we have grown as specialist scholars, we have shrunk as human beings?

Rachel Naomi Remen, M.D., who teaches in the school of medicine at the University of California San Francisco, addresses this same issue in writing about the training of doctors:

> It took me many years to realize that medical education is not an education at all: it is a training. An education evokes wholeness and attends to integrity, while a training specializes, focuses, and narrows us. And in specializing, we disavow parts of our wholeness. We sacrifice our wholeness for expertise. . . . During a visit to a historic graveyard I saw a tombstone which said: "Here lies George Brown, born a man, died a

gastroenterologist." Now, I come from a medical family. In two generations of my family there are nine physicians and so I was inspired by this
epitaph. It never occurred to me that this was not a step up.[5]

Certainly not all medical doctors nor all scientists, nor all inquirers in
any field, have followed this paradigm of valueless and commitmentless
inquiry. But the exceptions have very often been lonely voices in their
fields. Rachel Carson, Aldo Leopold, Barbara McLintock, Robert Oppenheimer are some of the names that spring to my mind. But too many have
been happy to comply with Tom Lehrer's parody: "We just shoot the rock-
ets up, / We don't care where they come down. / That's not my department, / Said Werner von Braun."

Assumption 2: Knowledge, at its best, is represented by the disciplines—specialized, analytic, and, wherever possible, quantitative.

Education is usually structured to move from generality to specialization. The further we proceed in the university, the narrower our focus becomes. Becoming a specialist is, the assumption goes, the highest
accomplishment. Yet not everyone agrees with that assumption. Alasdair
MacIntyre, for example, has written:

> Undergraduate students move from general introductory courses . . . to-
> ward specializations of the major, while graduate students move from al-
> ready specialized courses in a number of sub-disciplines toward the
> narrowly focused research of their dissertations, perhaps an adequate
> preparation for a career to be spent exclusively in the same kind of re-
> search, but a remarkably inadequate education for anything else, includ-
> ing the life of a university teacher.[6]

Universities have changed a good deal over the centuries, but probably
most drastically over the last century. A century ago it was still the expectation that faculty would be learned in both the wide and deep sense. In the
contemporary university few are concerned to be. The only requirement
now is that one be some kind of specialist and have some facility in writing
grants. Faculty used to read widely and deeply. That is no longer the rule. I
know several faculty who read nothing but research journals in their specialty. They have never read the world's literature, nor its history, nor philosophy, and do not intend to. It used to be expected that faculty could
discourse with each other and help to realize the universe of learning their
community represented. Now faculty seldom speak beyond the boundaries of their subdiscipline and refuse to address any question, no matter
how deeply human, that falls outside that fence.

Alfred North Whitehead, writing in his classic *The Aims of Education*,
argued that education needs to have three stages. The first is the age of romance, the stage where we pursue studies that we find alluring. At this

stage we are drawn to study by the fascination of test tubes and lab coats, the romance of playing the cello, the apparent depth of philosophy or theology, the aura of erudition that goes with learning Greek and reading Shakespeare. But we do not get very far in the study of any of these things before we encounter the next stage of learning. This Whitehead calls the stage of precision or discipline, the stage of doing the hard and exacting work required to excel in any of those areas. This is the stage when many a dream is dashed on the hard reality of doing what is required. One does not become a scientist nor a musician nor a philologist by dreaming about it. Unfortunately, Whitehead maintained, most modern education stops at this stage. It is the stage at which we earn our doctorates and publish our first professional papers. But Whitehead thought that a third stage was just as necessary as the first two. This he referred to as the stage of generalization or synthesis, a stage where we put back together again what we sliced into pieces in stage two. The aim of this third stage is wholeness; it returns us to the human community of discourse, informed by our specialization and our particular discipline, but not confined by it.

Wendell Berry, in his essay "The Loss of the University," warns:

> Without a common tongue, a university not only loses its concern for the thing made, it loses its own unity. . . . when the departments of the university become so specialized that they can speak neither to each other nor to the students and graduates of other departments, then that university is displaced. . . . it cannot know either its responsibilities to its place or the effects of its irresponsibilities. This too often is the practical meaning of "academic freedom." The teacher feels free to teach, and learn, make and think, without concern for the thing made.[7]

Berry goes on to say that for a university "the thing made is humanity." In institutions that follow the secular paradigm the thing being made is, I fear, not humans but specialists.

Assumption 3: The best knower, and by implication the best student, is the specialized genius—the pure thinker or researcher, exemplified in the professor or ace graduate student: relatively disembodied, spiritless, disconnected, committed only to the discipline and to publishing significant papers in it.

Many of us have, somewhere in our educational experience, suffered from the alienation that the structure of learning in the disciplines has worked on us. I remember very vividly meeting again, after three or four years, one of my best undergraduate students. We had all been very excited when she had been admitted to a prestigious graduate school. After all, her success was a validation of us as her teachers, was it not? As we chatted I could sense that perhaps not everything was going well for her. So I inquired and this is what she told me. "Oh, it was such an exciting place to be studying with all those great scholars and teachers. As long as I was taking courses I just couldn't get enough of it. But then I was required to choose a field and topic for my dissertation. Professor X asked me what my field was going to be. I said, 'The history of religions.' She then asked, 'Yes, but which religion?' I answered, 'Islam.' She replied, 'Yes, but what period of Islam?' So I said, 'Medieval Islam.' She said, 'Yes, but where, when, who, in Medieval Islam?' So, I've been working for the last fourteen months on the early writings of this obscure writer. The further I go with it, the less interest it has for me. Now I do it only to get done with the damn thing. I think to myself, 'This isn't what drew me to the study of religion, this isn't what made me want to go to graduate school to begin with. These aren't the deeply human questions that excited me earlier on. Do I have to sacrifice this connection in order to be a successful professional scholar? If so, I'm not sure I want it.'"

I sympathized with her predicament and said, "This is the same reason that many of us have deliberately chosen to teach undergraduate students at a smaller institution rather than pursue a narrow specialty on a large faculty of a big university. It's those questions, those deeply human questions, as you put it, that can still be asked and pursued here. But, having made that choice, we are frequently haunted by feelings of failure and inadequacy. Deep in our psyches is this professional voice that tells us, 'You're not a real scholar, you're not a real success as an inquirer because if you were you'd be a specialist at a big research university. That's where it's really at.' We all hear that voice."

Assumption 4: Academe can be broken into three distinct tasks: (a) research, i.e., real knowledge making; (b) the communication of knowledge; and (c) facilitating the growth, the development of students. Those who do the first of these three are the stars of the secular academy—the research professors. Those who do the second are the underlings of the academy, the graduate assistants and the not-so-stellar faculty. Task (c), if it is done at all at a secular university, is thought to be below faculty attention. It is relegated to the student services personnel or to the counselor's office or some such "non-academic" workers.

One of the most significant differences between the secular and the Lutheran paradigm is that the latter questions this distinction, this separation, and the evaluation it implies. *The Lutheran approach is that knowing is essentially linked to the sharing of knowledge which is essentially linked to human becoming.* Where they are separated a counterfeit and a caricature of each occurs, represented very well by the contemporary research university. The essential linking of knowing, teaching, and human becoming I call the *paideia* paradigm. This will be discussed more fully in the chapters that follow.

Previously I quoted Wendell Berry's assertion that in a university the thing made is humanity, or at least that it ought to be. But he goes on to point out how rarely this occurs. He writes, "But the thing made by education now is not a fully developed human being; it is a specialist, a careerist, a graduate."[8] Borrowing a metaphor from Samuel Johnson, Berry argues that a university ought to be like a living tree with a stout trunk and many branches. He writes:

> From the trunk it is possible to "branch out." One can begin with a trunk and develop a single branch or any number of branches. . . . [But] the modern university, at any rate, more and more resembles a loose connection of lopped branches waving about randomly in the air.[9]

We will challenge the secular paradigm further in later chapters of this book where we sketch out what the Lutheran approach is to knowing, human becoming, the disciplines, and scholarship. For the present let us be aware of the assumptions operating in this modern secular paradigm, be careful of the power these assumptions have over us, notice how much of our thinking is influenced by them, and recognize that there are many reasons to be highly suspicious of them.

A Known World Too Small to Live In

The paradigm of knowledge embodied by the secular universities of the world has, for the most part, left us with a very reduced and confined world. A world, in fact, too small for humans to live in. That's why most academics cannot relate their own disciplines to other domains of knowledge, to solving problems in the practical world, or to real lives, their students' or their own. Academies have become good at cloning specialists, but not good at educating whole human beings. Most, in fact, would not even pretend to know how to do so.

Page Smith, in his provocative book, *Killing the Spirit: Higher Education in America*, quotes Walter Moberly:

> If you want a bomb, the chemistry department will teach you how to make it, if you want a cathedral the department of architecture will teach you how to build it, if you want a healthy body the departments of physiology and medicine will teach you how to tend it. But when you ask whether and why you should want bombs or cathedrals or healthy bodies, the university . . . must be content to be dumb and impotent. It can give help in all things subsidiary, but not in the attainment of the one thing needful. In living their lives the young are left the sport of every random gust! But for an educator this is abdication . . . .[10]

Most of our Lutheran colleges and universities, on the other hand, embrace a vision of education that is explicitly aimed at serving the world and educating whole humans toward their own full humanness. This implies that they also challenge the epistemological paradigm that informs most secular institutions. But few have done that explicitly. It is a large part of the argument of this book to initiate that challenge.

Hard, Shaping Questions

Wendell Berry concludes the discussion I quoted above by suggesting that a university may recover itself by the therapy of asking itself some very hard questions. I register my agreement with that proposal by quoting his questions at length:

> If, for the sake of its own health, a university must be interested in the question of the truth of what it teaches, then, for the sake of the world's health, it must be interested in the fate of that truth and the uses made of it in the world. It must want to know where its graduates live, where they work, and what they do. Do they return home with their knowledge to enhance and protect the life of their neighborhoods? Do they join the "upwardly mobile" professional force now exploiting and destroying local communities, both human and natural, all over the country? Has the work of the university, over the last generation, increased or decreased literacy and knowledge of the classics? Has it increased or decreased a general understanding of the sciences? Has it increased or decreased pollution and soil erosion? Has it increased or decreased the ability and willingness of public servants to tell the truth? Such questions are not, of course, precisely answerable. Questions about influence never are. But they are askable, and the asking, should we choose to ask, would be a unifying and a shaping force.[11]

I would like to think (and later will argue) that such questions are particularly appropriate for the kind of education that grows out of the Lutheran tradition. It may be that the persistent asking of such hard questions will itself shape a particular outlook and education of a certain quality. Berry is not the only one to suggest that this may be the case. Mark Schwehn in his essay "Lutheran Higher Education in the Twenty-first Century" suggests that four questions will "come to dominate discourse about higher learning in the Western world over the course of the next century."

> Here are the four questions. First, to what extent, if any, can universities credibly remain integral and coherent communities of learning without transcendent horizons? Second, can higher learning in America retain its vitality if it loses the plurality of institutions that collectively advance it? Third, can the persistent decline of liberal learning relative to so-called

vocational preparation be arrested without some kind of imaginative re-conception of the whole relationship between liberal education and preparation for vocation? And finally, a question that in some ways en-compasses all of the others: can a liberal democracy continue to be served by a higher education that exalts ideas of freedom, enlightenment, pro-gressive development, problem solving, and the relief of humankind's es-tate without commensurate attention to the meaning and significance of the overwhelming facts of human mortality and finitude? Or, to put the matter more bluntly, can higher learning remain credible in the next cen-tury in the face of the facts of the past century, if it continues as a kind of subtle denial of death?[12]

It is Schwehn's argument that Lutheran higher education is particu-larly well positioned to take these questions seriously and to begin to an-swer them. I agree with him and would go so far as to say that this capability, but in particular taking such questions seriously, is the Lu-theran gift to higher education embodied in our understanding of what it means to be human, what it means to know, and how both are done in community. A very large part of what now passes for higher education is the avoidance of such hard questions as Berry and Schwehn articulate. What is there about the basic assumptions of a university that would make it avoid such hard questions?

I was invited to dinner at the home of a family whose twin sons were both seniors at a large public university. Over coffee at the end of a meal we all became engaged in some rather deep discussions—about peace and war, about human life and its orientation to violence, about all our com-plicity in things that we were very much opposed to. At the end of the dis-cussion the father said to his sons, "This sort of discussion makes me envy you boys." "Why?" they asked. "Because the university is a place where you get to pursue deep and important questions like this in a community of people who take such things seriously." "You've got to be kidding," the boys responded almost simultaneously. "We never have serious conversa-tions at the U, particularly in classes!" "Serious questions," the other twin added, "require depth, commitment, reflection, and judgment. None of which are practiced very much in the classes I take. It's almost as though the classes are so fact- and method-oriented in order to avoid deep and im-portant questions. By far the deepest discussions I've had have been with friends over a beer or here at home."

I believe there are ample resources and reasons in the Lutheran tradi-tion to turn toward the hard and deep questions, questions about what it means to be human, about how we are to be in the world, about the nature of evil, about what we are called and gifted to do, about what we may hope. The encountering of such questions and a community that takes them seriously can occasion remarks like one I was pleased to hear from one of my senior students: "I came to this place to get a degree; but in the process, and to a certain degree in spite of it, I received an education."

Expressions of Faith-Relatedness in Higher Education: Four Prototypes

Institutions of higher education that are related to faith traditions may embody that relationship in various ways. Most do so in more than one of the ways I will distinguish. Thus, in practice, these distinctions are not as clear as they are in theory. Still, these characterizations may be helpful in understanding the dynamics of any given institution. I will sketch four prototypes here. They correspond to my experience of such institutions. But it is possible that there are types (besides combinations of the four) that I have left out.[13]

Type A. There are institutions whose religious identity is established and maintained by the presence of an identifiable religious community. The most obvious examples of such institutions are Roman Catholic schools founded by a religious order of monks or nuns who maintain their presence and influence there. I interviewed for a faculty position at such an institution many years ago. When I asked the dean about the relation between the faith orientation of the institution and the expectation for faculty he said, "Oh, there isn't any connection at all. The brothers take care of the religious identity of the place and that frees the rest of us to pursue our own studies without having to worry about the religion thing." Similar thinking may occur in any institutions where the assumption is that the religious identity is the task of a particular school, department, or office, or particular segment of faculty, administrators, or students.

Type B. There are institutions that embody their religious identity in the behavioral expectations of the members of the community. Such institutions may make very explicit the way they expect students (and faculty and staff) to behave. Most often these expectations are in terms of what students are not to do—consume alcohol or drugs, smoke, dance, visit members of the opposite sex in their rooms, but sometimes there are other behavioral expectations—observing a dress code, attending chapel, taking part in service projects, treating others in a caring way, participating in community-building activities, etc.

Type C. There are institutions that embody their religious identity in theological conformity. Such institutions make explicit what the orthodoxy of the community is, and expect persons attending and working there to affirm it or at least not challenge it. They may ask people to sign an oath of allegiance promising not to teach things they know to be in conflict with its central tenets. A student graduating from such an institution is expected to know and endorse the theological tradition and the worldview it implies.

There are institutions where religious identity is addressed through educating "in a Christian context." In many cases this phrase was inserted in catalogues or mission statements because it asserted some vague connection to the faith tradition but implied nothing. But I think it is also possible to understand "Christian context" in a more substantial way. "Christian context" could refer to the presence of a religious order (as in type A) or, conceivably, to a pattern of behavior promoted by the institution (as in B). Context may also refer to the ethos of the place, or to the history and traditions of the institution. Some institutions are "ivy" in this sense, so is it not conceivable that an institution could be Christian or Jewish or specifically denominational in a similar way? This identity may express itself in the architecture of the institution, the holidays it celebrates and the way it celebrates them, the way worship is emphasized and organized on the campus, the way the institution and the public think of the typical student at such an institution, and so on. Another way to talk about this is to say that the religious identity is part of *the culture of the institution.* There are Quaker institutions that fit this pattern. Their Quaker-ness may manifest itself in silences respected, values expressed in process, the way decisions are made, the values embedded in curriculum, as well as many less obvious ways.

Type D. There are some institutions where religious identity is embedded in the epistemology and pedagogy of the place, i.e., in the way knowledge is thought about, defined, valued, pursued, and communicated, and in its anthropology, the way human being is understood. We know that institutions may differ in their epistemologies, but we are not used to thinking of these differences as embodiments of religious identity. Still, I believe they can be so in a very important way. For a very long time some Roman Catholic institutions had the philosophy of St. Thomas Aquinas as the centerpiece and cornerstone of their curriculum (which would have made them type C institutions). No one could get an undergraduate degree in any subject without taking many courses in Thomistic philosophy. In many ways it was *the core curriculum* at these institutions. At contrasting institutions the function of a core curriculum is, almost by definition, to provide students with a diversity of academic outlooks and worldviews. The idea that one would require students to study any single author or viewpoint to such a degree would raise the strongest objections. These differences in view not only suggest a difference in the evaluation of the thought of St. Thomas, or John Calvin, or some other particular thinker, but a difference in epistemological principles. One institution may make their orthodox worldview the center of their curriculum and the main focus of learning. But another institution, no less connected to a religious tradition, would not even consider doing so. Whether they would consider it or not is dependent on the epistemology derived, in many cases, from theological premises.

Several persons who have written about the relation of colleges and universities to their faith traditions have lamented the fact that many of these institutions of type A, B, or C have "lapsed" and simply gone over to being secular institutions with only a nominal connection to their original religious traditions. This certainly has happened and continues to happen. But there are many cases where people may have supposed that an institution has lapsed because they look at only one or two of the categories typified above. If college X now allows dancing and mixed-gender dormitories where previously it did not, one might be led to suppose that it has lapsed and that the faith tradition has now become quite irrelevant. But perhaps what has happened there is something else entirely. Perhaps, for example, the institution has intentionally decided that those behavioral prohibitions are really not authentic expressions of its religious identity *and never were*. The change, therefore, rather than suggesting a loss of interest in the religious tradition, may in fact be a sign of its vitality. College Y may have earlier in its history taught a single theological viewpoint but now intentionally exposes its students to a wide range of religious expressions and theological views. Have they lapsed from their faith tradition? Perhaps they have, but not necessarily. While some might describe them as "teaching a variety of religious viewpoints in spite of being Lutheran," one might also describe them as teaching this same variety *because* they are Lutheran. Change, and particularly change toward liberality, is not always a sign that an institution has abandoned its faith tradition. In many instances *such change, such "lapses," may evidence the vitality of the tradition in a place*. It may be the tradition itself reappropriated that has led to questioning the assumptions on which the institution previously operated. More questions need to be asked about an institution to determine if this is the case. Maintaining that "theologically shaped anthropology and epistemology" may be legitimate expressions of faith-relatedness allows for the possibility of seeing a vital faith orientation at work in institutions where we might otherwise have supposed it was missing or waning. It allows us to be surprised to find a faith tradition alive and functioning where many may have supposed it had died off or become irrelevant.

Hidden in Plain Sight

A few years ago I was invited to speak at two conferences. One was a gathering of faculty and administrators from southern Baptist universities, the other a conference of administrators and trustees from northeastern Roman Catholic colleges. They both wanted to hear about how Lutherans do higher education. Why, you might ask, were they interested? I asked myself the same question when their invitations came to me, and I was quite amazed to learn the answer. Here is a paraphrase of what they said: "We are in the situation of losing what we have assumed has given us our religious identity. [In the case of the Baptists it was the loss of the *de jure* connection to state and national Baptist conventions; in the case of the Catholics it was the loss by aging and attrition of the religious orders that had founded and maintained them for so long.] You Lutherans are part of a religious tradition that has had neither of these, yet you have maintained a connection to your founding faith tradition and have created strong and lively places of learning because of it. How do you do it?"

My immediate inclination was to say, "Are you sure you're talking to the right person? I teach at a Lutheran university!" But after realizing this was no mistake, I began to take the invitation seriously. My second temptation was to expound, "We do it by means of an informing theology that is understood and applied by the faculty and administration of our institutions and passed on to our students." But could I honestly say that? Would that not imply that we were institutions of type C, which like Calvin College have deliberately shaped our curricula around an explicit theology and Christian worldview? I could not claim that, nor did I have a desire to. For it was not that we, as Lutheran educators, had wanted to follow that model and had failed, but that we did not follow that model because it would not have been right for us. And the wrongness of Lutheran institutions pursuing such a model, as I suggested above, would have been *an epistemological wrongness*. So, what I said at that time was as follows:

> What makes our institutions Lutheran is a vision of the educational task itself that is informed by a tradition of theological themes and principles embodied in practice. Mistaken assumptions that we often make about the nature of "religious" education make us look for evidence of our Lutheran-ness in the frosting and the decorations. I believe that it's in the cake itself. We are Lutheran by means of our educational vision, a theologically informed orientation that manifests itself in what we do as we learn and teach together and our understanding of why we do it.[14]

In other words, even though it did not occur to me to put it thus at the time, we are Lutheran institutions *by virtue of being informed by a theo-*

logically shaped anthropology and epistemology. This shapes our approach to knowing, to teaching, to being a community of learners.

In some ways the faith-relatedness of institutions of type A, B, and C is easier to explain. Their faith-relatedness is visible and quite easily identified by the presence of certain people, certain behaviors and practices, certain belief systems and worldviews, certain elements of the culture. But to see the faith-relatedness of an institution of type D one must examine carefully the whats and whys of the curriculum and pedagogy of the place. For some reason this is the last place many would think to look, in spite of the fact that it is the heart of any institution that claims to be engaged in learning and teaching. For such institutions—and I am claiming that Lutheran colleges and universities are among them—*faith-relatedness is a gift located right in the center of our efforts to learn and share the truth and grow in response to it.* We are Lutheran colleges and universities because of our educational vision, a vision about what it means to be human in the world, given the task of knowing and communicating what we know, thereby shaping a service to the world. I think something like this is what Joseph Sittler intended when he wrote:

> Any effort properly to specify the central and perduring task of the Church-related college must pierce through and below the statements of purpose that often characterize public pronouncements. . . . The Church is engaged in the task of education because it is dedicated to the truth. That dedication alone is its true nature and function. If its proposals, memories, promises, proclamations are not related to the truth, it should get out of the expensive business of education. For at the heart of the people of Israel and the people of the new covenant is the conviction that these traditions embody the profoundest and most comprehensive visions of human life and of the whole of the created order. If [our] commitment to the faith is not one with our commitment to the truth, no multiplication of secondary consolations or benefits will suffice to sustain that commitment for [our] own integrity.[15]

I do not know any Lutheran colleges and universities that have taken Sittler's challenge very seriously. Up until now we have been preoccupied with other tasks. Our colleges and universities were started by immigrant Lutherans largely in order to preserve traditions, maintain identities, and also to acquire the culture of the new world. The struggle between new and old identities occupied many of our colleges through their first decades. Then came decades of struggle for identity in an increasingly secular culture. Some made their identity by becoming like elite institutions they admired, some by being different from those same institutions. These tasks have occupied most Lutheran colleges since the Second World War. I think it is time to think again about why Lutherans should be engaged in the task of higher education. Do we have something of importance to say? Do we have an approach to the tasks of learning and teaching and human becoming to offer the world? I think we do, and I believe the world is in great need of it. This combination of gift and need makes this our vocation.

What I learned in trying to advise Baptist and Catholic educators is how gifted we are as Lutheran institutions. Yet it is a gift many of us have undervalued because, for the most part, it is a gift we never noticed we had. Like some wedding presents, this is a gift many of us have never unwrapped. Others have noticed our giftedness and have asked us to share it with them. That may be a wake-up call to all of us, to realize the value of this gift hidden in plain sight.

II.
Luther, Lutheran Theology, and Eight Focal Theological Themes

Theology can be a fortress within which we hide and prepare for battle. It can also be a prison in which we confine our children.... But it can also be like the piazza of an Italian town, a crossroads at which we meet and converse with each other and celebrate with doors and gates open, sharing the rich wine of life.

—Joseph Sittler

Luther and the Reformation[1]

On All Saints Eve of 1517, Dr. Martin Luther, Augustinian monk and professor of biblical studies at Wittenberg University, posted ninety-five theses for debate on the Wittenberg Church door. The theses, written in Latin and intended for a learned audience and academic debate, explicitly challenged both the practice and theory of selling indulgences, i.e., documents that promised, for a fee, freedom from temporal punishment for past and future sins, freedom from penance, and liberation from purgatory. Implicitly Luther's theses challenged the whole penitential system of the church and the idea that "credits" could be earned by pious acts. Against this Luther argued that there was nothing humans could do to insure their own salvation or make right their relation to God. Redemption, in Luther's view, is God's work and God's gift. Luther argued that his own view was based on Scripture and that he would recant it only if someone were able to show him otherwise. Those with whom he debated repeatedly refused to address this issue, arguing instead that indulgences were based on papal authority.

Thus began a process that would shake the foundations of Western Christendom and change the history of the church and Western Europe forever. This challenge to debate was never intended to fracture the church, much less to start a new denomination within it. Luther's intention was criticism toward reform. His detailed study of the Bible had led him to believe that the church had strayed far from the theology and structure envisioned in Scripture. So with the intention of having his perceptions tested publicly, he made the invitation to debate. Some of the theses he posted he had first penned as essay topics for his students. Neither Luther nor his friends who advised him against such a public challenge had any notion about the scope of the dramatic events that were to follow from this invitation to debate.

Arthur McGiffert in his book *Luther: The Man and His Work* says about Luther's speaking out on the issue of indulgences:

> Had he been a humanist [like Erasmus] he would have laughed the whole thing to scorn as . . . beneath the contempt of an intelligent man; had he been a scholastic theologian, he would have sat in his study and drawn fine distinctions . . . without bothering himself about the influence upon the lives of the vulgar populace. But . . . he had a conscience which made indifference impossible, and a simplicity and directness of vision which compelled him to brush aside all equivocation and go straight to the heart of things.[2]

It is tempting to tell Luther's whole story here. It is such a great adventure, a tale of courage, close scrapes, loyalties and betrayals, shaking the foundations, building again. Luther is such a vivid, multidimensional, explosive, trash-talking character. But I will leave you to pursue that story on your own.

The Reformation had far-reaching consequences for the shape that institutions and culture would take in the modern world. Philip Jenkins, in his recent article "The Next Christianity," writes:

> [The Reformation] was more than a mere theological row. It was a far-reaching social movement that sought to return to the original sources of Christianity. It challenged the idea that divine authority should be mediated through institutions or hierarchies, and it denied the value of tradition. Instead it offered radical new notions of the supremacy of written texts . . . interpreted by individual consciences. . . . there arose such fundamental ideas of modern society as the state's obligation to tolerate minorities and the need to justify political authority without constantly invoking God or religion.[3]

The Reformation as Educational Inspiration

From just the little bit that we have said about Luther here, and without getting into theological particulars, we can already discern important principles that have left indelible marks on the Lutheran tradition.

The Reformation was a movement begun in the university, by a professor, that ended up changing the world—ecclesiastically, theologically, politically, socially, historically. Lutherans have been engaged in transformative education ever since. I will venture the bold claim that there is no denomination in Christendom for whom the university is more important and more essential than it is and has been for Lutherans.

Luther's challenge to debate was an act of *faithful criticism*. Many people cannot even believe that such a thing is possible. If one is faithful to a tradition, they suppose, then one must not be critical of it. If one is critical doesn't this show, automatically, that one cannot be faithful? Yet this is precisely what Luther did, he criticized the church as an act of faithfulness. He had no intention of destroying the church, but he did want to correct its course. Throughout his life, and long after he had been publicly condemned by Rome, Luther called on church leaders to hold a council to publicly discuss these issues. As a consequence, this principle of faithful criticism has been embodied in the tradition. Lutherans believe that the Reformation was not a one-time event, but one that must continue: *ecclesia semper reformanda*, the church must continually be reformed. Rather than seeing questions and issues as settled once and for all, Lutherans tend to see things in continual process, in need of continual critique and correction.

Lutheranism was born in the process of criticizing the church, the highest and most powerful authority in existence in its day. As a consequence, Lutherans see all human institutions as in need of continual correction and critique, their own church among them. Lutherans are and have always been a critical and self-critical lot. This has resulted in our often being contentious, but it has also made us healthfully suspicious of established orthodoxies, even our own. Many Lutheran colleges and universities were founded in America to preserve ethnic identity among Lutherans here. But at least an equal number were founded because some group of Lutherans disagreed fundamentally with some theological tenet of fellow Lutherans who had founded a school not more than thirty miles away. Lutherans take theology seriously. With some historical distance on these disputes we may be tempted to say we sometimes take it too seriously.

It was Luther's learning in Hebrew and Greek and his study of newly developed methods of historical criticism that made possible the reading of the Bible that fueled his criticism of the church. Lutherans have, as a consequence, valued learning that has such liberating power. Some denominations in Christendom have been largely anti-intellectual, finding that learning has often led to a questioning of beliefs; they have seen this as a threat to the faith and found it frightening. Lutherans have, obviously, not gone that way. Instead Lutherans have valued the disciplines and liberal learning and *have embraced critical thought as an expression of faithfulness.*

I remember discovering these Lutheran traits in college when I began to read the works of Søren Kierkegaard. Kierkegaard embodied many Lutheran traits: he was exceptionally learned, engaged in faithful criticism of his culture and the intellectual trends of his day as well as the established church, and wrote in a way meant to be edifying, i.e., intending to be of service to his readers, not merely in pursuit of a disengaged academic erudition.

Thinking, inquiry, the pursuit of truth have always been linked, for Lutherans, to service and transformation of the larger society and culture. Lutherans turned away from the model of cloistered and detached learners. Luther spent a good deal of time shut up in his own version of an ivy-covered tower, hidden away for his own protection, but what he did there—translating the Bible into the vernacular, writing theological and practical treatises, arguing with church leaders and princes—had tremendous impact on society. The university, for Lutherans, has thus always had this multidimensional aspect. It is a place to get away to, a place of safe haven if necessary, a place of intellectual freedom certainly. But this freedom does not imply academic detachment nor social disengagement. Lutherans value telling the truth boldly, even when it gets them in trouble to do so. But beyond that, the university is also *in service* to the larger society. And the service that the university renders is often challenging and transformative, telling a truth and leading people to fulfillment beyond what they supposed they needed.

Luther and Lutheran Theology

Luther's activities, theology, and character are certainly the inspiration for Lutheran theology. But Luther has never served as the authoritative source for the theological tradition in the same way that Aquinas has for Roman Catholics and Calvin has for Calvinists. There are several reasons for this that are worth noting.

Luther was not a systematic thinker and writer but a rhetorical and polemical one. He did not write anything like Aquinas's *Summa* or Calvin's *Institutes*, works meant to summarize in a coherent way their author's theological viewpoint. Luther wrote a tremendous amount, but his works are rhetorical in the sense that they address a particular audience about a particular issue that arose in a particular context. A very large proportion of Luther's writings, for example, are sermons and letters. Luther's writings are more like Paul's epistles than they are like the usual German three-volume systematic theology. Joseph Sittler has noted: "There is, to be sure, a sense of the term systematic thinker before which Luther would not qualify—which, in fact, he would not understand."[4] Luther's works are also polemical; very often he is writing against someone or some view that he thinks is in error. It is important to keep these things in mind when reading Luther, and not quote his work as definitive on some issue without noting to whom and on what occasion it was written and how that may have shaped what Luther said.

Luther was extremely critical of his own theology just as he was of the work of others. Toward the end of his own life he referred to his own theology as "a bag of excrement." Elsewhere he says, comparing his own work to his contemporary, Philipp Melancthon:

> I do not think the Holy Scriptures have been treated with such sincerity and clarity for over a thousand years, for his [Melancthon's] talent is next to the apostolic age. . . . I am losing these years of mine in unhappy wars and would be pleased if all my works perished lest they become obstacles to pure theology and better geniuses. . . . I have done the rough cutting and Philipp has done the planing. But sometimes yet a badly knotted log calls for a blunt wedge.[5]

This self-critical attitude has kept Lutherans from enshrining Luther's work as normative. Lutherans have tried to preserve the spirit of Luther's work even where they have been critical of the letter of it. For Lutherans, quoting Luther adds substantially to a debate but it seldom settles one. I believe Luther would himself have been pleased with that treatment and would be displeased to see his writings used as the "proof text" for anything.

Luther was a very intemperate man, both in his personal life and in his writing. His joys, his sufferings (both physical and spiritual), his loyalties, and his betrayals all were of heroic proportions. As a consequence he often overstates things, calls names, and heaps invective on those he argues with (including himself). Reading Luther is a good dose of medicine for those who believe that piety is equivalent to being inoffensive and nice. Luther was neither.

The final reason that Luther is not an unquestionable authority for Lutherans is that, in some things at least, he was just plain wrong. He backed the princes and German royalty and roundly condemned the peasants in the revolt that he was, at least in part, the stimulus for.[6] He did not seem capable of seeing any justice in their cause. He viciously attacked Jews who did not convert to Christianity.[7] His rhetoric is thus at least partly responsible for the Holocaust, and for the fact that so many Germans were complicit or quietly obedient while the Nazis worked their program of extermination. Thank God there were some Lutherans who protested and resisted and gave support to the Jews. Unfortunately they could not quote Luther in support of their cause.

Lutheran theology has been and is, therefore, more like a set of variations played on some basic themes to be found in Luther. These themes have certainly inspired Lutheran thinkers, but they have also left them with a great deal of room for variety, creativity, and critique. One has only to examine the differences in the thought of Hegel, Kierkegaard, Grundtvig, Aulén, Bultmann, Bonhoeffer, Tillich, Pannenberg, and Sittler, among others, to see what a lively and diverse tradition Lutheran theological thinking represents. Luther's influence is not confined, of course, to Lutherans. It is particularly interesting to see how close to Luther's own views the Roman Catholic Church has come in some recent statements on justification and vocation, to cite just two issues previously disputed. The discussions in subsequent chapters will illustrate the variety of persons that I have found voicing variations on Lutheran themes.

Lutheran Engagement in Higher Education

As was mentioned above, the Reformation was born and took root in the university. The university was the host within which the movement grew, and Luther maintained his faculty status throughout his life. Though many things in his life changed, this was one that did not. So Lutheranism was not first a church that then decided it would be good to get into the business of higher education; it was first a movement in the university that later manifested itself as a confessing church. That Lutherans should have founded and supported more colleges and universities is, therefore, completely natural and fitting. Expanding on this connection, Robert Benne writes:

> From the beginning the reformation included a strong intellectual element along with the religious, aesthetic, and practical. In its decisive break with Rome, the Lutheran movement articulated its faith in a refined and systematic theological confession, *The Book of Concord*. As it developed it paid strong attention to the education of clergy into this confessional tradition. . . . This emphasis on an educated clergy is one of the defining themes of Lutheran identity. A second theme is the calling or vocation of all Christians. Christians are to act on behalf of their neighbors with faith, love and hope in the specific worldly roles they have been given. But they are also to act with competence. This means provision for the education of the laity as well as the clergy. . . . A third theme . . . is a high evaluation of human reason as a guide to earthly, civic life; in the words of Luther, "How dare you not know what can be known!" Luther-

anism teaches that while reason cannot achieve saving knowledge of God, it can reach trustworthy knowledge of our world.[8]

Since the education we pursue must prepare us to serve competently in the world, it is never sufficient for persons to merely receive a "religious" or "parochial" or "Bible college" education, narrowly defined. As a result of their education people will become doctors, lawmakers, teachers, therapists, engineers, administrators, and responsible parents and citizens. The education required for this must, therefore, be as rich and diverse, as disciplined and rigorous, as critical and world-engaging as any. Thus Lutherans steer their institutions between the purely secular alternatives on one side, and the world-wary parochial approach on the other. The college or university, in the Lutheran understanding of it, is a place where the gospel of Christ meets and engages the world. The result is a dialogue that attempts *to tell the whole truth in a way that serves well the deep needs of the world.*

Eight Focal Lutheran Themes[9]

The themes discussed here are Lutheran, but not in the sense that Luther or Lutherans invented them or that they are exclusively Lutheran. Some are common to both the Hebrew and Christian traditions. Some are common to many, if not all, Christians. I have chosen these eight themes not because they are the only ideas important to the Lutheran tradition, but because they meet two criteria: (a) They are ideas central to understanding the Lutheran tradition. Grasping the Lutheran understanding of these ideas gives an adequate, if not a complete, view of what the Lutheran theological tradition is and how Lutherans tend to think about things. (b) They are ideas that have implications for the way we know, the way we inquire, the way we learn, and the way we teach. They are, in other words, ideas central to a Lutheran approach to education.

In the present chapter I want to briefly explain the theological significance of these eight themes. In the chapters that follow I want to sketch their implications for anthropology (a view of what it means to be human), for epistemology (how we think about knowing and learning and teaching), and for how we, as colleges and universities, are called to educate whole human persons for the age in which we live.

1. Creation

Lutherans affirm God as creator of the entire universe, of all that exists. Someone reading this is likely to ask, "Does that mean that Lutherans are creationists?" My understanding of creationists is that they are persons who advance the creation account as a scientific theory or at least as a theory to rival scientific theories. Lutherans, by and large, are quite content to let scientists do their best work to answer the questions science can answer. It is very possible for a Lutheran astrophysicist to advance some version of the big bang theory and for a Lutheran biologist to argue some version of evolutionary theory. As a scientist she ought to pursue the best account that science has to offer. She certainly should not want to reject a scientific account just because it is not the same as a biblical account. Lutherans, generally, do not think that the Bible is an authoritative scientific text. They do not think that it is the task of theology to come up with cosmological accounts to rival the best that science has to offer.

Christians who are inclined to read the Bible as an authoritative scientific text do so, usually, out of two assumptions: (a) they want to honor the Bible, to affirm its truth, and (b) they think that scientific truth is the only kind worth bothering about. From these two assumptions flows their conclusion that we should read the Bible as an authoritative scientific text and affirm it as an alternative scientific view. If the creation accounts in Genesis are not scientific, they reason, what good are they? Isn't the only truth worth asserting scientific truth?

Lutherans do not draw the aforementioned conclusion largely because they do not make the second assumption mentioned above. They do not make that assumption for two reasons:

First, Lutherans are not inclined to enshrine science (or any discipline for that matter) as *the* paradigm of knowing. This does not mean that Lutherans think science is worthless. Far from it. Some very eminent scientists have been Lutherans, and Lutheran colleges and universities generally make great efforts to have excellent science faculty and facilities. For Lutherans, science is a perfectly appropriate human response to the created universe. We do God's creation honor by trying to understand it.

For Lutherans science is an extremely valuable but limited enterprise. Scientists pursue specific kinds of inquiries, based, like all human endeavors, on certain assumptions, shaped by particular kinds of tools, molded by human agendas and the institutions that embody them. Lutherans would be inclined to say that we should pursue science in the best ways we know how. Having done that, we should be critical of our means of knowing and modest about what we have come to understand in the process. When asked whether creationism should be taught in science classes in the public schools, I responded, "No, I don't think so. I think in science classes we should teach the best science we know. And we should teach it critically, admitting what we know, what we do not know, what we assume, and what we conclude on those bases. Where there is more than one theory that is viable we ought to admit that and explain the grounds for preferring one theory to another."

The second reason Lutherans are not inclined to accept the creationist premise is because we think that the affirmation of creation is a richer and deeper concept than any scientific theory. For lack of a better term, I would say that *when we affirm God as creator of all things we are making an ontological claim, a claim about the fundamental nature of reality and our relation to it.* What, exactly, are we affirming? The following seven things are at least part of the meaning of affirming God's creative work. They only begin to show how many dimensions this one theological idea has.

When we affirm creation we affirm:

(1) *That the world is real and important, a manifestation of the ultimate, God.* Some religions and philosophies have seen the world as an illusion; some see life in it as ultimately meaningless. People who affirm God's creation cannot see it that way. We take the world seriously. We are caught by the wonder of it. We want to scale its heights and plumb its depths. The ordinary is intimately and essentially connected to the ultimate. The world is not God, but it is good; it is good in its finitude. It is ours to wonder at and care for. Those who affirm creation are thereby called to affirm the world and find their rightful place in it. To persons who affirm God's creative act the universe is not a vast, meaningless emptiness. We may wonder at its vastness, but for us its vastness unlocks a depth of meaning, not a depth of meaninglessness. Contrast these two visions; the first by Bertrand Russell:

> Amid such a world, if anywhere, our ideals henceforward must find a home. That man is the product of causes which had no prevision of the end they were achieving; that his origin, his growth, his hopes and fears, his loves and his beliefs, are but the outcome of accidental collocations of atoms; that no fire, no heroism, no intensity of thought and feeling, can preserve an individual life beyond the grave; that all the labours of the ages, all the devotion, all the inspiration, all the noonday brightness of human genius, are destined to extinction in the vast death of the solar system, and that the whole temple of Man's achievement must inevitably be buried beneath the debris of a universe in ruins. . . . Only within the scaffolding of these truths, only on the firm foundation of unyielding despair, can the soul's habitation henceforth be safely built.[10]

Contrast to Russell the voice of the psalmist responding to the creation he sees:

> O bless the Lord, O my soul,
> Immeasurable is your greatness!
> You are robed with splendor and majesty,
> Dressing yourself with light for your white cloak.
> The deep heavens are the curtain of your tent,
> The great trees the ship in which you ride the ocean swells,

You ride the clouds like a chariot,
And walk upon the wings of the wind.
You established the earth on its foundations,
So it will not move from its rightful path;
You cover it with the sea as with a garment;
The sea and the mountains and the valleys
Move to the place you have assigned for them,
You have set them boundaries.

You cause the grass to grow for the cattle,
And vegetation for the labor of humans,
So they may bring forth food from the earth,
And wine to make the heart glad.

You made the moon for the seasons,
And the sun knows the proper place of its daily setting.
You have made the day and the darkness of night,
Sleep for humans and a refuge for the prowling beasts,
Who, in their way, seek their food from God.

O Lord, how many are your works!
In wisdom have you made them all;
I can do nothing but be amazed
And praise your name forever.

Bless the Lord, O my soul! (Psalm 104, selections)

(2) *That the world is good, loved by God, God's domain of creativity.* Some religions and philosophies have seen the world as basically an evil place, a place to be rescued from, a place opposed to God. There is ample evidence in both the Hebrew and Christian scriptures that this is not the dominant biblical view, even though there are some passages, influenced by Gnostic thought, that point in that direction. The creation narrative is punctuated with the line, "And God saw that it was good." John 3:16 begins with the assertion, "God so loved the world that he sent his only begotten son." This attests to God embracing the world in spite of its fallenness. So it is fitting for those of us who affirm the creation to enjoy it, savor it, celebrate it, give deep thanks for it. We sing, we dance, we explore, and often we are awed into silence. These are all ways in which we, as the psalm says, "taste and see how gracious the Lord is." Some have viewed the world as meaningless chaos, some have imagined it as meaningless repetition, and some have seen it as a battleground of opposing forces; the Genesis account envisions the world as divine creativity, a

work of depth, of beauty, of awe. One of my favorite authors, Annie Dillard, writes:

> My God what a world. There is no accounting for one second of it. . . . The whole of creation is one lunatic fringe. If creation had been left up to me, I'm sure I wouldn't have had the imagination or courage to do more than shape a single, reasonably sized atom, smooth as a snowball, and let it go at that. No claims of any and all revelations could be as far fetched as a single giraffe.[11]

(3) *That the world is God's; it is not the possession of humans.* Human beings are created beings like all the others. We have a kind of creatureliness that we forget at our peril. We are but one part of a larger community of creatures. The creation and our fellow creatures are not ours to destroy, but ours to enjoy. The wanton wasting of creation simply to suit our own agenda is blasphemy. It claims as ours what is only ours to use and enjoy. We would not destroy a friend's vacation home if allowed to use it. Yet too many of us are ready to destroy the world without any sense that we have to answer for it. Affirming creation puts us in our place as part of, not apart from, the natural world.

(4) *That humans are fundamentally of-the-earth.* The Genesis narratives relate that humans are created from mud, the only of all the creatures of which this is said. The name they are given, *adamah*, means "from the earth." Interestingly, there is also an etymological connection between the Latin-English word "human" and a word for fertile ground, "humus." Wendell Berry has commented that Genesis gives the following "recipe" for making humans: mud plus God's breath. What does this account communicate to us? I would suggest at least two things: It reminds us of our finitude—that the earth was here before us and will be here after us, and that our lives are basically "dust to dust." It reminds us to be humble (once again a humus-related word), or in the words of the Shaker hymn, "to come down where we ought to be."

(5) *That all humans, the Genesis accounts tell us, come from a single set of parents.* This implies that the differences between people (race, caste, class, nationality) that we are tempted to place so much importance on are not part of the created order. Fundamentally humans are one family, we are all the children of God, and any differences between us must be justified (if at all) by some other explanation than, "That's how God made it." Some creation accounts establish castes; some establish a king as the god incarnate. The Judeo-Christian creation account tells us that basic equality is the default setting for the human situation.

(6) *That we are created and called to be in conversation with God.* The Genesis narratives, in fact the whole of the Hebrew and Christian scrip-

tures, show us that to be human is to be in the presence of God. God calls us, and one way or another we answer, even when our answer is to hide. The Psalms illustrate the wide variety of forms that conversation took in the life of the Hebrew people. There are psalms of joy and praise, psalms of doubt and questioning, psalms of abandonment and lamentation, even psalms of accusation, putting to God hard questions that had to be voiced.

The Genesis account tells us that humans are created in God's image. Over the ages there have been many interpretations of what that means. Some have said it is human reason, or human creativity, or human freedom, or some other human gift that makes us image God. My own interpretation is that all of these things may play a role, but that we image God by virtue of our mutuality, our being-with, our being-in-conversation.

(7) *That God calls humans to be stewards of the creation.* God calls us, because of our special gifts, to be stewards of the creation. We are God's delegated caretakers. For this role we have been given certain gifts. We are responsible because we are, of all creatures, response-able, called to conversation with God. And perhaps we are stewards because we are, of all creatures, of-the-earth.

It should be clear from the above discussion that the affirmation of creation is much more than a cosmological theory. It addresses so many more concerns. It explains to us where we are, who we are, what our orientation is, how the world is to be regarded, how we are related to each other, how we are related to the Creator. I do not know of any scientific account that does that. Science, appropriately, has a different focus. Our affirmation of creation has the power to inform our lives. It makes clear that we are called to be in the world in particular ways, and not others. We are here to manifest wonder and care, to savor and plumb, to be a part of creation, earth-born siblings to all humans, responsible stewards in conversation with God.

2. Sin

If the first narrative in the Bible is about creation, the second is about sin. The first records the goodness of all creation; the second is about rebellion and alienation. It is about how we have departed from the original intention God had for us. It records the human rebellion against God. Humans disobey God, transgress the boundaries set for them, when confronted try to blame each other, and end up attempting to hide from each other and from God. The alienation that follows infects all of creation, not just human life. Nothing is quite the same as it was before.

Many religions and philosophies have something like the idea of sin operating within them. Frequently, however, these accounts are dualistic in nature. That is to say, sin is a way of dividing some people from others, or some things from others. A dualist might, for example, see the body as sinful and the soul as pure. Such a view often misunderstands sin as being equal to carnality and worldliness. Life, by such an account, becomes an attempt to separate soul from body so that when the body is destroyed the soul floats up to God.

Luther explicitly rejected such dualism. He rejected it, first, because it was unbiblical. God creates humans, in the Genesis account, as embodied creatures in the world, and having done so declares this to be good. We do not "fall" into embodiedness, or into humanity or creatureliness or finitude. God creates all these. Sin is not our being biological creatures. In fact, sin is, as Douglas John Hall has stated, "Our refusal to accept our own identity as biological creatures."[12] Second, Luther objected to dualism because he maintained that there was no part of our life that was not stained by sin. Therefore there was no part of our human life that was essentially more sinful than another. We cannot avoid sin by beating up on our bodies or by practicing celibacy or self-denial. Our own efforts to secure our own sinlessness themselves spring out of pride and are marred by sin. This is why Luther, once himself a devoted monk who, it was expected, through his exemplary life would earn not only his own salvation but accrue merits he could share with others, ended up rejecting completely the penitential system of the medieval church. Only God, Luther argued on the basis of Scripture, can atone for sin. All human attempts to do so are a rejection of God's redemptive work given as an undeserved gift to all humanity.

For Lutherans, therefore, sin is not a moral category but an ontological one. It is how we now are, not what particular thing we have done or not done. We do not avoid sin by being good, because our every effort to be good is itself sinful. Sinner is not a word that applies only to some. It applies to all. And, most important, it applies to us. Alexander Solzhenitsyn stated:

> If only there were evil people somewhere, insidiously committing evil deeds, and it were necessary only to separate them from the rest of us and destroy them. But the line dividing good and evil cuts through the heart of every human being.[13]

This lesson is clearly illustrated in a gospel story, John 8:3–9. Judges confront Jesus with a woman caught in the act of adultery. (Where is the man?) Having established her guilt, they are about to stone her to death, as the law indicates. In an attempt to corner Jesus in a conflictive situation (Does he respect the law or not?) the judges ask him what should be done. The story tells us he writes something with his finger in the dirt, but we're not told what. Then he says, "Let him who is without sin cast the first stone." The judges, and the crowd, we are told, go away angry. And it is easy to understand why. Jesus has taken from them something of great importance to them, the ability to appear righteous because they all, as a group, have been able to identify and punish someone else as a sinner. How often we feel good about who we are because we can find someone else about whom we can say, "At least I'm not one of *them*." We join in the abuse of others because we fear ourselves becoming the target of such abuse. How much evil in the world has been done by people trying desperately to establish their own righteousness!

Many Christians are tempted to identify sin with particular behaviors that "good people" have avoided. This temptation appears in things we do and in ways that we talk. We may say about an unmarried couple living together that they are "living in sin." A reflective Lutheran should not talk that way because, from the Lutheran point of view, *we are all living in sin*, whether we are married, single, sexually active, or celibate. Our sexual situation or orientation or practices do not make us more or less sinful. Any relationship may be self-serving, harmful, abusive, careless, and hateful. We are certainly not rid of all that simply because we have enjoyed a church wedding.

Sin manifests itself in so many ways: as pride, power, greed, hate and cruelty, putting others down, waste, destruction, self-abuse, neglect, spite, turning away from gifts. Sin, like an addiction, is not a problem we can cure merely by willing it away. And like an addiction it has not only the power to harm others, but to make us not even able to recognize our own good or pursue it. As in the case of an addiction, we may be able to avoid a particular behavior for a time, but that does not mean the problem has gone away. It is a stain that has soaked through the whole cloth. It is not just a disease but, like AIDS, a disease of our immune system. And, again like AIDS, it is a condition that is ferociously contagious, passing not only through the whole culture but from one generation to another. Following the comparison with addiction, Lutherans are more likely to see the church as like a twelve-step program than to see it as a gathering of the righteous. Each of us stands as a sinner in the midst of sinners. Yet, by the grace of God, we are redeemable.

Sin is a problem only God can cure. That is the whole point of the incarnation. God bridges the gap created by sin by becoming fully human in Christ. To make an effort to "earn" or "deserve" such a gift is, in fact, to reject it. The only proper response is thankful acceptance. That we find it so difficult to accept this gift is itself a symptom of our continuing sinfulness. Thus we are, as Luther put it, *simul justus et peccator*, simultaneously saint and sinner. We are saints because we have already been redeemed, and we are sinners because, in our continuing pride, we want to congratulate ourselves for being so gifted. St. Augustine characterized sin as *incurvatus in se ipse*: as being turned in on oneself, as being thoroughly self-focused and, the special temptation of the religious, as being self-congratulatory. For Lutherans neither ethics nor religiousness are ways to avoid sin. Both are sin-stained institutions. The twentieth-century Jewish thinker Martin Buber recognized this when he wrote: "there is nothing that can so hide the face of our fellow man as morality can [and] religion can hide from us, as nothing else can, the face of God."[14] The recognition of this is also what led Luther and many of his followers to be suspicious of both.

3. Grace

We stated above that sin is a problem only God can cure. The good news of the gospel is that God has done so in Christ. This gift is what Christians refer to as grace. If anything is the central recurrent theme of Lutheranism it is this: we are justified by grace through faith. We are not justified by our good deeds or efforts or virtues, nor by the evil we have avoided. Some Christians accept Luther's argument to that point, but then assert that we are saved by the correctness and fervor of our beliefs. For them, justification is not a function of good works but of right belief. Many have supposed that this is the Lutheran position as well. Luther's view was that our beliefs are as susceptible to sin as our actions are. Sin is part of the human condition, not just of this or that part or faculty. Luther wrote: "I cannot by my own reason or strength believe in Jesus Christ or come to him; but the Holy Spirit has called me through the gospel, enlightened me with his gifts. . . ."[15] So even belief is a gift of God, not something we accomplish through reason or will. It is not something we can take pride in or congratulate ourselves for.

This understanding of grace was absolutely central to Luther's thinking. It explains what upset him so much about the sale of indulgences. It is what led him to be critical of the monastic life, of private masses, of pilgrimages and reliquaries. All these things were human attempts to obtain credit with God. And all of them, Luther came to believe, were rejections of the free gift of God in Christ. Attempts to save ourselves by a pious life or by good works were, thus, a rejection of the gift. Good works flowed from the gift as the fruits of grace. As Luther put it, "A tree does not grow strong from its fruit, but it is recognized as strong by these fruits."[16]

Some of my university colleagues have argued that talk about sin and grace gives us a very negative and pessimistic view of humans. Wouldn't it be better to focus on what humans do well and what they do right than to focus on sin? Wouldn't it be better, they argue, to credit humans with their own redemption rather than seeing it as a gift from God? My response is fairly complex because it addresses a number of assumptions present in their argument. (1) Some account must be given of the evil that humans are capable of and the harm we do to ourselves, each other, and the environment. Greek tragedy, the teachings of Buddhism and Taoism, as well as Judaism and Christianity see this as a problem that runs through the heart of each of us. It is not something that is just true of "those evil people," even though we are very tempted to say so, but it is something that is true of us all. It would be irresponsible to pretend not to see it. The concept of sin is an attempt to deal with human nature realistically. (2) The evil we do is very often connected to the good we attempt to do. The bloodbath that was the French Revolution was born out of an attempt to achieve "Liberty, Equality, Fraternity." The hell that was Soviet Communism was born out of an effort to create "a classless society." Who knows what will be the name of the horror presently being created by our own efforts to secure "liberty and justice for all." Dualistic accounts of human evil just do not do justice to human history. (3) Interestingly, both the French and the Communist revolutions were efforts to get rid of evil in the world by getting rid of the persons and social structures that were identified as the cause of it. In neither case were the revolutionaries able to see the potential for evil in their own movements as they marched out to destroy the evil they found in others. It would be easy if we could rid the world of evil simply by destroying whatever form "the evil empire" takes in our own age. But what do we do when we recognize, as Walt Kelly's Pogo so plainly put it, "We have met the enemy and he is us"? (4) The Judeo-Christian view does not focus exclusively or ultimately on sin. Unlike Greek tragedy and, to a large extent, the Hindu idea of karma, sin is not the final word, only a very important one. The final word is grace, the unrelenting love and care of the Creator God for the creation. Life, as well as the cosmic drama, has more than one act: the first is creation, the second is sin, and the third is grace.

When I was younger I beat up on myself quite regularly for all sorts of failings. I would get very uptight when I had to perform in public. My fear was that I would make a mess of things or that my performance would be less than stellar. My worry about this was, of course, frequently the cause of my messing up. So in many ways my fear of failure was a self-fulfilling prophecy. I know this is not just a problem I have because I often have seen it in my students and colleagues. When I was in my thirties I met, after an absence of ten years, a high school and college friend who had gone on to become an accomplished soprano. She frequently sang at Carnegie Hall and with orchestras in Europe and the United States. When I saw her we talked for quite a while; about the past, about what we had done. Finally I asked her how she dealt with the fear of failure, with performance anxiety. This was her response as I remember it:

> There is no such thing as a perfect performance. I might be able to paste one together on tape, but a live performance of any song will have something the matter with it. Once I realized that, I relaxed a good deal. I also came to realize that the "goofs" weren't all my fault, and the good performances weren't all my doing either. When I perform I consider it a gift, given to me, to my accompanist, and to the audience by means of both of us plus the composer. I have a voice, a talent, an education, teachers who pushed and led me, a community of people who support me, opportunities to perform, students to teach; all of these are gifts. Being hypercritical and self-condemning is not the opposite of being a perfectionist. They are opposite sides of the same coin. When I perform I just try to remember these things.

When I asked her where she had learned this she said to me: "Thomas, I'm surprised at you. I learned it in church confirmation class studying Luther's *Small Catechism* just like you did." I didn't say it to her on that occasion, but I have certainly said to myself: "You obviously learned it better than I did."

I remember hearing from a freshman writing teacher a strategy she used to get her students past common freshman excuses: "I'm no good at writing," "I can't think of anything to write about," "I hate writing." She tells them to go off and write the worst short essay they can. She said, "They inevitably come back with really good and often very inventive stuff. They have such low confidence because they have such high expectations. Putting oneself down is not, you know, the opposite of egotism but a symptom of it. My students just have to get past their self-inflicted perfectionism. Then they can enjoy and develop the gifts they have."

The confession of sin is not the same thing as a preoccupation with one's own failure. Incanting "Woe is me. I am sh–t!" over and over is not confessing sin. It is practicing narcissism. This focus on self is one of the manifestations of sin, surely. But it is also a wallowing in it.

So to my university colleagues who have argued that talk about sin and grace is a real put-down for human effort and endeavor I would say that my experience is almost exactly the opposite of this. Grace, giftedness, the admission of our own sinfulness, all these things have liberating power. That is why any discussion of grace in a Lutheran context is incomplete without an exploration of our next theme, freedom.

4. Freedom

Luther wrote about freedom in his famous treatise, "The Freedom of a Christian":

> A Christian is a perfectly free lord of all, subject to none. A Christian is a
> perfectly dutiful servant of all, subject to all. . . . Freed from the vain at-
> tempt to justify himself . . . [the Christian] should be guided in all his
> works by this thought alone . . . considering nothing but the need of the
> neighbor. . . . This is a truly Christian life. Here faith is truly active
> through love, that is it finds expression in the works of the freest service
> cheerfully and lovingly done.[17]

Luther understood freedom as the consequence of grace. We are freed
from the necessity to work our own redemption. We are freed from trying
to climb the staircase to God's love, because God came all the way down.
This means that we are freed from the captivity of hierarchical dualisms
one usually finds in religions. We have no need to transcend the bodily in
service of some "higher" spiritual realm. We have no need to deny the
secular to serve the sacred. We have no need to depart the natural to serve
the supernatural. Luther was adamant that we are called to serve where we
are, in the stations in which we find ourselves—thoroughly embodied,
concrete, earthen, and particular. We are also freed from our self-
constructed and self-maintained hierarchies. So we may be called to be
women, not "not quite men"; to be children, not "not quite adults"; to be
students, not "not quite careered"; to be secretaries and custodians, not
"not quite executives"; to be laity, not "not quite clergy"; even to be (*pace*
Luther) philosophers, not "not quite theologians."

The fact that we are embraced by God means we are freed to be fully
and honestly human. We are freed to be eating, drinking, excreting, sexual,
working, sweating, hoping, fearing, crying, nurturing, and thinking beings.
Piety, in this Lutheran view, is not a denial of part of our own reality but
rather an embracing of all of it. We are freed to come before God not pure
and unspotted but in our honest wholeness. Rabbi Harold Kushner, in his
book *How Good Do We Have To Be?* offers the following commentary:

> My candidate for the most important word in the Bible occurs in Genesis
> 17:1 when God says to Abraham, "Walk before me and be *tamim*." The
> King James Bible translates it as "perfect"; the RSV takes it to mean
> "blameless" . . . . Contemporary scholars take the word to mean some-
> thing like "whole-hearted." My own study of the verse leads me to con-
> clude that what God wants from Abraham, and by implication from us, is
> not perfection but integrity. . . . That, I believe, is what God asks of Abra-
> ham. Not "Be perfect," not, "Don't ever make a mistake," but "Be
> whole."[18]

As a consequence of this gifted freedom there is no part of us or our life
that we must not embrace because it is "lower" or "unclean" in some
phony pious sense. As a consequence, when we do our work we may work
fully engaged, alienated neither by the dirtiness of hauling garbage, the

chaos of teaching fifth grade, the smell of the nursing home, nor the mess of politics.

5. Vocation

It should be obvious that Luther's understanding of grace and freedom will have implications for his understanding of work. Before Luther the word vocation (Latin: *vocatio* and German: *Beruf*) had been applied only to people who had a "religious vocation," people called to be priests or monks or nuns. Luther challenged that usage and the view of human work it presupposed, that some are doing God's work but others are not. Luther argued that the station of every Christian was a calling from God to serve the needs of our neighbor wherever we are as we are able. It isn't that we need to serve God separately from our other work. We serve God through our service to each other. Luther used the word vocation, therefore, to apply to the work and duties of every person. The fish-pickler, the shoemaker, the schoolteacher, the mayor, the street cleaner, the prince, the pastor, the parent, even the student—each of these has a work and a responsibility given to her or him by virtue of this station. I said "even the student" because we often suppose that students are *preparing* for a vocation but we seldom think that *they already have one*. Yet that is exactly what Luther asserts. God calls each student to be a good student and to serve, by being so, the school, the community of learners, the development of one's gifts, and eventually the wider world.

Darrell Jodock offers the following explanatory expansion of vocation:

> I mean by vocation an over-arching self-understanding which (a) sees oneself not as an isolated unit but "nested" into a larger community and (b) gives ethical priority to those behaviors that will benefit the community.[19]

As a consequence vocation has to do not only with what it is we do, but how we do it, and with what understanding we do it. Each of these dimensions has the power to change the others. We may be led to do a different thing, or to do things differently, when we re-understand what we are doing as a divine calling. Similarly our performance of an ordinary task can lead to a new understanding of what needs to be done, as well as why we are called to do it.

In some of Luther's sermons he becomes quite upset by the old habits of his parishioners. They still think that they ought to be doing something peculiarly religious, perhaps by working at the church, by going on a pilgrimage, or doing some penitential works. Luther tells them to return to their workaday duties. Neither they nor God nor their neighbor will be served by their pious deeds. But probably there is someone who needs shoes, or needs bread, or needs legal counsel. "Return to your work," Luther says, "that is what God calls you to do."

In the section on freedom we noted that God's grace leaves us free to focus on the task at hand. We do not have to keep our eye on some extraneous transcendent punishment/reward system. So we are left to care for, and focus on, and take an intense interest in those things that are right in front of us. The service of God is present, just as in a sacrament, in the concrete and particular. "Purity of heart is to will one thing," Kierkegaard wrote as the title of one of his works. We needn't keep one eye on God while working in the world; we can keep both eyes on the needs of our students, our children, our clients, on the tasks of farming, planing boards, or cleaning up the kitchen. We serve God inasmuch as we serve these things. Vocation does not require double vision nor double-mindedness.

This Lutheran understanding of vocation may be evidenced in the musical manuscripts of J. S. Bach, several of which I got to view when they were on exhibit in the United States at Yale's Beineke rare book library. As Bach completed each work, whether it was a motet for the Sunday worship or a concerto for the court or a two-part invention for his children's keyboard practice, he would sign, "J. S. Bach, *Ad Majoram Gloriam Dei*" or "*Soli Deo Gloria*." All of these works, the religious no more than the nonreligious, were done in service to the neighbor and thereby to the greater glory of God.

6. Sacrament

Some early followers of Luther were eager to throw away everything associated with the Roman Church. In their fervor for reform they wanted to destroy all that reminded them of the traditional church: the distinction between laity and clergy, vestments and symbols, paintings and statues, and even in some cases church buildings themselves. In spite of being a courageous reformer in many ways, Luther was also conservative and moderate in others. He argued that even where theological argument pointed one way that practical concern for the experience of common people might point in another. So on many issues Luther tried to preserve the patterns that tradition had established.

The Roman Church had maintained there were seven sacraments. Some reformers questioned all of them. Luther used the test of Scripture when it came to examining the issue of the sacraments. What had Christ instituted? What served as a means of grace? Luther argued that using those two tests there should be fewer sacraments: baptism and the Eucharist, the meal in which Christ's body and blood were shared. The traditional Roman understanding of the Eucharist was that the bread and the wine of the meal were literally transformed into the body and blood of Christ in the process of the Mass. Some reformers, by contrast, argued that the language of the words of institution—"This is my body," "This is my blood"—should be understood only symbolically. The Eucharist was, by this reading, simply another occasion to remember Christ's saving grace. Luther argued that Christ's words meant what they said, that Christ was present in the bread and wine. But rather than seeing the Eucharist as the working of a transformation, i.e., what *had been* bread *was now* the body of Christ, Luther saw it as a both/and. For him no magical transformation had taken place. What was bread was still bread and at the same time the body of Christ. It was the real body and blood of Christ, as Luther put it, "in, with, and under" the real bread and wine.

Luther addressed the nature of the sacrament by using the same principle that Christians use in addressing the incarnation. Christ is both truly and fully human and truly and fully God. He is not really one and only apparently the other, as some had argued, nor is he first one and then later the other. The assertion of the incarnation is truly a simultaneous assertion of opposites. Jesus is fully God by being fully human. At this point Christians have been willing to say that logic's principle of noncontradiction must take a back seat. Lutherans would say the same thing about the Eucharist. A paradox or tense conjunction expresses reality more faithfully than any single proposition can.

Though the historical arguments about this issue may seem to contemporary Christians like verbal hair-splitting, the Lutheran affirmation of this both/and has had far-reaching effects in shaping Lutheran thinking. Because of this affirmation Lutherans continue to do several things. (1) They continue to question the absoluteness of apparent opposites: sacred/secular, heaven/earth, the divine/the worldly. So, when asked, "Is it this or is it that?" Lutherans are very likely to answer, "Yes." (2) It has fostered a tendency among Lutherans to find the transcendent in the ordinary, the eternal in the temporal. This can be witnessed to a certain degree in Lutheran architecture, hymnody, art, and literature and in the ways Lutherans understand vocation. (3) It has nurtured in us a kind of earthiness, a reverence for the ordinary that is not so pronounced in more "heaven-bound" forms of Christianity. (4) It has kept us in ecumenical conversation with other sacramental traditions. (5) It has made us suspicious of logical consistency as an end in itself, and willing to explore things that can be affirmed only paradoxically or dialectically.

What is most important to me about sacrament is not to think of it primarily as a separate ceremony but as a way of seeing, a way of regarding all of creation. Sallie McFague expresses something like this as well:

The Christian eye usually does not need any help seeing God. [I'm not so sure of that as she is.] But it does need help seeing the world. . . . My idea of sacrament: holding on hard to the huckleberries, to see all things in God.[20]

Affirmation of incarnation and sacrament is a recognition of God present in the world. Lutherans are not so likely to be supernaturalists (seeing God as above nature) so much as we are sacramentalists—seeing God in nature, in history, in bread and wine and water and word, in the lives of humans, in the life of the church.

7. Theology of the Cross

Early in Luther's theological development he made a distinction that was important for a great deal of his thinking: He contrasted the theology of glory with what he called the theology of the cross. In some ways it is a theme that can be recognized as part of each of the others listed above. Perhaps the best way to explain it is by making the contrasts explicit. Though the distinction is basically Luther's, the language I've used to explain it here comes from many subsequent thinkers.

Theology of Glory	*Theology of the Cross*
Focus on God above the world	Focus on the love of God for the world, working *in* the world
Salvation seen as a rescue *from* the world	Redemption *of* the world, God's embracing the world
Focus on how good we can be	Focus on our own sinfulness
Focus on human progress, accomplishments: focus on penance, piety, pious works	Focus on how sinful we are even (especially) when we attempt piety
Focus on the triumphant Christ, neglect of the crucified Christ	Focus on the cross, grace by means of it
"Cheap grace"	"The cost of discipleship"
Separating ourselves from the suffering and marginalized	Solidarity with the suffering and marginalized
Christianity understood as a religion of security	Christianity understood as a religion of risk
Faith seen as an escape from doubt and despair	Faith seen as engagement of doubt and despair
A theology of answers	A theology of questions

Some contemporary Christian denominations have removed the cross from their church buildings and interiors. Their thinking is that some people will be offended by it. Church, they think, ought to be a pleasant place to be. Certainly an instrument of torture and death should not be displayed in such a place. Should we not focus instead on the positive, on the love of God and the good things God will do for those who love him? As though foreseeing such objections Luther wrote the following theses as part of the argument of his famous Heidelberg Disputation of 1518:

> 16. The person who believes he can obtain grace by doing what is in him adds sin to sin so that he becomes doubly guilty.
>
> 17. Nor does speaking in this manner give cause for despair, but for arousing the desire to humble oneself and seek the grace of Christ.
>
> 18. It is certain that man must utterly despair of his own ability before he is prepared to receive the grace of Christ.
>
> 19. A person does not deserve to be called a theologian who looks upon the invisible things of God as though they were clearly perceptible in those things which have actually happened (Romans 1:20).
>
> 20. He deserves to be called a theologian, however, who comprehends the visible and manifest things of God seen through suffering and the cross.
>
> 21. A theology of glory calls evil good and good evil. A theology of the cross calls the thing what it actually is.[21]

Lutherans see God's love for a sinful humanity in the cross. When God embraces us and our sinful world, that embrace takes the form of the cross. We might wish it were otherwise but that is the reality of it. An ad agent might advise Christians to choose a new logo, but this is the one the suffering and dying God chose. As a consequence the grace of God that comes to us is not an escape from difficulty—the martyrdom of the earliest Christians certainly demonstrated that—but the grace to find redemptive power in that difficulty. The Christian story is not an "and they all lived happily ever after" story. It is the story of Dietrich Bonhoeffer, of Martin Luther King Jr., of Nelson Mandela, of Mother Theresa. The Christian life is not a life of avoidance, pleasantness, and security, but a life of engagement, risk, and embodied hope. The glory of Christ is not the glory of the superhero who avoids destruction, but the glory of a God become fully human, fully one with "the least of these" who bear their own crosses in the world. As Douglas John Hall puts it, "what makes Luther's theology a theology of the cross and not . . . a theology of glory, is that the gospel is for him not the good news of *deliverance from* the experience of negation so much as it is the permission and command to enter into that experience with hope."[22]

Curtis Thompson rightly reminds us, however, that we ought not take the theology of the cross as the denial that God's glory is manifest. He writes, "There needs to be developed, I think, a renewed appreciation for the notion of glory that is both central to the biblical story and relevant to contemporary theological thinking. I define glory as the sparkling presence of God shining through human beings and the world of creation." He continues, "the theology of the cross points to a dialectic or tension. . . . But sometimes that theology becomes so onesidedly negative that it loses its tensive quality."[23]

What the theology of the cross affirms is that the same God who is the author of creation embraces that creation in a cruciform way that includes suffering, humiliation, and death. What it corrects is our inclination to be arrogantly religious, to use our faith to overpower, to set ourselves up as the righteous, etc. To worship the God on the cross is to be willing to take our place there, to see the world and ourselves from that point of view. That is not a world-negating view but a world-transforming one.

8. Faith

In some ways it might have made good sense to have faith be the first of the eight themes discussed, because all of the rest are connected to it in one way or another. But I put it last in the hope that these other discussions may have illustrated pretty well already what a Lutheran understanding of faith would be.

Faith is relational; specifically, it is the relationship of a person to God. This is implied by what we said in the discussion of creation, that humans are created and continually called to be in relationship to their creator. This relationship is the grounding condition of our humanity; everything else about who humans are, what they have done, what they have become, what they may hope springs out of the basic fact of this relationship. Discussions of sin, grace, freedom, vocation, sacrament all are chapters, as it were, of the overriding truth that we stand in relationship. This is why faith is closely related to openness as well as to hope.

Faith is holistic, i.e., it is the response of the whole person, not just a response of our intellect or will or emotions or some other part. That is why belief and our feelings can be part of faith but are never the whole of faith. That is why faith can survive the loss of belief and the struggles of belief, why it can survive depression and despair, why it can abide through terrible loss and profound confusion. Someone who doubts that should read the Psalms. They are a strong expression of the depth of faith in situations where despair and doubt and confusion are very present.

Faith is ultimate; it is not just one more thing that may be added to an already full life, but it is the ultimate grounding or orientation of life itself. Paul Tillich wrote about faith as "ultimate concern." It has to do with what we hold to be ultimately real, ultimately important, ultimately good, ultimately loved. Faith is that relational point where all the deepest questions we can ask intersect. Where there is no depth, where everything is given over to shallow and glib answers (no matter how religious they might be), there is very little faith. About faith Luther writes, "Faith is not the human notion and dream that some people call faith. . . . Faith is a living, daring confidence in God's grace, so sure and certain that the believer would stake his life on it a thousand times."[24]

Faith is in process. It can grow; it is nourishable. The same thing that expressed our faith when we were young may not adequately express it now. Since it has to do with the whole of us, and with the depth of us, it must grow as those dimensions of ourselves grow. Faith is intimately connected to who we are and who we are becoming. We do not arrive at faith as if it were a final destination; faith is a journey, a continuous experience of being on the road with a long way yet to go. Talk about God is not talk about some remote object, but talk about that which makes us who we are. Talk about faith is naturally connected to talk about grace and freedom and vocation. And faith is nourished by sacrament and all the gifts of the Spirit of God that dwells with us.

In some ways the contemporary world is not hospitable to faith. We have trouble with anything deep or holistic, to say nothing of things requiring life commitment. We live in a world of many specializations and specialties. We meet some of our needs shopping at one store, some shopping at another. We go to a doctor for medical care, to a psychiatrist for mental or behavioral problems, to a masseuse to be physically touched, to a concert to be entertained, etc. Where in all this does the whole person get addressed? We tend to see religious practice as one more specialty among all the others. Where do we address ultimate questions? Our society seems afraid of them; we entertain ourselves well in order to avoid thinking about them or talking about them. So we find we live in a world that is like a flooded parking lot: it is sixty acres in area but only an inch deep. Questions of faith have trouble being heard or understood because, to quote Tillich again, "we have lost our dimension of depth."

Gift and Task – I

The theological themes sketched here and the reformation process they generated (and that generated them) are a gift and a task. The gift is to be unwrapped, to be thankfully received and attended to. The task is to continue in openness to these themes in the tradition so that our thinking and living may be critically and imaginatively informed by them. If we do not bring these theological ideas out where they can be examined, discussed, argued about, imaginatively applied, then we fail to realize them as both gift and task. We need to structure both the necessary space and time for such discussions. To lose the relevance of such themes or to lose the ability to hold such informing discussions is truly the loss of something extremely valuable.

My purpose in this chapter has been to introduce the reader to some things about Luther, Lutheran theology, and some focal Lutheran themes. Some might be disappointed that my treatment of these important theological matters is so brief and sketchy. Doesn't each of these themes deserve a whole chapter? Indeed, I would answer; each deserves a whole book. But it is important to remember that this book is not mainly an essay on Lutheran theology. My interest in each of these themes is in their implications for the way they might inform a Lutheran understanding of university education. So each of these themes will come up again in the discussions that follow.

III.
Whole Humans—Toward a Lutheran Anthropology

And they heard the sound of the Lord walking in the garden in the cool of the day, and the man and the woman hid themselves among the trees of the garden. Then the Lord called to the man and asked, "Where are you?" And the man answered, "I heard you in the garden and I was afraid because I was naked. So I hid myself." And the Lord said, "Who told you that you were naked? Have you eaten from the tree that I commanded you not to eat?" Then the man said, "The woman you gave me, she was the one that gave me the fruit and I ate." And the Lord said to the woman, "What is this you have done?" And the woman replied, "The serpent deceived me and I ate." (Genesis 3:8–13)

Telling the Truth about Humans: How We Approach the Task

I have heard a story about Marco Polo writing back to his friends in Europe after first seeing a rhinoceros on one of his travels. What was it he had just seen? Polo wrote that he had seen a unicorn, but contrary to expectations it was not white, it did not have a smooth hairy coat, it did not have hooves and, finally, it would not be very likely to be embraced by a virgin. Polo proceeded by establishing the species (unicorn) and then describing the differentia (how this thing departed from the "normal" unicorn). This story, apocryphal or not, illustrates the truth that we do not bring an innocent eye to empirical investigation. Our language, our categories, our beliefs shape what we are able and willing to see (he was seeing a unicorn). Realizing this we should come to the project of knowing with care and honesty.

If this is true of our description of a rhino it is certainly also true of our attempt to describe the species of which we are a part. When Spanish explorers encountered the native peoples of the Americas they didn't know for sure whether they were seeing human beings. This issue became a matter of debate, not to be settled by a mere recital of facts. Did the natives have the same problems with the Spanish? Likely so. What shaped their seeing? What shapes ours?

When we tell the human story what do we include, exclude, focus on; what do we assume to be unimportant? Is the human story a story of continual progress? It has certainly been told that way. Is it a story of continual degradation from an ideal state in the distant past? It has been told that way, too. The closest we can come to telling the truth about such a subject is to admit, as clearly as we can, what the assumptions are that inform our seeing. In an important sense that is what we were doing in the last section of the last chapter, where we explicated focal theological themes: connectedness to creation, sin, grace, freedom, vocation, etc.

Telling the Truth about Humans: Some Testimonials

Earlier we noted that God's grace frees us to tell the truth. As Luther put it, "A theology of the cross calls the thing what it actually is." So what is the whole truth about humans, about ourselves? If we set out to tell that truth today could we speak with the optimism of an earlier age?

> Nature has set no limit to the perfection of human faculties . . . the perfectibility of man is truly infinite.
>
> > —Marquis de Condorcet (1794)[1] (written just days before his suicide while imprisoned by his former friends and colleagues of the French Revolution)

> What a piece of work is man.
>
> > —Alexander Pope (1733)[2] (How different that line sounded not so long ago in the musical, *Hair!*)

> The Golden Age of the human species is not behind us, it is before us. It lies in the perfection of the social order. Our fathers did not see it at all. Our children will one day arrive there. It is for us to clear the path.
>
> > —Henri, comte de Saint-Simon (1789)[3]

Once in a while, one still encounters such optimism:

> I'm not the least worried about environmental problems. When the necessity arises, science and technology will once again come to our rescue. For example, if this planet becomes unlivable, we'll just colonize another one. And as far as garbage goes, interstellar space is an infinite landfill.
>
> > —Science professor, Concordia College (1983)

The free market is the means to complete human happiness. With com-

plete market freedom we'll be able to get whatever we want at the price
we're willing to pay. So the only impediments to complete human freedom are those who would limit market freedom in some way or another.
All human striving boils down to economics. Why isn't this as clear to
everyone else as it is to me?

—Student essay, Capital University (2001)

Many recent writers, however, seem to be less clear about humanity
and its prospects.

If someone had described the events of the 20th century to reasonable
Europeans even as late as 1914, they would not have been believed. In fact
they would have been thought quite mad. For it was almost universally
assumed, though not all of the world's problems had been solved, that we,
the human species, had turned the final corner in pursuit of science, sanity, welfare, peace, and justice. This was not the first, nor the last, time
that we have been seriously mistaken about what seemed eminently reasonable.

—François Furet (1995)[4]

There is a question in the air, more sensed than seen, like the approach of
a distant storm, a question I would hesitate to ask aloud did I not believe
it existed unvoiced in the minds of many: "Is there hope for man?" In another era such a question might have raised thoughts of man's ultimate
salvation or damnation. But today the brooding doubts that it arouses
have to do with life on earth, now. . . . For the question asks whether we
can imagine that future other than as a continuation of the darkness, cruelty, and disorder of the past; worse, whether we do not foresee in the human prospect a deterioration of things, even an impending catastrophe of
fearful dimensions.

—Robert Heilbroner (1974)[5]

From Pamnwitz the engineer to Broniewski the poet, the idea of humanity that we have inherited is both fragile and harmful, mortal and murder-
ous, leaving us with two urgent tasks: to preserve the idea of humanity
and to make sure the idea does not kill. . . .

—Alain Finkielkraut (1999)[6]

Now it is less evident than before that man is the superior creature of nature, that his place is to be the dominator and the king. Now it is less evident that all evolution really is evolution, that is to say, an improvement.
. . . In the natural order, evolution merely represents the modification and
adaptation of beings to different conditions, but it doesn't seem to ascend
toward the formation of a superior type of being—and even if it does, man

does not appear to be the miraculous offspring of this large and troubled process.

—William Ospina (1995)[7]

Our last century has had such a litany of war and genocide that we may have become numb to it.

> The bloody massacres in Bangladesh quickly covered the memory of the Soviet invasion of Czechoslovakia, the assassination of Allende drowned out the groans of Bangladesh, the war in the Sinai desert made people forget Allende, the Cambodian massacres made people forget Sinai, and so on and so forth until ultimately everyone lets everything be forgotten.

—Milan Kundera (1982)[8]

And many of our excellent poets sound the same tragic chord, such as T. S. Eliot: "Twenty centuries of human history / Distances from God and brings us closer to dust,"[9] or Wislawa Szymborska: "Our twentieth century was going to improve on the others. / It will never prove it now."[10]

Telling the Truth About Humans: A Creature of Extremes

What does it mean to be human? The only responsible answer to this question must take into account the extremes of human history. To be human is

> to have a history of wars, wars to end wars, and wars to prevent wars;
>
> to have destroyed the civilian populations of entire cities, annihilating people by the millions;
>
> to have repeatedly denied the full humanity of entire populations because of their gender, race, nationality, or beliefs;
>
> to have destroyed the livability of large areas of the earth;
>
> to have knowingly and carelessly annihilated thousands of other animal species;
>
> to have murdered, raped, tortured, and horribly abused each other;
>
> to have grown incredibly rich by exploiting each other and the resources of earth;
>
> to have thought of ourselves all the while as the most rational of all earth's inhabitants and the one set of earth inhabitants among all deserving of divine attention, salvation, or eternal reward.

And at the same time to be human is

> to have generated a few individuals who were willing to live and give their lives for freedom, human rights, peace, the rights of other species, and the care of the earth;

to have inquired about the universe beyond our immediate perceptions;

to have produced cognitive constructs that allow us to predict, and sometimes to know and even understand, the world of which we are part;

to have traveled beyond our home planet and probed our solar system;

to have created deep and joyous modes of human expression in many media;

to have generated modes of worldwide information transferal, sorting, and storage;

to have occasionally achieved sustainable mutually beneficial life patterns with each other and with other species;

to have probed the causal workings of our own bodies, including our own genetic structure, etc.

Such a listing could go on and on. But even a brief list like this one allows us to see that humanity has been capable of going very far—in terms of harm *and* benefit, destruction *and* construction, hatred *and* sympathy, pain *and* joy, narrow-mindedness *and* imagination, shallowness *and* depth, self-congratulations *and* self-criticism, greed *and* service, control *and* liberation.

What Have We Become? A Reflection on the Last Century

R. G. Collingwood commented that "the chief business of twentieth-century philosophy is to reckon with twentieth-century history."[11] And the questions that history poses are very difficult indeed to answer. How was it possible that a country, previously known for the poetry of Goethe, the music of Beethoven, and the philosophy of Kant, all of which affirmed the unity of humankind, should now be known for its wars, ethnic cleansing campaigns, its death camps and human butchery? How was it possible that a philosophy that argued for human liberation, human equality, and a classless society should inspire the imprisonment and mass murder of millions of citizens? How could two completely opposite political outlooks result in almost identical human carnage? And, lest we fall to the temptation of thinking that these things exemplify *their* problem, not ours (after all, we opposed both of *them*, didn't we?), we should face the very real possibility that we here in America will be seen as "the evil empire" of the twenty-first century. And, lest we should see such evils as only a European and American problem, we have only to remember the massive murdering that has been done in the name of ethnic cleansing and religious wars in countries only recently liberated from colonial rule. It is as though people all over the globe could not wait to be free from colonial interference in order to immediately begin killing each other.

We used to think that if we changed the structures of society human problems would be solved. If only we got rid of the poor or the rich, or of the stupid or the well-educated, if only we could get rid of "them," problems would be solved. We used to think that if we liberated people and provided them sufficient freedom, then all their problems would be solved. We used to think that if people's basic material needs were met then problems would be solved. Not so long ago we imagined that if people were properly educated, learned the scientific method, and shed all their superstitions then all our problems would be solved. Some still today think that if only our enemies could be eliminated, if only the axis of evil could be destroyed. . .

Learning from Tragedy

It has been a perennial flaw of us humans to blame our enemies for our problems. I do not think this is believable any longer, yet I hear it spouted weekly in one form or another on the news. On a few occasions in human history we seem to have been able to see beyond such a view. In *The Iliad*, for example, the story is told not as a good guy/bad guy tale but as a tale of tragedy for all concerned. Good and noble men on both sides fall in the dust of battle. In the telling of the tale we come to see the valor and the failures of all of them and weep the death of both Trojans and Achaeans. If anyone is to blame for all this death and destruction, in the Homeric view, it is the gods. This tragic view has some things to recommend it. It certainly is superior to the childish good guy/bad guy chauvinism we hear in most of our movies, a lot of our fiction, and from many of our national leaders.

The view I find most applicable to our twentieth-century situation is the one so aptly captured in the biblical book of the prophet Amos. It shares with Hellenic tragedy several important characteristics. Amos opens his prophetic address by announcing that God intends to destroy the city and the people of Damascus. One can almost hear the cheers of the crowd in Jerusalem who heard this, "Yes! Finally those people in 'Sin City' are going to get what they deserve. The evil empire will be brought down. Three cheers for the Lord!" Then Amos goes on to announce the destruction of the Ammonites, and Gaza, and Tyre, and Edom, all neighbors and traditional enemies of the Hebrew people. Once again the cheers must have gone up around the square. "We knew the Lord would finally punish the wicked! We just can't figure out what has taken him so long. When will the fires begin?"

Finally at the very end of his list Amos announces the destruction of Judah and Israel and the destruction of Jerusalem. Where are the cheers now? The irony of Amos's speech is fierce. The people of Israel and Judah are included in the list of those to be punished by God. Their hate-fueled cheers of moments ago must be burning in their ears. We, like those people of ancient Jerusalem, are all for the destruction of the bad guys, the sinners, as long as we suppose that we are the good guys, the righteous ones. The distinction between us and them is very clear in our minds. But what can we think when we find ourselves on Amos's short list? "Because you have grown rich on other's suffering, because you seek security more than justice, because you wage war and call it peace, because you waste and destroy the earth, because you love your machines more than your children, I will lay you waste, declares the Lord God of hosts."

The "we" of the title of the section above, "What Have We Become?" includes myself and my readers, people mostly in or striving toward the middle class, educated North Americans. Many of us are the inheritors of the European Enlightenment, shaped to some degree by the immigrant experience, our ancestors having "made it" in this new land, but molded largely by the American idea of success, security, and technical and economic progress. We possess or dream of possessing homes, cars, pickups, SUVs, TVs and video players, computers, cell phones. We believe that who a person is, is largely determined by what she or he owns. We shop and consume incessantly in the hope of really "being somebody." We wear brand-name clothes and shoes and display company logos to achieve prestige, identity, and "coolness." Our kids spend countless hours per day captured by our machines—plugged in to TV, CD, or video games. By observing our behavior, if not our words, it would be easy to tell that we regard consumption as the real end and purpose of life. All kinds of other things—work, relationships, education—are understood as means to consumer fulfillment. This shapes our judgment of ourselves and of others, our economics, our legal priorities, our social structure, and even our approach to international relations. It is the "American Way of Life" that we go to war to defend if our fuel and other material resources are threatened.

We Americans have liked to think of ourselves as a peace-loving people, but we are very willing to bring war to other people's homelands. We value security and think it is achieved by keeping other people insecure. We value prosperity and comfort, and part of that comfort is not seeing the suffering our lifestyle may bring to others. We have traveled to the moon and with our space telescopes explore the vastness of the universe. We have explored the interior of the atom and of our own genetic structure, yet in spite of this incredible ability to see, we live as though we could not see beyond the ends of our noses. We live wastefully with very little concern for the fact that few on the planet can live as we do, or that our own life-style is unsustainable, a very temporary thing. Neil Postman has said we are "the worst informed but best entertained" people to ever live on the earth.[12] We value freedom, sometimes fanatically, but are thoroughly conformist and fail to see the irony of this. In one of my classes a couple of semesters ago a group of nine athletic young men regularly sat in the back row. They all wore baseball caps backwards, wore tank-top shirts, and brought to class pop cans into which they spit frequently, since they were all chewing tobacco. One day before class I asked them why they all followed this pattern. Their answer amazed me: "Just to be different." I'm sure this desire for rebellious individuality is also what creates the lines outside of tattoo and piercing parlors across the country. But it isn't only our kids who fall for such stuff. How many successful ads promise us true freedom and individuality if we will only rush down to the store and buy "before they're all gone"?

The amazing thing is that most of us, like the young men in my class, do not see the irony in any of this. In some cases the irony is comic and stupid and fairly harmless, but in many cases the irony is tragic and the harm is incalculable. How have we become so narrow and shortsighted? How have we become so shallow? How have we failed to notice that the economists are not right and that these consumerist attitudes are not virtues?

Paul Tillich, writing in the middle of this last century, analyzed human shallowness as a direct consequence of our ways of knowing and manipulating the world.

> [One source of human shallowness] is the concentration of man's activities upon the methodological investigation and technical transformation of his world, including himself, and the consequent loss of the dimension of depth in his encounter with reality. Reality has lost its inner transcendence or, in another metaphor, its transparency for the eternal. . . . God has been removed from the power field of man's activities. He has been put alongside the world without permission to interfere with it. . . . The result is that God has become superfluous and the universe left to man as its master. . . . Man is supposed to be the master of this world and of himself. But actually he has become a part of the reality he has created, an object among objects, a thing among things, a cog within a universal machine to which he must adapt himself in order not to be smashed by it. But this adaptation makes him a means for ends that are means themselves, and in which an ultimate end is lacking. . . . Man has ceased to encounter reality as meaningful.[13]

But many of us have found a way of coping with all of this, and that is by so limiting our view of ourselves and reality that we do not notice the loss. We focus our attention on the parts of reality that we can manage and deny the rest. Like savvy attorneys in court, we only ask questions the answers to which will fit our view of things. Intellectually we call this reductionism; psychologically it would be called repression. Tillich adds, "This is the neurotic way out which becomes psychotic if reality disappears completely."[14] It is concern about this dose of reality that Carlos Fuentes has in mind when he writes, "High on the agenda for the 21st century will be the need to restore some kind of tragic consciousness."[15]

There have been many kinds of human failures before—failures of knowledge, of foresight, of power; economic failures, political failures, social failures. But I believe that when the history of our species is finally written, the modern period, beginning with Descartes and Bacon and running through our own age, will be noted as *the greatest philosophical failure* of all time. *It is the intellectual reduction of reality and the human that we are living out*, and the full consequences of this reduction have not yet been seen or totally imagined. Tillich's claim that all of this is rooted in our ways of knowing the world and ourselves will be more thoroughly explored in the following chapters.

The Human Image: The Lie of Mastery

Douglas John Hall, one of the most significant theological voices of our time, sees the human species in the process of a struggle. "It is a struggle," he writes, "for a new image of what it means to be human. . . . It is a revolt *against* the most dominant answer to that question given in the modern epoch, that to be human has to do with mastery. And it is an openness *for*, a struggle towards, a quite different answer to that question." Hall continues:

> There is a growing recognition that the human image elaborated by the greatest minds of the past three or four centuries, the image of human mastery, is ultimately annihilating. Increasingly, it is understood that the end of the process that seventeenth century sages began to call "progress," with humanity at its helm, is the denigration and extinction of humanity; that the mastery of nature must inevitably mean the mastery of human nature, the subjection of our own being to the manipulative techniques we have applied to everything else. What is "blowing in the wind" is the terrible premonition that we are being killed by our own vision of our destiny as lords of nature and history!
>
> The idea of mastery is inspired by our desire to transcend nature, to be free from its necessities, to use it for our own ends. However, if to achieve this freedom we must subject ourselves to the political necessities implicit in the implementation of mastery itself, what have we gained?[16]

To put it more concretely, isn't our image of paradise to be able to eternally roam the Mall of America with an infinite shopping cart and credit without limits? Can we even imagine greater freedom than that? Notice how hard it is to see this as an un-freedom, as a total control of mind and spirit. We have sold our soul for a MasterCard account that will never notify us of the bill we have rung up and the interest it has accrued. The sign that this is so is that we do not even miss what we have lost. We have even learned to doubt that such things as souls exist.

Hall continues his argument:

> All the same, the concept of mastery contained an enormous lie from the outset: We simply are not masters. We are neither wise enough nor good enough to be masters. . . . just at the point where human mastery has become a real possibility, the world shows terrible evidence of our lack of wisdom and our lack of goodness. It does not require great powers of observation or insight for anyone today to draw the conclusion that the self-appointed masters of the world have almost ruined it. Moreover, that those in whom the concept of mastery was most inculcated, namely, the northern peoples of the Western Hemisphere, have contributed more than all the others to this ruination.[17]

The alternative to this image of the human as master of the universe Hall refers to as *receptivity*. Hall explains:

> Behind the move toward receptivity as a style of being, there is that profound, half conscious awareness that the preservation of the species depends upon it: that, unless we turn from mastering to serving, from grasping to receiving, from independence to interdependence, we will not last very long on the face of the earth.[18]

The Human Image: Living in Hope

At the conclusion of her book *Who Are We? Critical Reflections and Hopeful Possibilities*, Jean Bethke Elshtain poses the question, "What does it mean to live in hope?"[19] Her answers are so relevant to the topics of this discussion that I want to summarize her insights here. Citing Bonhoeffer, Elshtain argues first of all that we have an obligation to "preserve the preconditions within which factual truth can be recognized," and the conditions within which its force can be felt and regarded. More than a few times in the last century peoples have lost the ability to hear and care about the truth. She believes, and I agree, this is something we are very tempted to do again. Hope, therefore, cares about the truth and creates places where it can be told and be heard and where the giving of solid reasons is expected. "Christian hope," she states, "enlivens reason." She continues to explain that we should "be prepared to offer a reasoned defense of [our] position and to engage interlocutors from a stance of preparedness and openness tethered to an insistence that there is some truth to be found."[20]

Elshtain makes clear how a care for the truth also implies a care for language. She writes:

> Once one acquiesces in euphemisms like "pacification" for harrying and hounding peasants, destroying and looting their homes, and forcing them to become desperate refugees; or "compassion" for killing helpless, imperfect human beings, . . . or "community" for signs in cyberspace, one is on a fast track to the radical loss of meaning that so characterizes our age. . . . When words implode, so do worlds.[21]

Elshtain goes on to say that Christians, those who live in hope, must display in the manner and modes of their own lives what incarnational living in the world is all about. She lays out what the dimensions of such living are: "We are called to cultivate citizens who make visible before the world the fullness, dignity, and wonder of creation—the horror, then, at its wanton destruction."[22]

We are also called to recognize and protect the value of the idea of persons, an idea in the modern world that is about to disappear, as it devolves into an object of knowledge or manipulation on the one hand or into an essence-less subject on the other. Elshtain sees the idea of person, modeled on our understanding of the Trinity, as fundamentally a being-in-relation. She bemoans the ways, in our modern world, that real relationship has devolved into social contract. It is the Christian's task, therefore, to fight against this "one-dimensional, flattened view of human being that a totalizing ideology requires and feeds on. By contrast, the incarnational mind struggles to embody that which is concrete and before us and calls out for recognition, notice, attention."[23]

Elshtain concludes:

> Finally, citizens who are Christians and called, therefore, to live in hope must assure that their churches play a critical role as interpreters of the culture to the culture. This is a critical civic task. There are few such public sites available, especially in the era of media saturation. Remember the complex position of the Christian as pilgrim, poised between the twin poles of *amor mundi* and *contra mundum*. This means one is gifted with the task to transform a wounded culture—not as a messianic project but as a work of grace and love.[24]

What better site from which to begin such a project, and to live out such a hope, than from a Christian university or college prepared to hear and speak the truth because informed by the freeing grace of God?

The Human Image: Toward a Lutheran Anthropology

From all that has preceded, can we begin to piece together a view of the human growing out of a Lutheran theology? I believe we can. Even though the details of it are very open to discussion there are still some general things that can be said that are specific enough to be interesting and deep enough to have profound implications. We will structure this discussion around four themes: the value of humans, the calling of humans, the problem with humans, and finally, the human prospect.

1. The Value of Humans

The psalmist poses the question for us:

> When I consider the heavens, the work of Your fingers,
> The moon and the stars, which You have fixed,
> What is man that You take thought of him?
> And the son of man that You care for him?
> Yet You have made him a little lower than Elohim,
> And crown him with glory and majesty!
> You appoint him steward over the works of Your hands;
> You have put all things under his feet,
> All sheep and oxen,
> And also the animals of the field,
> The birds of the heavens, and the fish of the sea,
> And whatever passes through the paths of the seas.
> O Lord, our Lord,
> How majestic is Your name in all the earth! (Psalm 8:3–9)

In our contemporary world, when we have even more reason to marvel at the sun, the moon, the stars, the galaxies, the unfathomable expanses of cosmic time and space, we have even more reason to wonder about who we are, why we are here, and what our being here is all about. Reviewing our own history, we have more reason than the psalmist to wonder why God would bother with us at all. The Judeo-Christian traditions respond to that wonder, affirming that humans are part of God's creation, a part that God is particularly concerned with and in dialogue with. Like a parent and like a spouse, the two metaphors the Bible most often uses, God cares about us, frets over us, covenants with us, is disappointed in us, rescues us, and continues to embrace us. It isn't because we deserve this attention. Just as a parent loves the infant that she has borne, the love doesn't flow out of anything the baby has accomplished. Rather, it is the other way around, the relationship comes first and the personality of the child grows out of the soil of parent love. So it is with humans. So the first part of this anthropology is to affirm that we, humans, are God-loved. That is a simple thing to say; it may have even become platitudinous to many of us. But it is really quite an amazing thing to say as well. For the claim is this: the creator of the universe takes a loving interest in us. All of us!

This vision has the power to bring us to regard ourselves and each other in a new way. Emmanuel Levinas states:

> Monotheism is not an arithmetic of the divine. It is, perhaps, a gift from on high that makes it possible to see man's similarity to man beneath the continuous diversity of individual historical traditions.[25]

And the Apostle Paul stated the insight in a Christian vocabulary in such a thoroughly radical way:

> There are no more distinctions between Jew and Greek, slave and free, male and female, but all of you are one in Christ Jesus. (Galatians 3:28)

Many philosophers and political theorists have written about human dignity, human rights, human equality, human justice, and the moral necessity to care for each other. But why should we? Why shouldn't humans be treated as we treat other animals? Why shouldn't we use them merely as means to our own ends? Why is there anything wrong with slavery? Why not use humans for pack animals, or draft animals or, for that matter, as animals to be eaten? At this point we resort to the language of human dignity, human rights, human consent, etc. But what is all that rooted in? I think that a careful examination would show how much of our morality as well as our political axioms have grown out of this biblical conception of the human. The human is a living soul, in conversation with and cared for by God.

Aristotle, certainly one of the greatest moral theorists of all time, maintained that slavery was the worst human life imaginable simply because a slave could not act toward her own self-fulfillment. No one asks a slave, "What would you like to accomplish with *your* life?" The slave's life was not his own. The slave was a means to the master's self-fulfillment. But in spite of this judgment Aristotle did not argue for the abolition of slavery because he believed, on empirical grounds, that some people were not capable of directing their own lives toward self-fulfillment. The best they could do, he thought, was to have their lives directed for them by someone naturally superior to them. This benefited not only the master but, in the case of "natural slaves," the slaves themselves. Lest we congratulate ourselves too quickly for being beyond such antiquated thinking, we have only to notice how often we defend social, economic, and political inequalities with much the same argument. We may not argue for slavery anymore. At least we don't use that word. But many inequalities in the world are justified on the grounds that "they don't deserve any better," or "they wouldn't be able to make use of a good education if they had it," or "they don't know what's good for themselves," or "they need someone to manage their affairs for them."

How could Thomas Jefferson possibly have penned the words, "We hold these truths to be self-evident, that all men are created equal, that they are endowed by their creator with certain inalienable rights. . ."? Wasn't it obvious to him that people are not observably equal in any way? What, then, was he writing about? What moved him, again and again, to try to abolish slavery? What kind of equality did he see? What kind of equality does all this talk of human rights and dignity presuppose? I do not know any satisfactory answer to this question (that is, an answer that does not beg the question) except to say that we are all equal *in the sight of God*, and that God-relatedness is the ground of our inalienable rights and our dignity, our intrinsic value as persons.

My five children are not equal in musical and artistic talent, athletic accomplishment, financial worth, common sense, knowledge of math, science, economics, or the law. They are equal only in the sense that they are equally cared for, equally worried about, equally important to and loved by their parents. That nonempirical relational equality is nonetheless real.

So, to conclude, we begin our anthropology by saying that humans are valued. Their value is not equal to their utility. Humans are not just means to ends, but ends themselves, as Kant put it. They are valued because of their relationship to the God in whose presence we are all children, all brothers and sisters. There are things that distinguish us, of course, but our fundamental relatedness underlies and ultimately overrules those differences.

Humans, as a consequence of this relatedness to God, are not one-dimensional creatures, and we should resist every attempt to make us such. Think of the humanity-denying work of these epithets: "vermin," "beasts," "wild," "vegetables," "savages," and in more academically respectable circles, "labor force," "occupants," "contacts," "suits," "geeks," "chicks," "deviants." But most of all we must be aware of the ways in which our disciplines reduce the human to data, to resources, to subjects, to objects of different manipulable sorts. Students tend to think of their education as merely a means to economic ends because that is the way they have learned to view themselves, mainly as economic functions, and therefore valuable only for their abilities to produce and consume significantly. In this contemporary world, many of us fail to value ourselves. If truth be told we, like manikins, are valued for what we *have*, not for what we *are*. We become objects on which other objects (logos, brand names) can be displayed. For many having and being are assumed to be the same thing.

2. The Calling of Humans

As humans we are *called by God*. God has expectations of us. These expectations are as multidimensional as our identity. God invites us to answer his call with our lives. We are first of all *called to be creatures*, to recall our basic connectedness with the rest of the creation, appreciating and celebrating it. Second, we are *called to be human*, to be creatures in conversation, responsible because response-able to God. Third, we are *called to be stewards*, caretakers of the world that does not belong to us but to God. Fourth, we are *called to be brothers and sisters* with other humans, working for peace, for justice, for the basic respect that all humans need, that enables all human becoming, working to realize the kingdom of God that Jesus witnessed to as present in our midst. Finally, we are *called to serve* where we are, those we are given to serve, with the gifts we have available to us for service. We are called not to be some generic human, but *called to be our particular selves* and to realize that self in particular and concrete service to the needs of particular others.

3. The Problem with Humans

Sin is precisely the denial of the elements of the calling listed above. Sin is the denial of our creaturehood and the assertion of our self-creation, the denial of our fundamental relatedness and the assertion of our independence, the denial of our responsibility and the assertion of our being answerable to no one, the denial of our stewardship and the assertion of our ownership and mastery. As Douglas John Hall puts it, echoing Luther, "Sin is humanity's refusal to accept our own nature."[26]

As humans we live in sin, in alienation from the God who loves us. This alienation manifests itself in many ways, in our misrelation to nature, in our misrelation to ourselves, in our misrelation to each other. And each of these is also a misrelation to God. Though sin takes many forms, its basic reality is rebellion born out of the desire to be the owner, not the steward; to be the master, not the one who serves; to be the focus of attention, not one essentially related. We strive to do all this because we cannot accept ourselves as God-loved. So we try to establish ourselves by our own accomplishments rather than finding ourselves in relationship as cared-for as well as one-who-cares.

My longtime friend and colleague Don Luck has suggested that the human condition is like addiction in many respects. As long as we think of sin as something that those "others" do, as the problem that "they" have, we have not made even the first move. As with an addiction, the first step is to recognize that one has a problem—in a deeper sense, that one *is* the problem. The second step is to recognize that, as a consequence, it is not a problem that one can willfully, by one's own resources, solve. People I know who have been involved with twelve-step recovery programs say that the person who promises to solve the problem and "never do it again" has not really understood the depth of the difficulty. He will, they predict, "crash and burn" before he is ready to reach out for help. Sin, like addiction, requires remorse and repentance and forgiveness. But beyond all that it requires help. Only the person who has gone beyond being able to help himself, Luther maintained, can accept the help that has been there, offered as a gift from the beginning. The miracle is that addicts, never free from their addiction, can live beyond addiction. The miracle is that humans, never free from sin, can live beyond it. That is the dynamic of sin and grace. If we recognize and admit our alienated condition then we must be particularly alert to things in our own behavior, in our own thinking, and in our own history that have lead us into disaster. Like addicts, we must be constantly alert for those things that most tempt and spell disaster for us.

4. The Human Prospect

Frequently the analysis of human problems is followed by a statement about "what we must do now." Philosophers have thus proposed a new worldview, reformers called for a new moral vigor, politicians a new program, revolutionaries for the overthrow of those in power, etc. But what I have argued in the foregoing pages is that we have very good reasons to be skeptical and suspicious of such salvation attempts. The theological source of that skepticism and suspicion is our recognition of sin. The historical source is our recognition of the horrible evils that have been justified in the name of noble ideals and projects.

Does this imply, then, that we retire in hopeless and helpless despair? No, not at all. Because ours is a *caring* skepticism we cannot abandon thinking, imagining, envisioning, reforming. But because ours is a caring skepticism we cannot be naive or blind either. Because ours is an *engaged* suspiciousness we cannot retire from the world to complain bitterly about it while attempting nothing. We cannot abandon our particular places in an attempt to become "a citizen of the cosmos," as did Diogenes the Cynic.

Dietrich Bonhoeffer returned to his ministry in a Germany that he knew was thoroughly corrupt and headed in disastrous directions. There he labored until (and even after) he was arrested, trying to realize a new humanity in the midst of horrible inhumanity. Martin Luther King Jr. led boycotts, marched in marches, dreamed dreams, and spoke hard truths. But he did not do any of this naively or arrogantly. Both embodied the tense conjunctions of caring and skepticism, engagement and suspicion, realism and hope that were necessary.

Returning to and following one step further the addiction analogy employed earlier, no one needs to be more realistic about his condition than an addict. But this grim realism does not move one away from hope; instead it is the only path toward it. This is the difference between optimism and hope. Douglas John Hall explains:

> Christianity, at its roots, assumes that the human situation is such that we cannot save ourselves. It is, therefore, closer to the pessimistic than the optimistic disposition, in terms of its analysis of the human condition. Finally, however, it surpasses the "childish categories" (Heidegger) of pessimism and optimism. . . . Unlike the pessimistic disposition to existence, Christianity does not end in withdrawal or resignation. . . . It does not describe the darkness, but the light that can only be seen in the darkness.[27]

As a consequence, I think we have to refer to this view, informed by the Lutheran understanding of sin, grace, and the theology of the cross, as *realistic hope*. We can move into our own future only by telling the whole truth about ourselves, by noticing that we, as humans, still have the same tendencies and temptations that have lead us so horribly astray already, and by accepting God's grace and "being there" for each other. Luther would say that humans have a prospect only insofar as they put themselves in service to God. When we attempt to go on our own, to be the masters of our own ship, to run our own lives, to shape history by our own bright ideologies, we are doomed to repeat, at best, the worst horrors of our own past. Perhaps we will go down in history as surpassing the holocausts already devised. God have mercy on us!

The Educational Problematic: For Us by Us?

Suppose we were given the task of educating this human creature, intentionally shaping the creature's self-becoming. What would one do? How would one do it? That, by itself, is a task so daunting that I am tempted to respond to the challenge by saying what my friend Sig Royspern many times has said: "I'd sooner stay home and hit myself with a stick." But the truth is, that is not the half of it. For not only must this human creature, this embodiment of extremes, be educated, it must be educated by its own efforts. The education we would accomplish is to be *for us*, but it also has to be *by us*. The human creature has been left the task of educating itself. What is the likelihood that that will turn out well? Is it too obvious to say that we have to enter into this project with our eyes wide open? That we must do it self-critically, with an acute awareness of our most common fallacies and temptations? That we must enter into it humbly and carefully, knowing the many times we have quite thoroughly botched the job? That we have to enter into it prayerfully? Yet in spite of all these hesitancies it is a task we also must do boldly, for if we do not do it we leave the job of education to the culture, to those who have a particular agenda to serve by doing it. And I, for one, think that would be and has been a horrible mistake.

Sometimes humans have been pictured as a good/evil duality, as two personae confined in one body like the little angel and devil we see in thought balloons of cartoons. If that were the case, then an excellent education would be to establish the right order within the person. This is something like what Plato suggests in his *Republic*. There he pictures justice as the proper ordering of parts of the *psyche*. One part rules over another and they together rule over the unruly third. A good education helps to establish this order, and a good state, with its laws and institutions, helps maintain it. Freud suggested something quite similar in his earlier writings.

But what if Luther was right, that we are *simul justus et peccator*, not only both saint and sinner but *both at the same time and in the same respect*? What if, for example, human accomplishments and human destructiveness are not expressions of opposite parts of the human, but expressions of the same thing? What if it is the best part of us that goes wrong? Is that the meaning of the story about Adam and Eve in the garden who ate the fruit from one tree that was the tree of the knowledge of *both* good and evil? What would follow for our understanding of human knowing, human learning, human teaching? Let me suggest three things we need to seriously consider.

(1) The powers of human imagination are necessarily linked to the powers of abstraction. An architect imagines a building as floor plan or section. In order to do so she must abstract from many aspects of humanly experienced space. A physicist imagines masses in gravitational fields. In order to do so he must abstract from many aspects of the bodies considered. These aspects are irrelevant to his study, though they may be very relevant to him in some other facet of his life. This is not how he experiences the world, but it is how his science requires that it be seen. An economist imagines the world as a network of realities measurable in monetary units. This imagined world is an abstraction of certain features from among a continuum of features including ones the architect and the physicist (and the economist herself in a different context) find relevant. Only certain measurable features of the world enter into an architect's, a physicist's, or an economist's way of imagining. The world thus imagined

is simplified and clarified. The relations between focal quantities are expressible in formulas. The economist's quantities do not fit as variables in the physicist's formulas; the physicist's do not fit the economist's formulas either. Different features of the same thing (e.g., of steel girders or the midday sun) may appear in the imaginatively clarified worlds of all three thinkers.

Human imagination and focused attention allow us to perceive and interpret the world in many patterns. The variation in those patterns of imagination/abstraction make possible such widely diverse things as space flight and short stories, computers and mythology, skyscrapers and pornography, relativity physics and the works of Shakespeare, chemistry and ethics. Because each is an imaginative reconstruction of the world, it is an abstraction of the world. Because each focuses something in, it also focuses something out. Because each expresses a way things are, each also expresses a way things are not. Each is able to tell *a truth* because each does not tell *the truth*.

Herein lies one of the sources of our difficulty as humans. We have been so highly and perhaps naturally impressed by what we have been able to see and understand from our imagined/abstracted points of view that we have become seduced into thinking that these abstractions are reality itself. So we have created religions on the basis of our mythologies, and schools of thought on the basis of our disciplines. We have declared alternative views heresies, reduced others' ways of thinking to nonsense, and persecuted those who have not occupied our thought-world, calling them savages, uncivilized, and uneducated; calling those who did not know our stories and languages illiterate and barbarian. We have turned these abstracted worlds into playing fields on which all must play in order that we can win and they will lose. Their loss justifies their poverty and disenfranchisement. They cannot complain. They had their chance. We have called it equality of opportunity.

Thus our accomplishments in imagining and abstracting have often been accompanied by claims for the comprehensiveness, absoluteness, and exclusivity of the views based on them. The appropriate response to this realization is not to abandon or accuse this human ability to imagine and abstract. The proper response to learning that tools can be dangerous is not to stop using them. The proper response is to be much more critical of our own claims to exclusivity and comprehensiveness. We must realize that it does not follow from the fact that my view reveals *a* truth about the world that alternative views must be presumed false. Monet painted many pictures of Rouen Cathedral. Each of them does not refute the others. He was not a failure for not being able to paint *the* picture. Our failure lies not in imagining and abstracting, but in taking our imaginings and abstractions as *the* truth, the whole truth, and nothing but the truth. It isn't that we need to find a newer, truer view. We need to find the power to criticize ourselves honestly and then go on to celebrate the variety of our own and other's limited successes. Let us be happy we have as many paintings of Rouen Cathedral as we have without lamenting the fact that we do not have *the* picture of Rouen Cathedral, whatever in the world that might be.

When applied to human life patterns—political, social, economic—these absolutized abstractions become ideologies. Robert Conquest refers to our tendency to think in terms of them as "ideolatry." He writes:

> The huge catastrophes of our era have been inflicted by human beings driven by certain thoughts. And so history's essential questions must be: How do we account for what has been called the "ideological frenzy" of the twentieth century? How did these mental aberrations gain a purchase? What was the sort and condition of the people affected? Who were the Typhoid Marys who spread the infection?[28]

He later continues:

> But the world can no longer afford the rise of revolutionary-ideologues, any more than it can afford nuclear war—in part because the takeover of states by ideolaters must lead to gross inhumanity, and may lead to nuclear confrontations.[29]

So we must recognize this tendency in ourselves, this perennial temptation to absolutize our own ideas and outlooks and institutions. We have done this in politics; we have done it in religion; I fear we are doing it now in economics. I vividly remember a particular scene from Jacob Bronowski's TV series, *The Ascent of Man*. In one of the latter episodes Bronowski is shown squatting in a shallow pond of water, scooping up water and mud in his hands. As he does so he speaks these words:

> There are two parts to the human dilemma. One is the belief that the end justifies the means. That push-button philosophy, that deliberate deafness to suffering, has become the monster in the war machine. The other is the betrayal of the human spirit: the assertion of dogma that closes the mind, and turns a nation, civilisation, into a regiment of ghosts—obedient ghosts, or tortured ghosts. . . .
>
> This is the concentration camp and crematorium at Auschwitz. This is where people were turned into numbers. Into this pond were flushed the ashes of some four million people. And that was not done by gas. It was done by arrogance. It was done by dogma. It was done by ignorance. When people believe that they have absolute knowledge, with no test in reality, this is how they behave. This is what men do when they aspire to be gods.[30]

(2) Many human virtues are, as Aristotle long ago pointed out, the mean between extremes. Temperance, one of Aristotle's examples, is by definition the mean between debauchery and abstinence. Courage is the mean between cowardliness and foolhardiness. Finding this mean is not an automatic nor easy thing. It involves some experience, trial with the possibility of error, and practice. Family loyalty is generally a good thing. A certain amount of it is a necessary part of a functioning family. But family loyalty can clearly be carried to an absurd, even criminal extreme. The Mafia is probably the best example of this. Team loyalty can be a fine thing. Playing hard for one's team makes the level of competition exciting and exhilarating. But such loyalty carried out to an absurd degree ends by justifying gang warfare. National and even racial loyalty likewise can be a good thing, but if not tempered it can be carried to destructive extremes—fascism, loyalty tests, witch hunts, and nationalistic war-mongering among them. Perhaps every good thing can be pushed to an insane extreme. This is true of love, cleanliness, fear, carefulness, masculinity, femininity, property, and the desire for clarity, certainty, success, purity, and security. In all of this lies the making of many a great tragedy.

What is it about extreme cases that make them tempting to us? First of all, they require less thought. Extremes are clearer, less ambiguous, more easily identified, less easily misunderstood. We may, for example, morally object to some extreme forms of censorship. But we may also object to some extreme forms of pornography. Rather than carefully thinking through the issue to find a workable middle ground, we are apt to not want to think about it at all. So we take the extreme routes of no thought and no action, thereby leaving the issue in someone else's hands. Whose hand is that likely to be? It will be someone who feels strongly enough about the issue to do something about it, a person who occupies the one extreme or the other. The person who does try to sort through an issue like this makes herself vulnerable to attack from both sides. There is a kind of "moral purity" that the extremist position enjoys. From the extremists' point of view the person searching for a workable mean is "soft on pornography" and "soft on censorship" simultaneously.

There is also a certain kind of emotional momentum that drives us toward extremes. If we begin by thinking that thinness is good we may end up being anorexic. If we begin by thinking eating is good we may end up overweight. It is as though once started in a direction we cannot stop till we reach the extreme. Children sometimes say, "If I can't have it all I don't want any!" The frustrated adolescent whose model-building or homework project doesn't work out may destroy what he has made in a rage. As William James expressed it, "The best is often the worst enemy of the better."

We often celebrate extremism in our heroes and myths because extreme cases are colorful and interesting. Paul Bunyan harvested every white pine in the north woods; John Wayne is 100% man; Superman has every power; St. Francis gave away all his worldly goods; the people on our side are completely good and the enemy is "the evil empire." Such thinking is clearly childish fictional excess, but unfortunately it is fictional excess that ends up shaping our attitudes and actions and, in some cases, our national policy. It is fortunate that there are some *responsible* storytellers to remind us that beasts can also be beauties and beauties can be beasts, that Darth Vaders can also be our own parents, that yesterday's enemies can be tomorrow's bedfellows.

(3) Of the many virtues that we have discovered, passed along, and been educated in, the most important and most neglected may be what I would call the *critical virtues*. The first requirement of rationality is that a person be corrigible, open to correction. Yet we often celebrate the virtues of belief and obedience, being true do-or-die believers, asking no questions, convincing ourselves of our own wonderfulness and of the wonderfulness of our ways of looking at things. We have not learned to take criticism well; even less have we learned to seek it out. We enter into arguments not to learn but to convince. We enter into the rhetoric of business not to inform the free market but to subliminally sell. We enter into political debate not to inform the electorate but to create smoke screens and control the voter. We have become cynics about our own political process because we do not maintain a critical standard there. We have become cynical regarding our news media because we do not maintain a critical standard there, either. The best-selling national newspapers run headlines about movie stars' love affairs and drug problems, nine-headed babies, and Elvis reincarnations. We blame our media and blame our politicians, but we have only ourselves to blame. We have to say to ourselves, and to those who promote this nonsense and those who profit thereby, "We won't accept this!"

A person who deliberately misleads customers does not support the free market; he erodes it just as a counterfeiter does. An office seeker who deliberately misleads the electorate cannot possibly believe in "government by *consent* of the governed." Such a politician is, in fact, a hater of democracy. It is far from clear to me why we tolerate either behavior. But we are in much worse shape than this—we not only tolerate it but have come to *expect* it.

More than anything else *we, as human beings, need to be critical of our own abstractions, particularly of all those abstractions that claim ultimacy*. Is there an image of success that steers my life, that tells me what I, as a man or woman, ought to look like, what I ought to wear, how I ought to act, when I can feel good about myself and when I ought to feel awful, out of it, uncool? Does it dictate to me that I am too fat, too thin, too dark, too light, too old, too young, too female, too male, too serious, too playful, too emotional, too calculating, etc.? If there is such an image (and it seems to me there always is), we need to make it explicit and put it out where it can be criticized. Where does the image come from? Who is paying to have it put in front of us? Who profits from it and who suffers from it? What stereotype does it create or reinforce? What am I being sold? What will it end up costing? Who, finally, will pay that bill?

Our country may be arming for war or defense (there has never been a time in my life when it was not). What great threat are we avoiding? Who says it is a great threat? Who profits by there being such a threat? Whose behavior is thought to be unpatriotic, un-American, in the face of this threat? Will a war actually produce a beneficial result? Is there any historical reason to think that this is so? Will the loss of our men and women produce a great good or avoid a great evil? Is this evil enemy someone who only a short time ago was an ally? Have they recently been possessed by a demon? Have we?

Are certain beliefs and methods dominating my work or discipline? What argument can be made for their superiority over other beliefs and methods? Are people who disagree thought to be unprofessional? Are there certain ideas that make me fly into a rage? Why can't I discuss them rationally? What is it I find so frightening about them? Why should I find an idea to be threatening? Do I need to think in certain ways in order to get promoted, to be considered successful? Who profits from this orthodoxy? Who becomes an outsider or heretic thereby? What are the enforcement systems that I am complicit in?

In every aspect of our lives we are presented with partial truths that are promoted as the whole truth, abstractions presented to us as reality, images that are given to us as norms. We must in every case ask the hard, critical questions. We must ask these questions not only when we find ourselves in disagreement with these "truths," "realities," and "norms," but most especially when we hear no one disagreeing with them. Whenever someone begins by saying, "Everyone knows...," or "It's common sense that...," or "All right-thinking people agree...," it's time for someone to say, "Hold everything. No one is everyone without me! Explain this again."

Whenever we find the asking of critical questions to be unpopular, whenever we find orthodox belief and blind obedience to be the highest virtues, we are in serious trouble. We are about to beat someone over the head with our version of reality, truth, beauty, or goodness. We are in danger of becoming historical examples of humans willing to destroy for the sake of their abstractions.

Being open and being critical may not be the most exciting of human excellences, but I believe they are the most important, for these are what can prevent our other human excellences from becoming madness. A critical spirit and sharpened critical tools are necessary. We should acquire them, practice them, and teach them. We should learn to be thankful for criticism, even and especially when it comes to us. It is nice to be thought right, even when this thought is something of a delusion. But it is better by far to be learning—i.e., growing toward the truth, even a truth larger than our ability to process it.

Answerable Knowing?

The question should naturally arise: Isn't there a mode of knowing that goes past abstraction and the criticism of abstractions? Isn't there a mode of knowing whereby we can see *the* truth in all its fullness and complexity?

The history of ideas is full of attempts to find a view that is *the* view. As Immanuel Kant suggested, there may be something in the human psyche that drives it continually in pursuit of such a view of things. This driving toward a larger vision, a fuller reality, is certainly not a bad thing, provided that it is accompanied by the utmost humility and self-honesty. For our temptation, as we have seen, is always to claim that our own view, crabbed and abstracted as it is, is *the* view, is Absolute Reality and Truth itself. Then we are back where we were at our worst.

But imagine a concrete situation like the following: A parent, who has been abusive to his children and mate, by some miracle finally faces up to his own violence and the violence it has done. Perhaps he now sees this same violence in his children. Perhaps he also sees his own violence as a legacy from his parents' distorted view of life. They in turn had this as inheritance from their parents, and so on. This man now sees himself as one point in a whole network of causes and effects of violence received and violence done. We know that it is possible on rare occasions for such a man to see himself in a new way, as at once responsible person and victim, as standing in need of his family's forgiveness and standing in need of forgiving, as standing in the spotlight of his family's anger and disappointment and standing in the place where honesty and real love can begin.

The realization of such a person on such an occasion may come as close to the kind of truth and reality that we seek as any can. Here we have *a kind of knowing that requires radical honesty and self-knowledge, a kind of knowing that requires radical humility, a knowing of oneself as connected and as reconnecting, a knowing as mutual responsibility and mu-*

tual affirmation, a knowing related to forgiveness, compassion, and the hope for new community.

One could have such a realization as a person who has done violence to one's family. One could also imagine it as the realization of a person who has done violence to other races, to other species, even to the planet itself. In each case what we might be able to come to know is what kind of violence our modes of knowing are, what kind of being we are among other beings, and to know ourselves as having new possibilities held out to us by others to whom we hold ourselves out as a new possibility.

This kind of knowing does not escape any of the problems and limitations of human knowing. Its power comes from admitting and in some way realizing those very limitations, for it is the interconnectedness and acceptance of ourselves as connected and mutually limited that we will realize. But this kind of realization leaves us with new possibilities. To love someone is to behold them simultaneously as how they are and as how they can be. And love has tremendous transformative power.

The example I have used to describe such a possibility of knowing/self-knowing is very interpersonal. But I believe the same kind of knowing/self-knowing can arise as one confronts the world and our ways of knowing it. We can, perhaps, even come to know ourselves as the knower, destroyer, favored child, monster, as well as responsible caregiver, lover, and nurturer of our planet.

What should we call such a knowing? Many names suggest themselves: "embedded knowing," "loving knowing," "transformative knowing" among them. There are things I like about each of these suggestions. But the one I prefer combines many of the features of the others while stressing the feature of the human wherein we reflect the image of God, and contrasts most vividly with epistemological paradigms that pervade our culture. So I have called it "answerable knowing." The dimensions of such knowing we will explore in the two chapters to follow.

Learning toward Human Maturity?

Immediately after the dropping of the first nuclear weapons on Hiroshima and Nagasaki, Norman Cousins, then the editor of Saturday Review, wrote an editorial titled, "Is Modern Man Obsolete?"[31] In that article he argued that the human species had reached a crossroads. The possession of weapons of such devastating power required the human species to now grow up. We could no longer carry on as adolescents playing good guy/bad guy war games. Now our weapons are capable of destroying all life on the planet. The bellicose behavior that might have been tolerable in a species that had used small weapons in isolated wars now had become disastrous—the human species, having invented such weapons, now needed to invent sufficient maturity not to play war any more.

What has happened? We have gone on playing war. We have produced and stockpiled increasingly sophisticated nuclear weapons. But we have not used them in combat situations since Hiroshima and Nagasaki. Is this a sign of our maturity or is it only a sign of our good luck? Realistically, perhaps, a little bit of both. We now know how close we have come to irrevocable nuclear holocaust. This issue has not gone away. Our readiness and eagerness to play war is still a fact more than half a century after Nagasaki. Our maturity as a species is still very much in doubt. We still have the possibility of acting like very spoiled children, armed to the teeth with technologically sophisticated means of mass death.

But this is only one crisis we face. Another one, and by far the more unavoidable one, is the crisis of the environment, for here we have only two possibilities as a species: grow up now and learn to live sustainably, or continue on the path of unsustainable life patterns that will lead to planetary disaster. In the case of the environment, unlike the case of our military history, luck will have nothing to do with it. There are only two ways to live anywhere: sustainably, or in a temporary state of unsustainability. We have been pursuing the latter course for some time now and have not quit accelerating in that direction. A few of us have tried to walk toward the back of that mindless parade, but almost none of my acquaintance have turned around and started to walk the other way.

So, what is required of us as a species? We must learn to live on the earth in sustainable patterns, not patterns that imply future disaster. We must learn to grow our food without depleting the viability of the soil. We must live without producing poisons that will eventually make the planet unlivable. We must recognize the interconnectedness of our lives with the lives of other animal and plant species on the planet. We must quit seeing the earth as our private resource and garbage bin. We must realize that most of our ideas of prosperity are fundamentally a form of greed, and that greed is a form of stealing. We must realize that our high standard of living is really a lie in the same way that living off credit cards is—pretending that those bills will not ever come due, pretending there is no bill to pay.

William Ruckelshaus has argued that never before in the whole history of the human species have we been required to make such a drastic change in behavior and values as the environmental crisis will require of us.[32] The twentieth century has been a century of incredible change. What we have not foreseen is that the biggest change yet is required—a fundamental change in the level of maturity and responsibility of the human race. What is the likelihood that such a change can be made? What is the likelihood that it can be made in time? Viewed objectively, the probabilities of change are not very high. We have not gone very far down the road toward change. Public and planetary welfare is still being sacrificed for private greed.

But fortunately we cannot view this problem objectively. Probabilities are not the realities of human life, because everything we value is tied up in the outcome. So we cannot talk about this problem as though it were something that hypothetically might happen to someone, sometime. My recognition of the problem, and the directions that human change toward responsibility must go, must be accompanied by the realization that these things must begin with me and my present mode of living. It isn't someone else's behavior I must change first. It is my behavior—multiplied times millions like me, so change must begin with me.

These two realities, continuing war and planetary unsustainability, by themselves provide us with a complex agenda for the education of the human race. We do, as a species, seem addicted to war-making and to the despoliation of the planet. Is recovery possible? I have a friend and former student who worked for many years as an addiction counselor. He told me, "If you asked me at the first meeting what was the probability that an addict could recover, I'd have every time said, 'one in a million.' But over and over again I saw miracles occur. The addict didn't cure himself and I sure as hell didn't cure him, but somehow it happened again and again. I did this for years and I still don't understand it any better than that. The only thing to say is, 'Miracle occurs here.'"

What is the task of knowing, of learning together, of teaching, that we must pursue given a world like this one, given humans like we are? How do we proceed? What gifts do we, as educators informed by the Lutheran vision, have to bring to this task? These are questions I have tried to wrestle with in this chapter and the ones to follow. We have no reason to be optimistic. In fact we have many reasons to be very pessimistic. But fortunately our lives as Christians are not fueled by optimism or pessimism. They are fueled by faith and hope in a God who works miracles, a God who loves us, a God who is present in our midst, a God who suffers with us, a God who can use the fallible efforts of people like my former student and like ourselves to transform lives and thereby the world.

Gift and Task – II

It is my contention that a holistic and realistic view of human nature is one of the gifts of the Lutheran tradition, particularly as it informs the work of higher education. The ability to take such a bold and honest look at human being flows out of Luther's idea that it is by grace that we are saved and by God's doing that we are loved, not out of any effort or avoidance on our part. It also flows out of Luther's notion of the freedom of the Christian, the Lutheran understanding of sin (particularly his claim that we are at once both saint and sinner), and his earthy understandings of both creation and vocation.

We realize this gift in our colleges and universities when we tell the whole human story in all its depth and breadth and when we ponder the meaning of human evil as well as human accomplishments. All of us, and all of our students, should know the human story and the foolishness, fallacies, the unbelievable cruelty and destructiveness that we have wrought. All should also know the great stories of human heroism, loyalty, responsibility, and caretaking that humans have been and continue to be engaged in. Freedom is one of our theological gifts, and honesty should be one of its academic fruits.

A second part of this gift is that in spite of this honesty, this radical truth-telling, we stand together as a community of hope, not a community of despair. This possibility, to tell the truth and to carry on, is a powerful witness to our students. If we lose hope, or if we turn away from our own reality because we cannot bear not to deceive ourselves, we send the younger generation a deep message of despair—that the world and our own reality can only be borne if we deny large parts of it. Hope, in the Lutheran tradition, is the living out of the faith that such denial, by the grace of God, is not necessary. God knows us for what we are and who we are and embraces us in our wholeness.

IV.
Toward a Lutheran Epistemology: Sources and Models

The modern divorce of the knower and the known has led to the collapse of the community and accountability between the knowing self and the known world. . . . We now have the power to magnify our distortion many times over, to destroy with our acts the community we have destroyed with our minds.

—Parker Palmer, *To Know as We Are Known*

The purpose of this chapter is an exploration of how we think about knowing, including a brief examination of several sources and thinkers who have shaped our ways of knowing as well as thinkers who, more recently, have suggested critiques of that paradigm. This exploration is meant to serve as a means to the goal of chapter five, to articulate a Lutheran understanding of knowing, a "Lutheran epistemology."

Epistemology

Epistemology is the study of the nature of knowing; it is also often called "theory of knowledge." Its tasks as a discipline are to give an account of what knowing is, what we do know, what we do not, how knowing is related to belief, to language, to practice, to the institutions that embody or pursue knowing, etc. Most students and, unfortunately, many faculty have never pursued the study of epistemology. They are not aware that they and their disciplines make epistemological assumptions. Many would not be able to make those assumptions explicit if they were asked to do so. They simply adopt, in an unreflective way, the methods and procedures of their disciplines without stopping to ask what theory of knowledge they are based upon. The same is true of most educational institutions. Though each embodies some philosophy of education, and every philosophy of education contains, usually implicitly, some theory of knowledge, few are the educators that can give an account of the epistemology they employ. Most of us acquire our epistemologies without examining them, simply by absorbing the general culture of which they are a hidden but extremely significant part.

Why should anyone fuss about epistemology? Isn't it, like most of philosophy, just a very abstract argument about things of little concern to ordinary people? We might wish that were so, but it is not. Our age, the modern age, the age of science, technology, religious doubt, and moral skepticism, has been shaped by an epistemology more than anything else. One may characterize the Enlightenment, in fact, as a move toward making a particular epistemology central to our thinking. This epistemology has influenced our thinking about everything, including our thinking about thinking. Parker Palmer, in *To Know as We Are Known*, says that

> epistemology can help us decipher the patterns of our lives. Its images of the knower, the known, and their relationship are formative in the ways an educated person not only thinks but acts. The shape of our knowledge becomes the shape of our living; the relation of the knower to the known becomes the relation of the living self to the larger world. . . . our epistemology is quietly transformed into our ethic. The images of self and world that are found at the heart of our knowledge will also be found in the values by which we live our lives.[1]

So, how do we think about knowing? What are the dominant paradigms that shape our conception of knower and known, world and self, and how did we come by them?

The Cartesian Paradigm

We live in an age and a culture that, at least until recently, has been almost completely shaped by the epistemology of René Descartes. That is a large part of what we mean by calling this age and this culture "modern." In many ways Descartes is the most influential thinker of the last four centuries. All students of philosophy study Descartes. When they do, it usually does not take too long for them to pose a very perplexing question for the history of ideas: "Why should this philosopher's views have become so influential when they were, in almost every respect, wrong?"

My temptation here, as a philosopher, is to devote the rest of the book to a discussion of Descartes. I will resist that temptation and will, instead, tell only enough of Descartes' story to make the response to him make sense.

Descartes lived and wrote in a world beset with religious wars and persecutions. It was also a world where Galileo's new science of physics had just begun to be known. Descartes, himself an accomplished mathematician, wished that all knowledge could attain to the certainty of mathematics. So, in pursuit of that ideal, he set off in search of a method that would produce such certainty and that could establish all knowledge following the paradigms of mathematics and physics that so impressed him. The epistemology that he articulated has shaped our modern understanding of knowledge, the development of the disciplines, and the shape of the modern university. Here, in outline, are two of its main points.

There is a clear distinction made between knowledge and "mere belief." The criterion for knowledge is certainty. Things can be claimed to be known only if they are clearly beyond doubt. Knowledge, given this standard, is a very exclusive category. We should, therefore, doubt everything that cannot be proved, demonstrated, verified beyond doubt. Nothing short of this can be claimed to be known at all; it is mere belief, and therefore epistemologically worthless. Descartes was convinced that unless some knowledge could serve as an indubitable foundation that all knowledge claims were doubtful.

There is a complete separation of the self as knower from the world as known. The world as known, including our own bodies, is, according to Descartes, completely describable in quantitative terms and translatable into the language of mathematics. The language of the self, the knower, is completely different. This is the source of our common distinction between objective and subjective, the source of C. P. Snow's "Two Cultures," and the source of the assumption so deeply engraved in many students' and faculty persons' thinking, namely that there is an unbridgeable gap between facts and values. As a consequence of Descartes' separation of self and world he left modern philosophy with the tasks of explaining how such a separated self could know anything about the *external* world. As late as 1926, Bertrand Russell titled his own attempt at answering this question *Our Knowledge of the External World* (emphasis mine), and new editions of the book were offered by him well into the 1950s. Amazingly, many academics still think in these ways about knowing the world. Their outlook is basically shaped by Cartesian metaphors. We were also left by Descartes to explain how selves could be related to the physical bodies that in some strange sense "contained" them. British philosopher Gilbert Ryle (*Concept of Mind*, 1949) characterized and critiqued Descartes' view as "the ghost in the machine." We are a subjective consciousness somehow trapped inside a mechanical body. The philosophical problem of freedom versus determinism owes much of its plausibility to Descartes' way of relating self and world, body and mind, as does a good deal of the language of contemporary psychology and many recent discussions of the nature of human consciousness and its relation to brain states.

Another implication of the Cartesian paradigm is that it emphasizes theoretical knowing, knowing where the separation of body and mind is most plausible. Yet much of our thinking is not theoretical in this detached way. It is connected to action, to working in the world and on the world, shaping it as it shapes us, working with others toward agreed ends.[2] The shaping of judgment is another kind of thinking that the Cartesian paradigm finds problematic. Judgments are made in contexts (spatially and temporally particular) toward some purpose, moving toward a best answer, in a community to which we are answerable. Stephen Toulmin, philosopher and historian of ideas, writes:

> For 16th century scholars [before Descartes], the very model of a "rational enterprise" was not Science but Law. Jurisprudence brings to light, not merely the link between "practical rationality" and "timeliness," but the significance of local diversity, the relevance of particularity, and the rhetorical power of oral reasoning: by comparison, all projects for a universal natural philosophy struck the humanists [e.g., Montaigne] as problematic. A hundred years later the shoe was on the other foot. For Descartes and his successors, timely questions were no concern of philosophy: instead their concern was to bring to light permanent structures underlying all the changeable phenomena of Nature.[3]

This is part of the legacy that Descartes left us. He also left us the belief that real knowledge tries to follow the pattern of physics, that a real discipline needs to be quantified in order to be scientific, that the sciences, when properly pursued, are completely value free, and that nature has no value except what value the human knower, the subject, may give it. He also left us the idea of disciplinary specialization, that the world is really separate realities knowable by unrelated disciplines that cannot be translated into a common language. We live, thus, not in a universe, but in a multiverse, appropriately studied in a "multiversity," where we acquire technical expertise in one area while finding ourselves unable to discourse with experts, or even students, in other areas. Since only such disciplinary specialization is real knowledge, nothing like wisdom, speculative or practical, is at all possible.

Many have maintained that the latter third of the twentieth century has seen the waning of this modern view and the replacing of it with a postmodern one, and to some degree that is true. But in this postmodern age we are still thinking in ways that are framed in Cartesian categories. Now, however, having lost some of the confidence and optimism of an earlier age, we are more likely to say that there is nothing but subjectivity, nothing but "belief systems" that we try to enforce as part of our own "power agendas," nothing but solipsistic subjectivity. Meanwhile we are still left in an isolated, fragmented world, unable to be persuaded by or even discourse with each other. Descartes established the paradigm for knowing, and we are now surprised that there are not any (or at least not very many) instances of it. Postmodern skepticism and relativism, rather than opening a new positive paradigm, are just the last of Descartes' philosophical descendants.

There have been some important voices in the last century critical of this Cartesian scheme, among them Michael Polanyi, A. N. Whitehead, Owen Barfield, Martin Heidegger, and Hannah Arendt. At the same time many of us have felt a kind of inarticulate dis-ease operating within institutions shaped by this epistemology. It is the (usually unarticulated) reason that many of us were attracted to pursue academic careers in faith-related institutions. But for the most part Western colleges and universities, including faith-related ones, have lived and operated within this Cartesian paradigm without seriously challenging it or presenting an alternative. This is so partly because we have so much invested in it, or at least believe we do. In some ways it has shaped our identity as teachers and scholars as well as the identity of our disciplines, and we tend to react very negatively when that identity is threatened.

The Challenge to Articulate an Alternative Epistemology

In his book *Faith and Knowledge: Mainline Protestantism and American Higher Education*, Douglas Sloan writes a history of Protestant efforts at higher education in America. In the preface he states, "The church's claim to have a legitimate voice in higher education depended on its ability to demonstrate an essential connection between faith and knowledge."[4] Sloan goes on to say that he thinks the mainline Protestant churches basically failed at making that connection. That left their institutions of higher learning with three alternatives: (1) Buy into the dominant modern culture of scientific reductionism. (2) Adopt a position of "antimodernism," i.e., religious fundamentalism and Bible literalism. (3) Adopt some version of what he identifies as the "two-realm theory of truth," that allows science and religion to coexist without meaningfully discoursing with each other. Sloan does not see fundamentalism as a real alternative. He writes, "the resurgence of fundamentalism is essentially a modern phenomenon and comes itself to be a prime example of modernism. . . . The reaction against modernity, thus, frequently becomes a major carrier of it."[5] And about the two-realm view he says that

> the two-realm theory of truth is better than nothing. It is better than to not preserve the memory of a realm of human selves, meanings and aspirations in an otherwise meaningless universe. It is better than not to

work at the revitalization of the humanities in order to keep alive the important questions. . . . But since our experience of the world is finally shaped by our knowledge, these efforts will always be on the defensive, constantly undergoing erosion, and ever a little after the fact, a bit too late.[6]

But Sloan believes that institutions shaped by such a view of truth finally devolve into secular institutions with a little religious trimming, including attention to "Christian values." Consequently Sloan thinks that it is a task of first importance to develop a coherent Christian epistemology that will fully inform our efforts at learning and teaching. "It is our ways of knowing that give us our world."[7] Though he makes some suggestions about where we might turn to look for help in beginning such a project, he does not take on the task himself in *Faith and Knowledge*.

In an earlier book, *Insight-Imagination: The Emancipation of Thought and the Modern World*, Sloan does make some suggestions toward a new epistemology.

> Thinking that is not sustained by interest (a feeling) cannot serve as a way of knowledge. Unfortunately, the separation frequently made between thinking and feeling often simply blinds reason to the influence upon it of all kinds of interests that have nothing to do with the desire to know. The narrowing of reason, and the cutting of it off from feeling, increases, rather than prevents, the possibilities of its being contaminated by irrationality. . . . Thinking as knowing requires from the beginning, therefore, both a heartfelt interest in the other and a respect, a reverence for the other and what the other has to reveal.[8]

And later he adds:

> Love and compassion move relentlessly to an apprehension of and engagement with reality, and, therefore, often appear cold and "unfeeling." And they are tough, they endure through changes of mood and circumstance, and tolerate no hiding or drawing back from reality. In love and compassion feeling becomes not only an organ of perception but also an organ of cognition in which experience and knowing are one.[9]

Sloan suggests that knowing, as we have conceived and practiced it, namely as a function of the calculative intellect, needs to be expanded to include an interweaving of feeling, love, insight, and imagination.

Polanyi's Critique

Michael Polanyi, Hungarian by birth, was rapidly promoted as a young scientist and appointed in 1920 to a prestigious position in the Berlin Institute of Physical and Electrical Chemistry. He resigned from his position there as chair of the division for physical chemistry in 1933, in protest of Nazi policies that finally culminated in the firing of all Jewish professors.

Polanyi then moved his family to Manchester, England, where the University of Manchester was enlightened enough to create a new chair for him.[10]

Polanyi's first interest was in science, but his concerns led him to write and speak also about epistemology and what he thought was an erroneous philosophical view with disastrous consequences. He was particularly concerned about the way in which science seemed ready to serve any master and become disconnected, in the name of objectivity, from the rest of life. He was particularly concerned to see that scientists could pursue their science completely blind to and detached from the social and political evils their scientific work was serving. Polanyi wrote:

> I believe that the doctrines derived from our erroneous scientific world view have in our days shattered our culture, casting much of the world into mindless servitude, while afflicting the rest with basic confusion.[11]

Not only was this worldview disastrous in its consequences, Polanyi maintained, but it did not come close to doing justice to the character of scientific thinking. Thus Polanyi set out to try to restate what knowing was. He wrote several essays and books on this subject, the most important of which was the text of his Gifford Lectures, *Personal Knowledge*. Polanyi's view is complex, and did not develop all at once, but I will attempt a very brief condensation of it here because it is such an important critique of the Cartesian paradigm.

Polanyi maintained that it was simply wrong to try to make scientific knowing completely value free. Science itself depends on and embodies values, the values of freedom, truth, and honesty, for example. Besides these values, science is also propelled by passions. He writes:

> I want to show that scientific passions are no mere psychological by-products but have a logical function . . . . The excitement of a scientist making a discovery is an intellectual passion, telling that something is intellectually precious, and more particularly that it is precious to science. And this affirmation forms part of science. . . . Science is regarded as established in spite of its passionate origins.[12]

There is also a kind of caring naturally connected to the desire to investigate the world. Without such caring, Polanyi argues, we wouldn't know how to focus our attention; we wouldn't know how to set priorities or determine what is and is not relevant to an investigation. The learning of such appropriate values and passions, Polanyi maintained, should be part of a good scientific education, yet philosophers writing about science had completely left them out of their account of the scientific method.

Polanyi thought that most accounts of scientific method were pure mythology, since they seldom corresponded to what real scientists actually did. Science, in practice, was more than just a process of verification and falsification. It was also a process of discovery that required both insight and a great deal of creativity. Scientific breakthroughs very often had a way of being perceived before they could be clearly articulated or experimentally verified. How was this possible? Polanyi wondered. Modern accounts of scientific knowing seemed to leave such things completely unmentioned, because they didn't fit the epistemological paradigm.

To explain this occurrence, Polanyi developed the idea of *tacit knowing*, illustrated by the ability we have to corner successfully on a bicycle even though we may not be able to articulate the physics of doing so. We know the physics in our bodies long before we know it in our minds, and we know it in our minds intuitively long before we make it explicit on paper or chalkboard. Polanyi concluded that a huge mass of tacit knowledge stands behind every successful attempt to make the knowledge articulate and explicit. As Polanyi put it, "We can never state everything we know."

Polanyi also pointed out that we know certain things by means of other things. Our attention is focused at one level (the *focal objects* that we *attend to*) by means of things at another level or levels (*subsidiary objects* that we *attend from*). Polanyi tells the story of getting a letter from an old friend. Later, while telling his son about it, the son asked, "What language did he write in? Was it handwritten or typed?" Polanyi said he couldn't remember, but he remembered the contents of the letter very well. He had focused on the message of the letter, not on the script and the language that had brought it to him. Because he was able to "dwell in" the language he could receive the message without attending to the other realities that brought it to him.

Polanyi said that many thinkers had made the error of confusing the focal with the subsidiary. They had wrongly inferred that since we attend by means of our senses, "sense data" must therefore be the proper objects of knowledge. For Polanyi, this mistake was the source of a good deal of error in epistemological theory. It was similar to arguing that since we know Shakespeare's *Hamlet* by means of "black squiggles" on pages, what we actually know when we read Shakespeare are such squiggles. This error was the source of reductionism of the sort seen in positivism, British empiricism, and much of the psychology practiced in Polanyi's day.

At the beginning of our discussion of Descartes I said that many of my students are amazed that a philosopher like Descartes could be so influential if he was so wrong about so many things. When I introduce them to Polanyi they are also amazed, but in his case about how someone could be so right and still be so little known. In every case I secure from them a promise, namely, to go back and tell their professors to read Polanyi. I encourage you to do the same thing. If you don't want to tackle his difficult work, *Personal Knowledge*, I suggest his very provocative shorter book, *The Tacit Dimension*.[13]

The modern period has been shaped and defined more by its epistemology than by its moral or political or social outlook. That epistemology surely got some things right, rescuing knowing from the dictatorship of the medieval church. The relative independence of the academic disciplines is one of the benign consequences of this epistemology. But in the process of freeing itself from the control of the medieval church modern epistemology has fallen off the other side of the horse, attempting to create a knowing that is object-defined, value free, and detached, and a known world that is quantitative, mechanical, meaningless, and one-dimensional. Lutheranism, founded in a premodern movement also critical of the medieval church, has shown no interest in reviving the medieval authority of church over all knowledge. But Lutherans also have no particular allegiance to the modern epistemology, and have frequently been critical of it in practice even if not in argument. It is not unusual for students reading Luther to comment, "He almost sounds postmodern." Indeed, in some ways he does. In any case, I believe Lutherans are in a particularly enviable position of seeing beyond the Cartesian paradigm, thoroughly critiquing it, and pointing toward some new ways of knowing linked to themes within the Lutheran tradition.

Reformed Epistemology

Nicholas Wolterstorff and Alvin Plantinga were, earlier in their careers, both professors of philosophy at Calvin College in Grand Rapids, Michigan, a college in the Dutch Reformed tradition. While they were there they published several books and essays that articulated positions that have since come to be identified as "reformed epistemology." In 1976, Wolterstorff published a small book titled *Reason within the Bounds of Religion*. The title is a reversal of an earlier title by Immanuel Kant, *Religion within the Bounds of Reason*, in some ways a classic of Enlightenment thought. Wolterstorff's argument is basically that there is no need for the Christian thinker to conform her thought to someone else's epistemology. The Christian thinker instead ought to make her epistemology conform to her faith. And this is what Wolterstorff sets out to do in his book. He writes:

> The religious beliefs of the Christian scholar ought to function as control beliefs within his devising and weighing of theories. . . . they also ought to help shape his views on what it is important to have theories about. . . . [Many of us] fail to see the pattern of our authentic commitment and its wide ramifications. We see only pieces and snatches and miss the full relevance of our Christian commitment to our devising and weighing of

theories. . . . Christian philosophy and theology are at the center not because they are infallible (obviously they are not) but because it is in these two disciplines that the Christian scholar engages in systematic self-examination . . . and the articulation of such control beliefs.[14]

A control belief is the most basic assumption on which the construction and critique of theories is based. Wolterstorff offers two examples: The control belief for the inquisitors' judgment of Galileo was that Scripture held authority over scientific theories. The control belief for positivists was the belief that all knowledge must conform to the scientific paradigm.

In a subsequent book, *Art in Action: Toward a Christian Aesthetic*, Wolterstorff puts his conception to work. In that book it is his purpose not to write about the relation between arts and the church but to think about the whole domain of the arts from a Christian standpoint, i.e., to write a theory of the arts as a Christian theorist. He sets out to do what, in his earlier volume, he said ought to be done. The Christian beliefs that are at work in Wolterstorff's theorizing about the arts are: (1) that persons and their actions are more important and more fundamental than objects; (2) that humans, through work in the arts, are called on to assist in God's work of redemption in the world; and (3) that we should use the arts to evidence the life of those to whom grace has been shown. The heart of Wolterstorff's argument is a critique of the contemporary art world, its institutions, and the way they have made us think about the arts and their paradigms in our society. Wolterstorff, by contrast, criticizes the idea of "fine arts," and promotes a view that recognizes the wide variety of uses of art while refusing to make high art and a "trickle down" theory of culture the paradigm. He argues on behalf of an idea of tribal art, an art accessible to everyone, which can "bubble up" through the cultural life of a people. In music, the performances of symphony orchestras represent the high arts, while blues and jazz and congregational singing represent the tribal arts. Why should we assume that high art and the aesthetic contemplation it requires is the "real art"? Why should we assume that high art's values should dictate aesthetic theory? He writes, "To make aesthetic contemplation *the* use of art is to separate art from life and turn art into a religion with high priests, temples, mysteries, and rites of initiation."[16]

To all who are skeptical of Wolterstorff's idea of theorizing with Christian control beliefs, I would recommend his book on the arts.[17] It shows, better than anything else I have seen, what critical and creative insights can come to someone who is willing to begin thinking with a different set of assumptions. Socialists can theorize with socialist assumptions, feminists with feminist assumptions, libertarians with libertarian assumptions. So why, Wolterstorff asks, shouldn't Christians be able to theorize with Christian assumptions?

The second philosopher who has been influential in shaping "reformed epistemology" is Alvin Plantinga. His argument, in brief, is this: Over the ages many people have tried to come up with arguments that attempt to prove, or at least demonstrate the likelihood of, the existence of God. All of these arguments argue to the conclusion that God exists based on some premises the truth of which is supposedly more obvious than that conclusion. Plantinga questions that assumption. What is it that makes a belief basic, i.e., makes it a belief one argues *from*, and what is it that makes other beliefs derivative, i.e., beliefs one needs to argue *to*? Why must the existence of God be one of the latter rather than one of the former? Plantinga, consistently with the teachings of John Calvin, maintains that the idea of God is planted in all humans. It is therefore *properly basic*. We err, therefore, in treating it as something that must be argued for to be believable. Belief in God is rational, Plantinga argues, even though it is a logical error to give reasons for it.[18]

For reformed Christians, *the tenets of their faith should function as premises to be argued from, not notions that need to be argued for.* Both Plantinga and Wolterstorff agree that Christian beliefs ought to function in this way. Rather than placing Christian belief somewhere on the edge of our thinking as something derivative and dependent on argument, they place it squarely at the center, as something that the epistemology and the theorizing of the Christian scholar depends upon and flows from. For someone like Wolterstorff, therefore, it makes perfectly good sense to talk about Christian psychology or Christian history or Christian economics. Once these theories have been worked out, it also would make perfectly good sense to teach them in the corresponding departments and courses at a place like Calvin College. And, consistent to their purposes, that is exactly what they have been doing there. Both scholarship and teaching at Calvin College have been shaped by this epistemology. Taking Wolterstorff's *Art in Action* as an example of such scholarship, we would have to admit that such scholarship has been amazingly fruitful.

Should Lutherans, then, adopt the Dutch Reformed approach to epistemology and inquiry in the disciplines? No, I don't believe so, even though there are some significant things to be learned there. So, why not? I think there are four important reasons:

(1) Calvinists have historically adopted a different stance to the institutions of the world than Lutherans have. Calvinists, seeing the world and its institutions as sinful, have set out to replace or transform them with Christian alternatives, following the pattern that Richard Niebuhr identi-

fied as the "Christ transforming culture" model. This explains, in part, John Calvin's attempt to set up a theocracy in sixteenth-century Geneva as well as the Puritan revolts in Britain and the early Puritan communities in the Americas. In some ways, the attempt to do Christian philosophy or physics or psychology springs from the same outlook.

Lutherans' relation to the culture has always been more complex and more ambiguous, probably more correctly characterized as "Christ in dialogue with culture." Lutherans also see the world and its institutions as sinful and imperfect, yet God-ordained. Luther argued, for example, following the Apostle Paul, for the freedom of the Christian. The gospel, in other words, frees us from the rule of law. Human laws, and the institutions and people that administer them, are sinful—sinful creations for sinful people. But, Luther points out, these laws are no less necessary for all that. Since we are sinful people we need laws that recognize that fact and direct our lives in response to that recognition. So, Luther advises, we must be obedient to and supportive of the laws and rulers of our society in spite of the fact that they too are sinful. Thus, while it is proper for Lutherans to be critical of such structures, we can be active users of them. We can be both active participants in them and reformers of them. Thus Lutherans are not as inclined to replace such structures with Christian ones. This difference in approach is clearly demonstrated in the contrast between Calvinist and Lutheran attitudes toward public education. Calvinists are more likely than Lutherans to set up their own educational institutions in place of the public ones that may already be present. In fact, Calvin College requires that their faculty send their children to Calvinist primary and secondary schools. Lutherans have established such schools as well, but they are much more likely to send their children to public schools where they are available, to become teachers and school board members in them, and to be engaged as supporters of them, as well as being critical of them.

(2) Luther understood, as we have said, that the institutions of society are sinful creations of sinful people. But Luther thought that the works of Christian people were just as likely to be sinful and in need of criticism as the work of non-Christians or the culture as a whole. That is, establishing something on Christian premises, whether a school or a government or a discipline, is no more likely to make it perfect. Christians sin, in Luther's view, even in their own attempts to be Christian. Luther would, therefore, be as skeptical of Calvin's theocracy as of any other form of government, and he would be as critical of the idea of Christian philosophy as of any other kind, perhaps more so. Following this lead it is not likely that Lutherans would devise Lutheran theories of the arts or of psychology or eco-

nomics, even though it is very likely that Lutherans would be able and engaged critics of those disciplines as they are practiced by both Christian and non-Christian inquirers.

(3) Whenever one bases an inquiry or discipline on a particular set of beliefs one runs a very large risk of creating, not a genuine inquiry, but an ideology. During Stalin's rule, biologists in the Soviet Union were ordered to pursue Marxist biology, i.e., biology based on Marxist control beliefs. I am no expert in this area, but according to secondhand accounts I have read, the outcome was not good biology. What happened over and over was that inquirers were limited, not only in the conclusions they could draw but even in the inquiries they could pursue. I am not claiming that this is true of the work of Dutch Reformed scholars. I am claiming only that it is a danger of such an approach. But, no less important, it is a danger for secular scholars as well. No inquiry proceeds without assumptions. No discipline operates without control beliefs. Any discipline could, therefore, turn itself into an ideology, particularly where it has "succeeded" in silencing alternative views and voices. Lutheran scholars are not likely to follow the Dutch Reformed model *as a program* if they are aware of the "temptation toward ideology" built into such approaches. But there is no reason why Lutherans could not pursue such inquiries *as a provocative thought experiment*. What would a Christian approach to economics look like? What might it reveal about the assumptions of economics as usually practiced? Are there insights to be gained from such an approach? We ought not suppose, in advance, that such an inquiry would be "bad economics." But we should be very suspicious *to establish* this, or any single approach to economics, as *the* economic theory. My guess is that any college or university is in bad shape if all their economists (or any discipline's scholars) think in the same way about most things.

(4). Lutherans are less likely than either Catholics and Calvinists to strive toward a single, comprehensive, unified theory or worldview. Both Calvin and Thomas Aquinas did attempt this, and their work has been normative for many in higher education. Luther did not approach things in that way and most Lutheran thinkers do not do so. This is not a failure on their part, I believe, but a detection of a kind of epistemological intuition lodged in the theological tradition.

So there are reasons—historical, theological, and philosophical/cultural—that leave Lutherans as appreciative critics of the Reformed as well as the Thomistic approach.

How should Lutheran scholars then approach inquiry in their disciplines? I believe that an outline of an answer is beginning to emerge. Scholars informed by the Lutheran tradition approach knowing critically, self-critically, suspiciously, self-suspiciously, experimentally, openly, inviting a variety of voices, boldly and humbly, relating knowledge to full personhood and contexts of action and community.

On the Relation of Love and Knowledge

Mark Schwehn, in a recent essay, made the following provocative comments: "at Lutheran colleges and universities, knowledge is linked to love rather than power" and "The future of Lutheran higher education will depend finally on its capacity to maintain a lovingly critical perspective, in both theory and practice, upon educational projects that place an exclusively high premium upon knowledge as power."[19] "Lovingly critical"—that's the combination I would focus attention on here. Can such a marriage of opposites possibly last and bear fruit?

This combining of knowing and loving corresponds to many experiences I and perhaps you have had, for I have had teachers and colleagues who were quite thoroughly enamored of their subjects of study: waterfowl, hand horn technique and practice, stream ecology, the works of Kierkegaard or Plato or Shakespeare, Renaissance music, Native American religions, engineering of wooden trestle bridges, native plant species, the poetry of Virgil, the illogic of Lewis Carroll, Shaker furniture and farming practices, the films of Akira Kurosawa, Bach's *Two and Three Part Inventions*, biochemistry, analytic geometry, the novels of Nikos Kazantzakis. Their love for what they studied explained why they were willing to devote such very large portions of their lives to pursuing these things, often at not insignificant cost to themselves. Their love for their subjects did not make them less excellent or rigorous as inquirers, but in all cases more so.

Parker Palmer addresses the relation between love and knowing in *To Know As We Are Known*. He comments that though we have argued about the ends of knowledge, we have ignored examining the sources of our desire to know. He argues that we cannot answer the former question until we examine the latter one. Yet these questions are of utmost importance. He writes: "Is our knowledge—the very knowledge that distinguishes human beings from the beasts—creating a world far less human, far more beastly, than the natural world itself?" He continues: "We have ignored the question of origins because we imagine that knowledge begins as neutral stuff—'the facts.'" We assume these facts are value neutral and that value comes into the picture only when we have to decide how our knowledge will be used. "We think that knowledge itself is passionless and purposeless, but I have come to see that knowledge contains its own morality, that it begins not in a neutrality but in a place of passion within the human soul."[20] The two dominant passions that Palmer identifies as motivating most modern knowing are curiosity and control. He writes:

> Curiosity sometimes kills, and our desire to control has put deadly power in some very unsteady hands. We should not be surprised that knowledge launched from these sources is heading toward some terrible ends, undeflected by ethical values as basic as respect for life itself. . . . If curiosity and control are the primary motives for our knowing, we will generate a knowledge that eventually carries us not toward life but death.

> But another kind of knowledge is available to us, one that begins in a different passion and is drawn toward other ends. This knowledge can contain as much sound fact and theory as the knowledge we now possess, but because it springs from a truer passion it works toward truer ends. This is a knowledge that originates . . . in compassion, or love.[21]

As we said above, the Cartesian paradigm of knowing separates the knower, the subject, from the known, its object. The aim of Cartesian knowing is, therefore, to be as objective as possible and to remove the subjective as much as possible from the picture. Palmer continues:

> If the problem with primitive knowledge was the over identification of the knower with the known, our problem [as modern knowers] is the estrangement and alienation of the two. In our quest to free knowledge from the tangles of subjectivity, we have broken the knower loose from the web of life itself. The modern divorce of the knower and the known has led to the collapse of community and accountability between the knowing self and the known world. This distortion is different in kind from that of the pre-modern world, but not in degree of danger. Indeed, it is more dangerous. We now have the power to magnify our distortion many times over, to destroy with our acts the community we have destroyed with our minds.[22]

An epistemology that links love and knowing de-absolutizes the distinction between subject and object. These terms may still be useful but the distinction they suggest is not absolute for the process of knowing involves both. Knowing is the embodiment of a passion, as such it bridges the subject/object trench. The effort to know is not there for everybody. Not everyone puzzles over the navigational systems of butterflies, the clustering of galaxies in space, the link between the physiology of seeing and the psychology of recognizing. But besides there being a passion for knowing, there can also be passions in knowing. The "Eureka!" of scientific discovery, the thankfulness at the insights and self-knowledge achieved upon reading Dostoevski's *Notes from Underground*, the excitement at seeing the pattern that connects, formulating a theory that explains, a wisdom that transforms, all of these testify to the falseness of the subject/object divorce embodied in the modern paradigm. Sourcing knowing in loving allows not only for a knowing where I can grasp something, but where I can be grasped by it. Knowing in such a case is fundamentally a mutuality of influence, a seeing empowered by imagining, a sight powered by insight, a knowing empowered by wonder, and the reverse of each of these as well.

Palmer, probably better than any other author, shows the importance of this for teaching and learning. He argues that conventional education (shaped by what he calls the "objectivist" paradigm) has a hidden curriculum. He identifies four practices that convey important assumptions about knower and known:

> First, in the conventional classroom the focus of study is always outward—on nature, on history, on someone else's vision of reality. The reality inside the classroom, inside the teacher and the students is regarded as irrelevant. . . . Second, . . . the heart of the knowing self is never held up for inspection, never given a chance to be known. A third feature of the conventional classroom is its tendency to isolate the knowing self. . . . So the conventional pedagogy is not only non-communal but anticommunal. The fourth effect . . . is simply the outcome of the first three . . .: we become manipulators of each other and the world rather than mutually responsible participants and co-creators.[23]

Palmer suggests that Christianity offers a different approach to both pedagogy and epistemology:

> The personal truth of Christianity, with its emphasis on the quality of our relationships, is usually understood as an ethic, an approach to living—not as an epistemology, an approach to knowing. I have shown how the objectivist epistemology becomes an ethic of detachment and manipulation. Now I want to show how the ethic of Christian personalism becomes an epistemology of participation and accountability.[24]

This relating of knowing to love is sure to strike the ears of many readers as very strange, if not completely foolish. We are used to thinking in terms of the Cartesian paradigm. We think about valuing as completely divorced from knowing, and we are so accustomed to thinking of ethics as completely alien to epistemology that the linking of these two will seem thoroughly wrong. For many of us this supposition may be, of all our mental equipment, the one most difficult to question. Yet a variety of other thinkers have also suggested such a wedding of knowing and love:

> It is a task to come to see the world as it is. . . . Love is the extremely difficult realization that something other than oneself is real. Love is the discovery of Reality.
>
> —Iris Murdoch (philosopher, novelist)[25]

> It [the loving eye] is the eye of one who knows that to know one must consult something other than one's own interests and fears and imagination.

One must look at the thing. One must look and listen and check and question. . . . The science of the loving eye would favor the Complexity Theory of Truth and presuppose the Endless Interestingness of the Universe.

> —Marilyn Frye (political scientist)[26]

For the most part, artists of all kinds are helplessly intelligent but only deliberately compassionate. The first morning of each Festival [the Franconia, New Hampshire Festival of Poetry], the participants are told that in workshops . . . if they have to make a flash choice between sympathy and intelligence, choose sympathy: for sympathy—and here is the whole point—will increase the depth of intelligence. Love keeps seeing more; contempt is very soon blind.

> —Don Sheehan (poetry festival director)[27]

The prevailing conception of science based on the disjunction of subjectivity and objectivity seeks . . . to eliminate from science such passionate, personal, human appraisals. . . . this whole idea of disinterested observation is silly. . . . Theories of the scientific method which try to explain the establishment of scientific truth by any purely objective formal procedure are doomed to failure. Any process of inquiry unguided by intellectual passions would inevitably spread out into a desert of trivialities. . . . The inquirer has to care! Only then is one able to sort out the good questions from the bad ones and the relevant facts from the irrelevant.

> —Michael Polanyi (physical chemist)[28]

No one can reach a creative solution of a problem which he does not approach *con amore.*

> —Agnes Arber (biologist)[29]

I agree with Palmer and the others cited here that it is extremely important to question the supposition that love and knowing have nothing to do with each other. I also agree with Schwehn, that the linking of knowing and love should be a natural connection for Lutherans, as well as other Christians, to make. At the same time there is no reason why seeing the source of knowing in love should make it less critical or less rigorous. If Murdoch and Polanyi are right, love allows us to pay more attention to how things are because it is not focused on using them for our own purposes. Knowing shaped by loving is, if anything, less subjective in the sense of being shaped by the knower's own agenda. Of course it is very subjective in the sense of engaging the knower as person. This is only one illustration of how these glib distinctions, subjective/objective, obscure by oversimplification a much more subtle truth.

An Epistemology of the Cross

Mary Solberg has written a book with a very provocative title, *Compelling Knowledge: A Feminist Proposal for an Epistemology of the Cross*. But unlike many books, where the most interesting work is done in the title, this one is provocative all the way through. What Solberg attempts is to weave together the concerns she finds in postmodern feminist epistemologies with concerns she sees expressed in Luther's conception of theology of the cross. The outcome she refers to as an epistemology of the cross, "a powerful resource that both describes and may facilitate a recasting of our focus and categories of knowing."[30]

Solberg appropriates the feminist critique of the epistemology of the dominant culture. This culture, for the most part both privileged and male, (1) has been built on the experience and categories of a few persons without soliciting the embodied experience of many, particularly those on the fringes of the culture. (2) It has focused on "objectivity," a notion that is meant to give us reliable knowledge of the world but results in a knowledge that is disengaged and morally unaccountable. (3) It has pursued all of this while pretending to be "value free" and to be advancing no agenda at all. Feminists challenge all three of these claims, asserting (a) the necessity to give the embodied experience of all persons, particularly the poor and the weak, a voice; (b) the need to replace the myth of objectivity with a more full-bodied ideal like truthfulness; and (c) the need to practice mutual accountability.

From Luther's argument for a theology of the cross, and in particular from Douglas John Hall's interpretation of it, Solberg appropriates the understanding that coming to the foot of the cross is "conforming ourselves to Christ." This movement to the foot of the cross requires that we see and assume solidarity with all who suffer and are marginalized, and that we come to see ourselves as complicit in creating and maintaining the world in which they suffer. This realization occasions a *metanoia*, a reversal, a repentance, a new self-knowledge that simultaneously opens up a new knowing of the world. Solberg states:

> "True theology and recognition of God," Luther wrote, "are in the crucified Christ." The cross reverses and puts right the way in which humans come to know who God is and what that implies for their self-knowledge and their daily living, in that knowledge, *coram Deo*. In this sense the cross becomes the epistemic fulcrum, the point on which true reality and the gift to see it, and name it, hinge. Luther's theology of the cross explicates this and in so doing equips the believer to call the thing by its right name.[31]

Solberg later explains:

An epistemology of the cross shares with feminist epistemologies the conviction that, to the degree that relatively undistorted and ethically defensible knowing matter, the place of the least favored—at the foot of the cross, in all its contemporary forms—is a better place to start than any place of domination could be. To be there is to be with those who "raise the deepest questions about what it really means to be human." There is much that simply cannot be seen or known—about how things really are, and about ourselves in relation to that reality—without *being there*.[32]

What Solberg constructs is a vision of knowing very different from the Cartesian and modernist paradigms. It is an account that replaces abstracted experience with *embodied and fully lived experience*. It is an account that replaces a concern for objectivity with a concern for *engaged truthfulness*; an account that replaces the voice of the expert with a franchise for all with a *prima facie priority to the previously dis-enfranchised*. It replaces dis-engagement with *accountability and answerability*. It replaces privilege, power, and being "above it all" with *disillusionment* and the *recognition of our own implication* in the structures and realities of the world that our knowing describes.

Such knowledge is "compelling," Solberg states, because it requires us to change, to act, and to stand in solidarity. Such knowing has three aspects: (1) seeing what is going on, (2) recognizing our own involvement in what is going on, and (3) doing something about it. "These three," Solberg writes, "are not discrete or sequential events or stages. Instead they stand in dynamic relation to one another, they may even constitute one another."[33]

The language of power, privilege, disenfranchisement seem best suited to talk about the knowing of other humans; knowledge, for instance, in the humanities or social sciences. But how does this work for knowledge of objects or knowledge of nature?

Solberg, citing the work of Lorraine Code, argues that the modernist paradigm set out to know everything the way we know physical objects, as quantifiable, mechanically causal, and thoroughly manipulable. Why should we not now try it the other way around, and try knowing the natural world in the richer way that we are able to know persons? Is it so impossible to think that a knowing of the natural world should also be truthful, accountable, and cognizant of our implication in the wasting and destruction of the world? An implication of Solberg's approach is that all knowing should be self-suspicious, aware of the consequences such knowing may have on what and whom is known and whom and what agendas such knowing serves. We have often pursued knowing on the myopic assumption that it served no master even though so much of it was bent on mastery.

Solberg, and the feminist authors she cites, critique power structures and agendas. But in pursuing this course do we run the risk of creating yet another power agenda? Solberg addresses this by fleshing out the distinction between the epistemology of the cross and epistemologies of glory.

> An epistemology of the cross does not issue its critique of power-knowers or their knowledge claims from a neutral space. . . . It identifies itself as an epistemological alternative, holding forth "over against" positive, power-defined knowledge; it challenges power defined as domination-over, refusing to be caught up in the terms such power dictates. In critiquing the epistemology of glory, an epistemology of the cross issues from a perspective learned from and with those . . . relegated to the margins or backwoods of the "dominant meaning system" (Minnich). In contrast to the transcendent, global claims power-defined epistemologies make—claims rooted as much in fear of real, creaturely limits as in addiction to mastery of the surround—an epistemology oriented to the cross insists on the partialness of what can be known by any of us knowers, and/or by all of us together. It lives, often uncomfortably, with ambiguity and doubt.[34]

What We Can Learn: Things to Avoid

Our culture's misadventures with the Cartesian paradigm should have taught us to beware of certain patterns of thinking embedded there: (1) An exclusivist approach to the definition of knowing. (2) A sharp and oversimple distinction between the objective and the subjective. (3) A tendency to see one kind of knowing as the paradigm for all others. (4) A tendency toward reductionism. Let us consider each of these, very briefly, in turn.

(1) The Cartesian paradigm, we have noted, begins by defining knowing as gaining certainty and then excludes everything else about which even the least doubt is possible. The ultimate consequence of this in the postmodern era is to say that there is no knowledge, strictly speaking, and that what parades as knowledge is just one form or another of subjectivity promoted as someone's power agenda.

Some very fine thinkers, David Hume and Immanuel Kant among them, operated with a severely restricted understanding of what could be known. Both Hume and Kant were sufficiently honest in their philosophizing to admit that they could not live and function within the world their epistemologies allowed them to know. Hume tells us that, to maintain his sanity, he often had to get away from philosophy altogether and take excursions, as it were, into the normally lived world, drinking beer and playing billiards with his friends. Kant suggested that there had to be a reality richer than the one his epistemology accounted for, and so hypothesized a noumenal (yet unknown) realm beyond the phenomenal one of our own experience, a realm we assume in practice but cannot access intellectually or empirically. In both cases these philosophers knew, and admitted, that living requires a richer and more multidimensional world than their epistemologies allowed. Not all philosophers have been that honest. But neither Hume nor Kant was willing to suggest that this shows that there is something deficient with their narrow accounts of knowing. In many ways their philosophical work was an attempt to cope with an inadequate epistemology. Had they been willing to begin with a richer (deeper and broader) account of knowing they might have come up with a known world large enough to live in.

Our own approach, I would argue, should be the opposite of Descartes' exclusivism. Let us begin by *looking at knowing inclusively*, by noting the wide variety of ways of knowing there are and then examine the variety of modes such exemplars embody:

Being able to recognize one's own camel in a herd of 200 camels

Knowing how to successfully turn a corner on a bicycle

Driving a car—safely getting where we wanted to go

A doctor diagnosing a disease

A teacher detecting that a student does not yet understand

A young man discovering that he is gay

A child learning to recognize that she is experiencing a headache (not as simple as it seems)

A person realizing that she was born (or do we only know this on someone else's authority?)

A person realizing that he will die (Tolstoi's Ivan Illich)

A student concluding on the basis of lab experiments that the unknown substance is aluminum oxide

A psychologist diagnosing a patient's problem

A physicist concluding that the earth is in motion

Knowing what time is in spite of not being able to say anything non-metaphorical about it (St. Augustine's puzzlement)

Einstein postulating that time is the fourth dimension

Shakespeare seeing deeply into the human psyche

A reader seeing deeply into Shakespeare

Annie Dillard experiencing "the tree with the lights in it"

A parent realizing deep love for his children

A child learning the language of his parents well enough to say, "I don't want to eat because I amn't hungry"

A student of Buddhism understanding the truth of the teacher's claim: "The self is a cultural construct, not a reality"

A young woman knowing her self well enough to set priorities for her life, turning down a proposal of marriage

A man discovering that some of his most basic beliefs about human fulfillment were false

A grandmother once again making flawless piecrust

A student finally "getting" a poem by Wallace Stevens

A witness to a crime testifying under oath

A couple dancing a samba[35]

(2) The Cartesian paradigm is based on the sharp distinction of objective and subjective together with a phobia for the subjective. Our earlier discussion of the relation of love to knowing addressed the oversimplification that the subjective/objective distinction is. All knowing, we asserted, is subjective in several senses: (a) It engages a subject. (b) It makes assumptions, categorical, historical, and perhaps personal; this is unavoidable. (c) It has a motivation, a passion, a kind of caring that empowers it; that is its *eros*, if you will. But none of this implies that it is not object-focused, or that it is prejudiced, not carefully observant, or non-trustworthy. Yet these latter are the evaluative sense that we often attach to the word "subjective." We should take great care in using such terms, realizing that the use of them also hides a particular prejudice and agenda.

(3) Given the exemplars of knowing listed above, it should be obvious that knowing covers a wide range of activities, of varying complexity, focused on different kinds of things, requiring different gifts, combining different kinds of mental and physical functions, and different senses in which one "comes to know." Why then should we have supposed that one of these sorts of knowing was *the* paradigm for knowing, such that those things that differed from it were deemed not cases of knowing at all? The answer to that question would take a long history to tell, but I hope it's fairly obvious that selecting a single instance or even a narrow range of these activities as "the only real knowing" is going to take quite an argument to establish. To my knowledge no one has ever successfully made such an argument. Has anyone even attempted one? Such paradigms were simply assumed. Even attempts to make such arguments usually assume exactly what they would most need to demonstrate. What all of this shows is a human inclination to reductionism, an attempt to reduce a complex phenomenon to a one-dimensional one, to identify all of reality with only one layer of reality, and to set one thing up as the model by which all others are to be judged.

(4) When my oldest son worked for Jet Propulsion Laboratories in Pasadena, California, he took me on a tour of the facility and showed me

the computer terminals that were receiving digital signals from the Galileo probe on its way to Jupiter and from the Hubble space telescope. He pressed a button and one machine printed out a page of numbers. My response was to look at the page dumbly and ask, "But what does it say?" From the computer room we walked into a room that had large photos projected onto screens. I recognized the pictures as galaxies. My son pointed out to me that some of them were galactic clusters. One photo in particular struck me. It looked like a starry sky, with thousands of stars pictured. My son pointed out to me that each of what I had supposed were stars was actually itself a galaxy. "Wow!" was my response. "This is what that sheet of numbers says," my son explained.

Now we can imagine someone arguing that knowing the digits is the real knowing in this example, or perhaps the knowing of masses and gasses and theories of galactic clustering, etc. But how about my inarticulate "Wow"? Is there also a kind of knowing taking place there? Is the response of wonder and amazement "mere emotion"? Or have I gotten to the level of badgering out a meaning of the poem that is this amazing universe? I think we can make a good case against the digital reductionists. After all, the Hubble telescope was sending back digits from the beginning. The problem was that the telescope was out of focus and the digits gave information that was not scientifically useful. So they sent up a team of astronauts to refocus it. It was, after all, National Science Foundation money that was paying for it.

But I don't think that things stop there. I read a recent article in *Newsweek* that questioned the money we had spent on the trips astronauts made to the moon. It posed the question, "Did we find out anything of sufficient scientific interest on those trips to justify the expenditure of billions of dollars?" I am a poor person to try to answer that question because I know so little about what was learned there. But I think there was one thing worth billions of dollars that was brought back from the moon, and that is the photos of our own planet, blue and green and reddish brown, cloud-swirled, "floating" in the immensity of space. The potential value of that image to the human species is immeasurable. But its value is not just scientific; it is poetic, and philosophical, and religious in the deepest sense of the word. In some ways too deep for the object-focused words of our ordinary language it is an image that addresses meaning on the highest (which is also the deepest) level, a level where we learn who we are and what it's all about. But I can imagine a colleague saying, "It's just matter in motion. No reason to get all emotional about it." This is the typical reductionist's response, to say that a reading that is at a different level than his own cannot be knowing, but is "touchy-feely crap." But it seems to me just as insane to abort asking questions of meaning about the universe as it would be to stop our inquiry of a work of literature once we had performed all the logometric operations. Students cannot begin to discuss a dialogue by Plato until they know what it says. But learning does not end there. I would say that's only where it begins. The truth of the work is not determined just by knowing what it says, or knowing how many times *anamnesis* is used, but by seeing how the text informs our seeing, our understanding of other things and of ourselves. A whole lot is missed if we suppose merely to "verify" or "falsify" Plato's *Meno*, or the Genesis story of creation, for another example. We should press our search for truth and understanding as far as it may go, and not be deterred by someone's claim that real knowledge will let us go so far and no farther. But there is no reason why such epistemological openness should not also be critical. Critical openness, like loving criticism, is just another example of "opposites" that the Lutheran tradition is able to bridge.

What We Can Learn: Some Things to Explore

A holistic approach to human being implies a holistic approach to human knowing, like those suggested by Sloan, Polanyi, Schwehn, Palmer, and Solberg, among others. Our account of knowing should give us a world large enough to live in. As such it will be a knowing that is embodied; a knowing connected to interest and feeling; a knowing engaged in doing and living fully connected to the world; a knowing aware of our own mistakes and mistake patterns, our agendas and fallacies; a knowing informed by care, love, forgiveness, and hope. Such knowing will be much more than a technique or method. It will be naturally connected to our own identity as knowers and to the basic values and concerns of our lives. It will be open, loving, practical, and at the same time very critical and self-critical—more critical and self-critical, I am convinced, than knowing within the Cartesian paradigm ever was. All of these themes we will explore further in the following chapter.

V.
Toward a Lutheran Epistemology: Framing a Rich and Fallible Account of Knowing

It is our ways of knowing that give us our world.
—Douglas Sloan

Problematic: On the Outrageous Idea of a Lutheran Epistemology

In some religious traditions it is fairly easy to state what the epistemological assumptions and implications are. This may be one of the things that attracts people to certain religious views, i.e., that they have unambiguous and simple (and also sometimes simple-minded) epistemologies. In some cases, in fact, the epistemology may define the religious view. The word "fundamentalist," for example, designates an epistemological more than a religious viewpoint. In the Lutheran tradition, however, the epistemology is neither unambiguous nor simple. In fact, my first inclination, when I began thinking on this topic, was to say that there is no such thing as a Lutheran epistemology at all, certainly not just a Lutheran version of Wolterstorff and Plantinga's Reformed epistemology. But when I attempted to articulate the reasons why such a thing is difficult or undesirable for Lutherans it was pointed out to me (by Bruce Reichenbach of Augsburg College) that I had come very close to articulating a Lutheran epistemology in spite of myself. So, I engage this project knowing full well that the outcome will be ambiguous and that many (including myself at moments) may be suspicious of the whole enterprise. I also enter into this project knowing that it will not be completed here. My hope is to have made some movement *toward* such an account, not to have completed the journey.

Three Senses of "Lutheran Epistemology"

There are at least three senses we can distinguish for the idea of Lutheran epistemology.

(1) The first denotes an empty class, namely Luther's writings on epistemology. Luther was not an epistemologist. Had he even been aware of the possibility he probably would have been as suspicious of it as he was of all philosophy (and merely theoretical theology, for that matter). Epistemological issues arose in the process of Luther's arguments about other issues, but I don't know of any cases where Luther turns to face these issues squarely and answers them unequivocally. Luther is, in many respects, a rhetorical thinker; he shapes his arguments to the occasion and to those he argues with. This can be very frustrating for anyone who reads Luther in search of theological system, to say nothing of looking there for a consistent philosophical one. (2) Lutheran epistemology, in the second sense, is an attempt to articulate the epistemology of Luther's arguments and the implications of his central theological principles. Luther both appeals to authority and thoroughly questions authority. Both of these have epistemological implications. What do Luther's thoughts about sin, for example, his view of humans as *simul justus et peccator*, or his views of grace, freedom, incarnation, sacrament, and vocation suggest for the way a Lutheran might do epistemology? (3) Finally, "Lutheran epistemology" might refer to the epistemological implications of the ways Lutherans have thought, acted, and institutionalized their thought and action in the world. Here a look at Lutheran thinkers of different sorts would be appropriate, particularly those who may have addressed or come close to addressing epistemological issues. But it is also instructive to look at Lutheran higher education and the way it has been organized over the years, not because everything Lutherans have done must be "authentically Lutheran," but because there may be some discernible patterns we have followed that we now wish to be much more intentional about.

The first of these senses, denoting, as we said, an empty set, does not deserve extended discussion. But each of the other senses, I believe, does deserve serious examination, an examination I intend to initiate here.

Luther's Arguments and Theological Principles:
Some Epistemological Implications of Faithful Reformation

1. Sin. Luther, like some other reformers, had an acute sense of sin. Unlike many thinkers in the Christian tradition, Luther did not identify sin with particular parts or functions of the human person but with human life as a whole. The best that humans can do is therefore as tainted with sin as the worst. Luther saw this embodied both in himself and in the church he tried so hard to reform. We are *simul justus et peccator*. I take the "simul" here to assert that we are not only "at the same time" but also "in the same respect" saint and sinner. So, for example, sin is a pervasive ontological condition, not a locatable moral one. We do not avoid sin by being virtuous. Our very intention to be virtuous may be as motivated by our sinfulness as anything is. Friedrich Nietzsche's later suspiciousness of the motivations that lie at the heart of ethics, science, and truth-seeking is, I believe, very Lutheran in that respect.[1]

Jean-Claude Guillebaud in his recent book, *Re-Founding the World: A Western Testament*, also expresses a view of knowledge that comes off sounding very Lutheran. He states:

> [T]he reign of reason is not unlike that of the market: it is only a liberating factor when it recognizes its own inadequacies in advance, and never loses sight of its limitations. Reason is only reasonable when it is modest. . . . modern science, deprived of its capacity for self-criticism, is perfectly ready to adapt to the latest forms of fanaticism, tyranny and totalitarianism. Techno-science, itself incapable of producing human values, is perfectly compatible with a barbarism that rejects them.[2]

A consequence of this view is the understanding that all human thinking is not only fallible, by virtue of being limited, but also flawed, by virtue of its being a child of human pride and rebelliousness. This problem is not avoided by thinking rightly, for even the best of human thinking is riddled with sin. Luther points out that we are frequently at our worst when we suppose we are at our best and our best when we are at our worst. There is in Lutheran thinking the possibility of recognizing "the sin of virtue." Regarding not only ethics, but all of our thinking, therefore, we ought to be very suspicious. It is extremely unlikely that we have got things right and it is extremely unlikely that, even if we have, that our "will to truth" is not itself a disguised ploy for power or self-justification.

2. Faithful Criticism. Luther certainly maintained the absoluteness of God and the absoluteness of God's truth, the gospel of Christ. But he would have argued against the absoluteness of any human interpretation of the truth—including his own. Though Luther argued vehemently (and often viciously) with his opponents, he also often invites them to debate, to argue their case and to show him where he has erred. Until quite late in his life he repeatedly called for a council to debate the issues he had raised. Luther did not rule out the possibility that he was wrong, but he refused to recant until someone had demonstrated it. As a consequence there is no human institution nor tradition that Luther was not ready to question, including the hierarchy of the church and its official pronouncements and traditions. It is not that these things carried no weight in Luther's thinking, but that the weight they carried was still questionable. At least they carried little compared to the weight he placed on the authority of Scripture.

3. Gospel as Foundation. This might leave one supposing that Luther was a biblical foundationalist, that he reduced every issue ultimately to what the Bible had to say about it. But this supposition would also be a mistake. Luther was quite willing to critique the text of Scripture at places where it stated things contrary to what he took to be the truth *in* the Scriptures, namely the gospel of God's redeeming activity in Christ. So he was willing to call the book of James "an epistle of straw," and to criticize individual passages in both the Old and New Testaments where they did not agree with the gospel.

So, if Luther was not a biblical foundationalist, and he did not believe in the infallibility of pope or hierarchy or tradition or theology done by any human, would it be proper to call him *a gospel foundationalist?* That may be as good a term as any, as long as we don't hide the difficulties of this position beneath the label. The gospel is found in the text, according to Luther, but obviously not without an interpretive reading of the text. The text, in turn, may be judged by the gospel found there. What, then, is the epistemological status of the gospel? It is the standard by which the text is judged, but in some sense it too is the result of a fallible process of theological reflection and textual criticism. So, while it makes some sense to refer to Luther as a gospel foundationalist, in another sense it does not make sense to talk about him as a foundationalist at all. The gospel is to function as a transcendent ideal, never fully reached, yet a point from which one may, at least theoretically, critique every actual reading and interpretation of the gospel. This double understanding of gospel, as on the one hand a transcendent ideal and on the other the product of fallible human processes, leaves us with a radical ambiguity. On occasion the gospel serves as an unshakable foundation, the "rock" on which the church itself stands. But on occasion it is itself open to reformation and reformulation. Yet it endures "even when steeples are falling."

Faithful reformation (being willing to question as an act of faith) is a core Lutheran experience even if it is not epistemologically simple. One could, I believe, trace many of the subtleties of later European philosophy (including Kant and Hegel) to the attempt to do justice to the epistemology embedded in this non-simple and non-univocal Lutheran stance. This pattern of thinking—that we criticize from a point of view that also stands in need of criticism—comes as close as anything to being a Lutheran epistemological principle. Some refer to this as the reformation principle (*ecclesia semper reformanda*). I prefer to call it the principle of faithful reformation. It makes it possible to understand Luther's criticism of church and tradition as an act of faith. Many people in Luther's day as well as our own have had difficulty understanding criticism as faithfulness and prefer a "love it or leave it" dualism. It is not surprising that those who look for epistemological simplicity and security in their theology are not happy (or not long happy?) in the Lutheran camp.

4. *Affirming Tense Conjunctions.* Complex epistemology is also revealed in many of Luther's other concerns. Luther translated the Bible into the vernacular and put it in the hands of the common folk for edification and interpretation. On the other hand Luther encouraged the development of a well-educated and strictly trained clergy, the main tasks of which are textual interpretation and text-focused preaching. Is the text to be trusted to a vulgar reading or not? Is the presence of the Holy Spirit sufficient to guard against gross misinterpretation or not? These questions are still being debated today. They pop up in forums on parish education and in curricular debates in the seminaries. Should our seminarians first be grounded in the reading of the text and then learn theology or should they, having first become well grounded in theology, only then learn to read the text? The Lutheran response to this either/or question continues to be "Yes," affirming the ambiguity at the heart of the Lutheran experience. So the debate rightly and faithfully continues.

Lutherans have sometimes called such ambiguities by a positive name and celebrated them: thus Hegel's idea of dialectic, Kierkegaard's notion of paradox, Tillich's affirmation of mystery that overcomes dualisms. Of late even some Roman Catholic theologians have gotten into the pattern, as in the case of Karl Rahner's principle of the existential transcendent. Are these ways of making a virtue of intellectual laziness, or is there something to recommend this approach of affirming both sides of an opposition?

One can say this, at least: affirming ambiguity is not something that Lutheran thinkers have pulled out of the hat only once. They do it so frequently that it has become, in some ways, an identifying principle of Lutheran thinking. We affirm humans as being both saint and sinner; we affirm the sacrament as both real presence and as nourishing food, not first one then the other by miraculous transformation, but both together—in, with, and under each other. We affirm Christ as fully God and fully human, not just partly the latter to guarantee the fullness of the former, but fully human in order to be fully God. And we affirm these things because we do not hold logic to be the final arbiter of all things rational and because we detect a wisdom in the transcendence of what often appear as opposites. E. F. Schumacher speaks of such a wisdom in his classic, *Small is Beautiful*:

> All through our lives we are faced with the task of reconciling opposites
> which, in logical thought, cannot be reconciled. The typical problems of life
> are insoluble on the level of being on which we normally find ourselves.
> How can one reconcile the demands of freedom and discipline in educa-

tion? Countless mothers and teachers, in fact, do it, but no one can write down a solution. They do it by bringing into the situation a force that belongs to a higher level where opposites are transcended—the power of love.[3]

Whether one is inclined to call it dialectic or paradox depends on whether one sees the contradiction as finally overcome in a higher unity. But the most important point is that Lutherans appeal again and again to the idea that the highest truths are to be expressed in such (at least apparent) contradictions. Is this willingness to affirm contradiction, then, a Lutheran epistemological principle?

There are definitely dangers involved in making it such. If we become too facile at affirming contradictions we can use this facility as an excuse for lazy thinking, just as we can if we say "it's all a great mystery" too early and too often. Consequently I become suspicious when I hear such things, particularly too early in a discussion. Yet I still find myself affirming these *tense conjunctions* of things supposed to be absolute either/or issues. Perhaps that's the secret—the conjunction must be tense, the tension of the paradox must be felt, the contradiction must be recognized and preserved and suffered, even in the faith that affirms it. We should never become glib spouters of contradictions. This is why we as Lutherans should never become glib users of theological language at all. The doing of theology in a Lutheran context should always be a realization that our categories (and our mental equipment) are not adequate to the realities we affirm. Theology, for Lutherans, is a humbling occupation, as it ought to be for everyone. This should have profound implications for the way teaching and learning occur in our colleges and universities as well as our seminaries. This humility should not, however, make us timid inquirers but bold ones. We need to be bold enough to explore the truths embodied in what many would consider contradictions, and bold enough to be critical of ourselves in the process.

From Lutheran Theology to Epistemology to Educational Praxis

What I wish to argue and demonstrate is that the theological themes examined earlier have epistemological implications, shaping what I will call epistemic principles, and that these in turn have implications for educational praxis, shaping higher education in the Lutheran tradition. But we would be mistaken in assuming that one can only get to this epistemology or this praxis by means of these theological principles. So, though these epistemic principles are, I will argue, authentically Lutheran, they are not, in every case, uniquely or exclusively Lutheran. But unless one is a marketing manager trying to define the "market niche" of a Lutheran institution, that is not something one ought to be terribly concerned about.

Though I am presenting this as if it were a deductive model, reasoning from theology to epistemology to educational praxis, that is not the logic of discovery in every case. Just as frequently we discover the importance and relevance (and even the meaning) of our theological principles by reflecting on our praxis. So sometimes our thinking needs to pass from theology to praxis and sometimes from praxis to theology. Learning takes place in both directions.

Eight Epistemic Principles

1. Wonder – What difference does it make to us as knowers that we affirm that God is the creator of all that exists? When I ponder that question the image of one of my most valued college teachers, Reidar Thomte, comes to mind. He spent his academic life reading and teaching the works of Søren Kierkegaard. It didn't matter much what the title of the course was that he taught, we all knew that before long it would become a study of whichever of Kierkegaard's works he was puzzling through at the time. When a braver student than I asked him, "Don't you ever get tired of reading Kierkegaard?" he responded, "Not in the least. Every time I read him I find a new dimension to his thinking, a new connection between his works, a new way to think about things. I've been reading Kierkegaard for nearly forty years and feel like I have barely started to understand what is there for the person willing to dig a bit." I don't know exactly what that attitude of Thomte's should be called, but I think perpetual wonder may come as close as anything.

A present colleague of mine, Phil Whitford, spends countless hours crouched in a wetland or swamp observing migratory waterfowl. His idea of a great weekend is twelve hours outside in a blind in the rain. While most of us would call this lunacy, Whitford talks of it in terms of love. Once again, wonder is an appropriate term for what is going on.

Wonder is openness to depth. It is attentiveness, interest, caring, a willingness to look at things afresh, a willingness to learn, be stretched, be surprised, be captured. Frederick Franck, explaining a Japanese concept kindred to wonder, writes:

> *Kami-sabi* [refers to] the perception of a sacred presence in all things. . . . *Kami-sabi* demands that total openness by which one escapes from "the grave of custom" as Thoreau called it. It is the profound "ah!" of firsthand seeing.[4]

A brief examination of the etymology of "wonder" reveals a loose kinship with the root for "wound" and "to be wounded." This fact may help us make sense of this comment by Sam Keen:

> Every wonder-event requires a cognitive crucifixion; it disrupts the sys-

tem of meanings that secures the identity of the ego. To wonder is to die to the self, to cease imposing categories, and to surrender the self to the object. Such a risk is taken only because there is the promise of a resurrection of meaning.[5]

Wonder thus contains at least three elements, perhaps we could call them cognitive stances: openness, expectation, and a willingness to be wounded, i.e., a willingness to grow.

Isn't this the epistemic stance that the affirmation of creation implies? Given the richness of a world that physicist Freeman Dyson described as "infinite in all directions," how do we come at it? We can experience wonder at the smallest, most ordinary things as well as at the vastness of the universe. We are naturally awed at the stars, the galaxies, and the clusters of galaxies. We are awed at the calculus at work in the atom, at the chemistry at work in genetics, the electricity at work in our own thinking, and the who-knows-what at work in the global navigational system of butterflies. Wendell Berry writes:

> [In the] outdoors, we are confronted everywhere with wonders, we see that the miraculous is not extraordinary but the common mode of existence. . . . Whoever has really considered the lilies of the field or the birds of the air and pondered the improbability of their existence . . . will hardly balk at the turning of water into wine—which was, after all, a very small miracle. We forget the greater and still continuing miracle by which water (with soil and sunlight) is turned into grapes.[6]

Besides calling this wonder, we could also, as Berry does, see it as openness to a sacramental view of reality, a view that realizes that the commonest flower or a trout in a stream or a hatful of berries can be "means of grace," putting us in the presence of their and our transcendent source.

In spite of this, wonder is not the common attitude toward the world. Many (perhaps most?) people do not experience it at all. Many find the world flat and boring, one-dimensional, customary, the "been-there-done-that" place. A colleague of mine at Concordia College had taken a group of students on an art history tour of Greece. The students had the opportunity to visit Athens, Epidaurus, Mycenae, Olympia, and Delphi. After a day exploring the latter, two of her students came to her and complained, "We paid a lot of money for this trip, and so far all we've seen is a lot of piles of f–ing stones." She told them that she was extremely sorry that was all they had seen, but went on to make it clear that was not because that was all there was to see.

Wonder is an epistemic stance, a way of opening oneself up to the length and breadth and depth of creation. It is literally a "coming to our senses." Informed by the affirmation of God's creation we pursue a knowing that is consistent with being wonder-awake. Such knowing practices openness, makes us willing to move beyond our present categories, makes us critical of ways of knowing that are reductionistic, one–dimensional, and shallow.

The loss of awake-ness to wonder is one of the grossest impieties as well as a great tragedy. There are many things I wish for my own children: a sense of humor, caring companions, and something to deeply care about are near the top of my list. But so is an abiding sense of wonder. I would even go so far as to say that we realize our humanness in proportion to our ability to wonder. That is why it is so tragic that there are so many lives where wonder is eclipsed.

There are kinds of knowing that are consistent with our affirmation that God is creator, just as there are ways of knowing that are not consistent with it. The latter seem to fall into three patterns: (a) Acting as though the universe is our possession, our object, our plaything to do with as we want, we shape our knowing to allow it to serve ever more self-centered and destructive ends. (b) Looking at the world as limited by our conceptual categories, we deny dimensions of reality that do not fit our conceptions. We pursue knowledge as though we were the creator and designer of all there is, and that reality is there to suit our needs and fit our categories. (c) Denying or forgetting our dependence and the interdependence of all things, we pursue atomistic analyses of nature and human realities. (d) Forgetting our role as stewards, we imagine that the world is ours to master and end up destroying the very creation we should appreciate and serve.

2. Openness – Openness has already been talked about as one of the cognitive stances necessary for wonder. The openness we talk about there is a cognitive openness, a being willing to see aspects or dimensions of the world one might have supposed were not there, or were there but not important enough to be seen. But there are at least four other senses of openness that I think are implied by the Lutheran approach to things.

One is openness to views other than our own. Since we affirm that sin is a universal human condition, we cannot make ourselves exceptions to it. We must, therefore, be very suspicious of our temptation to think of ourselves as the righteous and "them" as the sinners. As a corollary, we must be suspicious of our temptation to think that "we" have things right that "they" got completely wrong. We put this suspiciousness into practice by opening ourselves to the voices and insights of others. We do not do this uncritically, but we try not to do it prejudicially either.

For many students (and I'm sure for faculty as well) it is important to have understanding precede judgment. If it does not precede it, it certainly has little chance of following it. On the other hand, we should not fall into the opposite extreme either, the extreme of making no judgments at all, of being judgment-phobic. Openness is therefore an attitude (or is it a practice, or perhaps a virtue?) with epistemic significance. It shapes what we see and hear as well as how we see and hear it.

The second is openness to the reality of those who have been marginalized and who suffer as a consequence of the power structures we are complicit in. This is a special case of the first sort of openness, but one deserving separate mention. In almost every situation, and certainly in academic discussions, certain voices are given primacy of position while others are very seldom heard. What would happen if the voices of the poorest people in a community could be heard in the classrooms of our law schools? What would happen if the voices of the very aged could be heard there? What would happen if the voices of those same people could be heard in our classes on health care? How would we have to rethink things in economic theory if we heard the voices who have been harmed the most by economic developments of, say, the last twenty years? Part of our commitment to openness involves us in guaranteeing that such voices are represented and heard.

The third is the openness of the community of discourse we create as communities of learners. Community is a precondition of being critical, a precondition of finding and speaking one's own voice. Community is, I believe, a precondition of real education in the sense of a learning that we are willing to let in to develop and transform us. I may be able to memorize a list of facts from a textbook even if I do not trust the instructor or my fellow class members or the textbook, but I cannot enter into an inquiry that connects to my own identity, my own worldview, to the things I care about the most, under those conditions. The creation of community exhibits openness, exemplifies openness, and enables openness. Without such a sense of community we will simply avoid talking about anything that really matters. Some people have suggested that community takes away the critical edge necessary for learning. I would say the opposite. Serious and engaged (as opposed to cynical) criticism requires a sense of belonging, ego-safety, and support. It is my experience that at least some of our Lutheran colleges are able to offer such a functioning critical community of this kind. It is a real gift where it occurs, better than a whole flock of prestigious faculty.

The fourth form of openness is the commitment to truth. It is this openness that makes the other three possible and gives us the *eros* necessary to pursue them. It is such a commitment that leads us to hear the other, critique ourselves, practice community. Without such a commitment we end up playing some form of self-serving academic game. With such a commitment we are capable of more. Iris Murdoch expressed it thus:

> We need to return from the self-centered concept of freedom to the other-centered concept of truth. We are not isolated free choosers, monarchs of all we survey, but benighted creatures sunk in a reality whose nature we are currently and overwhelmingly tempted to deform by fantasy.[7]

3. *Recognition of Connectedness* – Related to wonder as an appropriate response to the created order is the recognition of connectedness. If wonder makes us critical of reductionism, recognition of connectedness makes us critical of the way we separate and oversimplify. Denying or forgetting our own dependence and the interdependence of all things, our knowing is tempted to reduce the world to its simple parts. This has led us to a mechanical view of nature, a materialistic view of reality, and an atomistic understanding of ourselves and everything else. The affirmation of creation, on the other hand, suggests a systemic, even ecological view of nature, a sacramental view of reality, and a view of self and nature as essentially related. A simple, solitary, essentially unrelated thing (like Leibniz's monad, or the movie cowboy hero) is not the ultimate reality but the wildest abstraction. Yet atomism has been a dominating assumption, shaping our thinking in fields as far ranging as physics and economics. In order to know unrelated realities we have constructed unrelated fields of knowledge. David Orr points to this problem in *Earth in Mind*:

> A second danger of formal schooling is that it will imprint a disciplinary template onto impressionable minds and with it the belief that the world really is as disconnected as the divisions, disciplines, and subdivisions of disciplines of the typical curriculum. Students come to believe that there is such a thing as politics separate from ecology or that economics has nothing to do with physics. Yet the world is not this way, and except for the convenience of the analysis, it cannot be broken into disciplines and specializations without doing serious harm to the world and to the minds and lives of people.[8]

Systems theory and ecology are disciplines that focus on connection. I believe we need more studies like that. Any problem-focused study, as opposed to a discipline-focused study, will reveal such connectedness. A study of a city's transportation infrastructure, for example, will have to get into geology, engineering, politics, economics, history, and communications theory. It will have to include an understanding of energy sources, future potentials for carbon-based as well as alternative fuels, air and water pollution, and human psychology as well. How well prepared is the person who takes twelve courses in only one subject to deal with such a complex interrelatedness?

Joseph Sittler describes relational knowing:

> Reality is known only in relation. . . . There is no ontology of isolated enti-
> ties . . . whether we are reflecting about god or man or society or the cos-
> mos. The only adequate ontological structure we may utilize for thinking
> things Christianly is an ontology of community, communion, ecol-
> ogy—and all these words point conceptually to thought of a common
> kind. "Being itself" may be a relation, not an entitive thing.[9]

I would not argue, as Sittler seems to, that mono-disciplinary knowledge is worthless. I think the disciplines are very useful as tools for thinking about the world. But like tools, the individual disciplines are able to do
particular things well because they are limited. Those limitations are both
their strength and their weakness. A chisel can do its job well because it is
not also used as a screwdriver. Our mistake has come, not from the learning and use of the disciplines, but from assuming that their analytic approach was *the* paradigm of knowing and that the view of reality they
provide was *the* reality. The disciplines need to have a voice in the description of reality, but the recognition of connectedness as an epistemic stance
requires that they not have the last word in the conversation.

Seeing ourselves as part of the creation, in fact as the stewards of creation, connects our knowing to our doing. It realizes that growth in knowledge also requires growth in responsibility. It connects the knowing of
facts, the knowing of "how to," with the kind of knowing that cares, the
kind of knowing that results in responsible judgment. This is not the
model of knowing that currently dominates academe. It is one we must intentionally nurture if it is to grow.

4. Freedom – There are many mistakes we Western moderns have
made and continue to make, but one of the most serious and far-reaching
is a misunderstanding of freedom. Consider these two contrasting paradigms of freedom. Let's call the first one *the disconnected consumerist*
view: being bound by nothing, connected to nothing, free in that sense, I
make myself who I want to be, from nothing. Since I have no one to please
but myself, my whole life is devoted to the fulfilling of my preferences. Like
a store manikin my identity and value is determined by what I have. I am
what I own. I shop, therefore I am. Since there are always new things to
buy, the possibilities for recreating myself are endless. Since there is nothing (besides myself) to give the world (or myself) value, the world is frequently boring, irrelevant, unimportant ("The news depresses me"), and I
go from one extreme thrill to another trying to jolt myself into existence.
Given the prevalence of such a view it should not be surprising to discover
that the most frequent reason given by teens for violence is: "It was some-

thing to do." The most common response from their parents: "But we get over eighty channels on cable."

Consider an alternative view of freedom, for lack of a ready name I will call it *the connected self* view of freedom: Being called by those to whom I am connected (as I mature this may be an expanding circle), I discover my own identity as I discover what I love, what I care about, care for, am connected with. Hearing the call of others' needs and the call of truth, justice, love, and beauty, I am en-couraged and en-livened. I become who I am in the context of the call I receive. In place of freedom that says, "What shall I buy today?" this is a freedom that says, "Here I am, send me," or "Here I stand, I can do no other." Such freedom is vocational—dependent on vocation and intimately connected to the finding of identity. Luther said that we exist by being called by God, and we exist only so long as God continues to address us.

Freedom may not, by itself, be an epistemic stance, but it certainly does inform the way people think, inquire, and know the world. So what we want to focus on here is the possibility of freedom-informed thinking and knowing. As we saw earlier, the fact that redemption is a gift from God implies that we do nothing to earn it. Therefore we need not delude ourselves into thinking that we need to think purely, piously, parochially in order to please God. The gift of grace brings with it the gift of freedom. It is this freedom that enabled Luther to participate in all the enterprises that he also had been freed to be critical of. This illustrates well the double thrust of such a view of freedom—both a freedom-from as well as a freedom-to. This kind of freedom has epistemic implications.

In the December 1998 issue of *The Christian Century*, James Schaap wrote a provocative article about the difficulty of being an avowedly Christian writer. A reviewer of one of his novels told him she had liked his novel a good deal even though she had thought she wouldn't when the review was assigned to her. "Why does your novel say the word, 'Christian' on the back cover?" she asked him. "Now nobody is going to read it." The same novel was reviewed in the newsletter of the Christian Booksellers Association. The reviewer there did not recommend Schaap's book because it included characters who were homosexual, adulterous, and drug users. No bookstore that was a member of the CBA carried Schaap's book because it did not pass their standards for sanitized subject matter and inoffensive language. Among other writers the CBA will not carry are Flannery O'Connor (offensive language and despicable characters), John Updike (same reasons), Wendell Berry, Doris Betts, Madeleine L'Engle, and Larry Woiwode. Schaap comments that the most "offensive" book the CBA carries is the Bible.

God help us when the word "Christian" has come to be synonymous with "inoffensive," "sanitized," "asexual," or when "Christian" writers can only write about nice folks, in nice towns, doing nice things for nice reasons, in nice language. The freedom of the Christian is, among other things, a freedom from the suffocating and nauseating rule of niceness. It is a freedom to see the truth and tell it, not out of meanness, but out of a love of the truth. John Updike has written:

> God is the God of the living, though many of his priests and executors, to keep order and force the world into a convenient mold, will always want to make him the God of the dead, the God who chastises life and forbids and says No. . . . [As a Christian writer] I have felt free to describe life as accurately as I could, with especial attention to human erosions and betrayals. What small faith I have has given to me what artistic courage I have. My theory was that God already knows everything and cannot be shocked. And only truth is useful. Only truth can be built upon.[10]

Christians can be thinkers and inquirers in freedom and we can be inquirers and teachers toward freedom. Freedom is not only a shaping principle of our knowing, but of our teaching and learning as well.

5. *Critical Faithfulness* – In an earlier section I commented that Luther's efforts at reformation were best seen as an exercise in critical faithfulness. Luther was impelled to be critical of the practices of the church and the state of Christendom because he was so thoroughly committed to it. A less committed person might have been as critical, but the criticism would have turned to cynicism if it were missing a willingness to spend oneself on the improvement of that which was cared for. Thus many of us are critical of our governments, but few care enough to invest our lives in doing something about it. So we blame "them" for all our problems and sit on our hands.

Critical faithfulness, as an epistemic stance, requires that we fully develop our critical abilities and attitudes, but never as an end in themselves. The criticism must be joined to an attitude of active engagement. It is fairly easy, educationally speaking, to produce a class of "wise guys" who can shoot down everyone's argument and deflate everyone's project. But it is more difficult to join such critical abilities with a desire to make things better.

Children, at a certain stage in their development, start to play "the blame game." The symptoms of this condition are the frequent whining of the phrases, "It's not my fault, it's his fault," "I didn't start it, she did," "Well, he did it to me." What we hope, and work to enable, is that they will grow beyond this (not everyone does) and can learn instead to work toward solving the problem rather than establishing an ultimate beginning for it.

As long as Serbs blame Croatians and both blame the Muslims and the Muslims blame the Christians their problems will not be solved. The question is not how we can settle the question of first culpability in a conflict that has gone on for centuries. The problem that must be solved is how we can make things better, how we can move toward peace and justice from here on out. The culpability now lies with those who continue it, not with those, time out of mind, who started it. The problem repeats itself with Israelis and Palestinians, Protestants and Catholics in Northern Ireland, Muslims and Hindus in India and Pakistan, and so on.

There are many things that it is important to think critically about. What those things are will change from time to time as the urgencies of the world change. Yet there are certain patterns of criticism that need to be practiced perennially. I will identify just three of them here.

(1) Being critical of all human claims to ultimacy. Absolutism can take many forms. Absolutisms of ideology have resulted in a variety of totalitarian regimes in the last century, regimes that were willing to sacrifice everything (and everybody) in order to serve their particular agendas. Given the potential for destructiveness of such regimes, it is extremely important to practice criticism of all ultimate ideologies, including religions. Religions can become idols as well as anything else can. When we worship our religious identity, when we condemn people simply because they do not belong in the "us" camp, when we enthrone our own chauvinism, then we are worshiping an idol. All idols, all claims to ultimacy, need serious criticism and committed opposition. In our own American society, the consumer culture makes the most pervasive claims to ultimacy. There are more "true believers" in that church than there are in any other that I know of. That is why it needs a vigorous critique.

(2) Being critical of our institutions and the way they shape reality and value for us. Many times an institution is founded to meet a particular human need. Then, over time, it comes to serving itself, or the professionals within it, not those most in need of its services. This has happened to a very large extent with the legal profession and the criminal justice system. Originally formed to enforce the law and serve justice, the system now frequently serves the ends of increasing litigation and employing attorneys. The system has become so complex, so much a "game" understood and played only by insiders, that ordinary people, even if intelligent and well educated, cannot make use of it on their own. A couple I know asked an attorney to make a will and set up a trust fund for their children. When the document was completed, the couple, both of whom have earned doctorates, could not tell whether it said what they wanted it to. They hired another attorney to interpret the first attorney's work. Not surprisingly, the

second one told them that the document did not at all say what they intended and suggested they hire him to write them a new set of documents. They couldn't understand those either. The legal system is organized to make us need more services by attorneys. We all have many reasons to doubt that justice is served thereby.

Is the same thing happening to medical care? Does the increased use of the medical care system simply increase our dependence on it? Is the same thing occurring with education? Do schools simply make us more dependent on schools? Are there any that really take seriously the often advertised claim to make "independent learners"? Is it surprising that we have created a culture where what is desired is the certificate or the diploma, not the education? Since so much of our lives is shaped and controlled by these institutions, it is very important that they be thoroughly and frequently critiqued. Of course our own institutions of higher learning have to be included in that critique.[11]

(3) Being critical of our own modes of knowing. We should be critical of ways of knowing that are reductionistic, one-dimensional, shallow. We should pursue knowing that recognizes our fundamental connectedness and responsibility. We should be critical of knowing that separates, that oversimplifies, that object-ifies the known and abstracts the knower from living relationship. We should be critical of all reductionisms and all knowing that serves only to control nature without concern about asking, "To what end?" We should be critical of all knowing that is not also a form of caring. What kind of knowing makes possible the hydrogen bomb? What kind of knowing makes possible one person holding a patent on the four most toxic compounds the world has ever known? What kind of science disconnects itself from the use it will be put to, claims in the name of objectivity to have no interest in what happens to the world or its inhabitants? What kind of economics proceeds by not counting all the costs? What kind of history is written while completely forgetting the experience of three-fourths of the human race? In each case I think the answer is the same, a knowing that abstracts from the larger reality. Such knowing may be necessary, but it should also be examined very critically.

All of our thinking is limited. It is limited by the language we use, by the age we live in, by the disciplines we know as well as those we do not know. Our thinking is also very likely to be limited by our gender, race, ethnic and cultural heritage, economic class, and who knows what else. But sin, in the enterprise of knowing, is not about being limited. In most cases sin is the denial of our finitude, the attempt to absolutize it. Everyone who has ever done physics or written a law or thought philosophically or composed a poem has done so as a limited person with limited vision with limited tools. Yet some useful laws have been written, some instructive science and philosophy has been discovered, some inspiring poems have been written. In many cases the genius of a person or discipline is directly (not inversely) related to their limitedness. Physics does what it does well because it does not attempt to do everything. It errs not by being physics but when we claim that it is *the* picture of reality. Marx's critique of capitalism is sharp and insightful, but it becomes a horror when it is promoted as *the* meaning of life, history, politics. This is the meaning of totalitarianism: a limited thing that does not recognize its own limits. It is a theory, or discipline, or vision gone crazy. Wendell Berry, once again, aptly voices a warning:

> One of our problems is that we as humans cannot live without acting; we have to act. . . . Moreover, we have to act on the basis of what we know, and what we know is incomplete. What we have come to know so far is demonstrably incomplete, since we keep on learning more, and there seems little reason to think that our knowledge will become significantly more complete. The mystery surrounding our life probably is not significantly reducible. And so the question of how to act in ignorance is paramount. . . . If we lack the cultural means to keep incomplete knowledge from becoming the basis of arrogant and dangerous behavior, then the intellectual disciplines themselves become dangerous.[12]

6. Engaged Suspiciousness – A skeptic is a person who doubts the truth of things. Suspicion, on the other hand, doubts the motivation behind what we do.[13] As we mentioned earlier, Luther was suspicious of religious hierarchies, suspicious of self-serving structures, suspicious of ethics, philosophy, and theology, including his own. He was suspicious of many political authorities and even more suspicious of those who would lead rebellions against them. This suspiciousness did not make him a cynic who dissociated himself from all of these things, complaining about them while trying to maintain a distance from the whole enterprise. He was a person who led a rebellion, he was a person who wrote about ethics, he was a theologian, he was politically engaged. But he did all these things aware that his efforts were imperfect, because finite, and that they were flawed because he lacked the purity of heart he desired.

What does it mean to confess that knowing is a sin-infected undertaking? As our previous discussion indicated, it is possible to pursue knowing as a form of idolatry—an idolatry of self where we imagine ourselves to be God, the creator and possessor of all, and an idolatry of our means of knowing themselves. Absolutism can take many forms. One form is to claim ultimacy for our institutions; another is to claim ultimacy for our disciplines and our ideologies. To confess sin is to realize our temptation to do this and to be appropriately suspicious of our modes of knowing. Parker Palmer writes:

> In the language of the religious tradition, Adam and Eve committed the first sin. In the language of intellectual tradition, they made the first epistemological error. It was an error that has been repeated many times in human history, not least by those scientists of whom Robert Oppenheimer said, "The physicists have known sin." . . . Adam and Eve were driven from the Garden because of the kind of knowledge they reached for—a knowledge that distrusted and excluded God.[14]

As we said above, we must be critical of all claims to ultimacy, including those we make in the name of our religion. We also must be suspicious of our own motives for knowing and for claiming ourselves in possession of the truth. Whom does this possession of truth give us power over? Whom does it empower? What is it in this way of thinking that wants to become master? The recognition of sin in knowing makes us see the constant need of criticism and the development of the critical disciplines. It makes us see the value of corrigibility as well as the temptation of disciplinary myopia. But it also ought to make us aware of our own double-mindedness, that is, the way we serve one end while apparently serving another.

The recognition of sin in the project of knowing does not imply anti-intellectualism. To suppose that it does is to make a mistake that many Christians have made, the mistake of thinking that if one avoids sinful activity X, then one can avoid sinfulness altogether. That is not the Lutheran view. If it were, then Lutherans would never have established colleges and universities at all. If thinking is a sinful process we do not avoid it by thinking as little as possible. In fact, *we* do not avoid it at all. "Sin boldly," Luther is credited as saying. This is ridiculous advice for someone who supposes we can avoid sinning altogether. But this is not the Lutheran confession. Our efforts to avoid sin or protect our hard-won purity may end up being as sinful as anything. Isn't that the point of Jesus' story about the priest, the Levite, and the caring Samaritan? The point of the story is not just that the goodness of the Samaritan allows him to help. We also need to note that *the goodness* of the priest and Levite prevent them from helping. What does this imply for our thinking? What would an ethics constructed around this central Christian realization look like? What would a church constructed around it look like? Too often churches are communities of judgment rather than communities of people who all stand in need of forgiveness.

7. *Service/Vocation* – Inquiry, knowing, and learning continually shaped by the question, "How does this serve the needs of the world?" will

be appreciatively different from knowing not accompanied by such a question. I recently looked over the program of a national academic convention in the humanities. The pattern I observed was people presenting research focused on irrelevant minutiae of their disciplines. The purpose? To be able to add another line to their dossier, in some cases another publication to their list. In conversation with two colleagues, one in the natural sciences and one in the behavioral sciences, I was told the same thing about the papers at their national meetings. I admit that sometimes a useful discovery might come out of what appears to be trivial research. That could happen. But I would wager that in 95% of these cases it does not. What does go on is the scoring of points in an esoteric game, points that will be entered in some dean's or department chair's scorecard. The colleague in behavioral sciences told me that one of the characteristics of people who are autistic is this same kind of specialization. They create small, almost private worlds of their own that they become remarkably expert in—like memorizing timetables for trains in the New York subway system, and then they can't understand why everyone doesn't share their enthusiasm for it. What we have in academe is a culture of such autism which, we maintain, is "research productive." I tend to agree with the judgment of historian Page Smith, that such productivity is "essentially worthless . . . busy-work on a vast almost incomprehensible scale."[15] The Germans have an apt word for such academic experts: *Fachidioten*, "specialist idiots."

One of the sources of such a tendency to value research is "physics envy," the tendency to value disciplinary work that looks like physics, is empirical and mathematical, reports some facts that either confirm or refute some theory. This envy has shaped research even in departments of literature, where researchers look desperately for things to count that will support or refute the latest literary theory. "Whatever happened," one colleague at a major research university lamented in conversation, "to the idea that the study of literature was about the intelligent reading of powerful texts? Our best students, nowadays, believe that they read literature only in order to move on to advanced study in literary theory, on the assumption that this is what the discipline is really about. Their assumption is that only freshmen read literature with the idea that they will get something out of it."

Another source of such a view of disciplinary expertise is a particular understanding of the liberal arts. The original Hellenic idea of liberal arts was those studies that were so essential that no matter what one's particular role in life one needed to have pursued them. The pursuit of such studies was essential for free people, for citizens, in order to negotiate the complexities of life, to detect falsehood, to become part of the community of thoughtful people on whom community life depended. From that Hellenic ideal, however, the idea of the liberal arts devolved into learning that was, practically speaking, useless. A large part of that redefinition was the work of John Henry Newman in his classic, *The Idea of a University*. The sharp distinction between liberal and practical learning is central to that work. Liberal learning "refuses to be informed by any end, or absorbed into any art," he writes. It is liberal if "nothing accrues of consequence beyond the using."[16] So "liberal" had shifted from designating studies of social importance and essential life-usefulness, to meaning "free from practical employment." Is this also why we now use the word "academic" as in "academic question" to mean "of no practical importance"?

Derek Bok, the former president of Harvard, in *Universities and the Future of America*, laments:

> Our universities excel in pursuing the easier opportunities. . . . On the other hand . . . higher education has often failed to respond as effectively as it might, even to some of the most important challenges facing America. Armed with the security of tenure and the time to study the world with care, professors would appear to have a unique opportunity to act as society's scouts to signal impending problems. . . . Yet rarely have members of the academy succeeded in discovering emerging issues and bringing them vividly to the attention of the public. What Rachel Carson did for the risks to the environment, Ralph Nader for consumer protection, Michael Harrington for problems of poverty, Betty Friedan for women's rights, they did as independent critics, not as members of a faculty.[17]

I believe that such problems as we have noted above could be addressed by reconnecting the idea of knowledge and academic learning to social usefulness by means of the concept of vocation. This does not mean that we let the society dictate to the academy what it wants. In many, if not most, cases the thing society needs most is severe and thoroughgoing care-full criticism, as Bok's examples illustrate. Raising the questions, "Whom does this serve?" and "In what way is it a service?" about our own inquiries would reshape, for the better, a good deal of the "essentially worthless busywork" Smith mentions. Asking, as part of our efforts at knowing, "How is this related to the deep needs of the world?" might also move the academy in the directions that Bok envisions. These are, of course, the questions that inform the Lutheran concept of vocation. As we quoted Luther earlier, "the Christian should be guided by this thought alone . . . considering nothing but the need and advantage of the neighbor. This is a truly Christian life."

Affirmation of vocation makes us suspicious of hierarchy and rank, even while we are respectful of positions and responsibilities. Teachers may be respected for what they know, and do, and can communicate, but this does not imply that they are higher than their students or the other persons who keep the university running. We are tempted to be too impressed by what degrees, ranks, and specialties mean. We should be suspicious of such things. They may distinguish something useful, but they also may be ways of inflating ourselves and demeaning others.

Another facet of the affirmation of vocation is the need to critique our professions and the institutions that house and structure them. We are called, as Luther put it, "to work in the service of our neighbor to the greater glory of God." But it should be quite obvious that our work and our professions do not always do that. How often does the legal profession serve the needs of humans who most stand in need of the protection of law and justice? Instead it seems to me that it serves the ends of litigation, making us more dependent on attorneys and more cynical about the whole business. To what degree does the medical profession well serve the ends of health and the needs of those who need health care the most? To what degree do our institutions of education serve the learning needs of people? Here again we have an institution that tends to make people more dependent on the system and less enabled to learn on their own. There is more than one way a person may be learning-disabled. One may be disabled *from* learning, but one may also be disabled *by* learning. We should carefully examine the way we do our work, asking whether it really serves the deep needs of the neighbor or whether it is structured to advance some other agenda.

Learning shaped by the idea of vocation will be closely connected to service. *Theory must be critiqued by a doing that serves.* It is important for us to learn that sometimes our professions do not serve all that well. There may be no better example of someone who learned this than Robert Coles. He gives a vivid account of his coming to critical awareness of the harm that may be done by a way of knowing. He describes his experience as a young psychiatrist in his book *The Call of Stories*:

> A year after my internship, I was sitting with a young man who had attempted suicide (sleeping pills) and failed. . . . When I put that youth's "history" into a therapeutical formulation, the familiar phrases appeared, none of them surprising, each of them applicable not only to that person but to many, many others: "domineering mother" (and sister), "poor masculine identification," "aloof father figure," and so on. When I named his "defenses," his "hostility," the kind of "transference" (involvement with me) he'd made I was again consigning him (and me) to territory populated by many others. No wonder so many psychiatric reports sound banal: in each one the details of an individual life are buried under the professional jargon. We residents were learning to summon up such ab-

stractions within minutes of seeing a patient; we directed our questions so neatly that the answers triggered the confirmatory conceptualization in our heads: a phobic, a depressive, an acting-out disorder, an identity problem, a hysterical personality.

Some of these labels or categories of analysis are psychological shortcuts and don't necessarily mean offense to patients or diminishment of the user. On the other hand, the story of some of us who become owners of a professional power and a professional vocabulary is the familiar one of moral thoughtlessness. We brandish our authority in a ceaseless effort to reassure ourselves about our importance, and we forget to look at our own warts and blemishes, so busy are we cataloguing those in others.[18]

8. *Hope* – There are two relevant senses of hope because there are two ways in which the process of knowing can lead to hopelessness. The first is a failure to find meaning, a failure to connect the increase in knowledge to a growth of the self. The second hopelessness is a despair at ever making a positive difference in the world. Both forms of hopelessness are frequently induced by the collegiate academic experience.

Sharon Daloz Parks, researching the learning processes of young adults, writes:

> We human beings seem unable to survive, and certainly cannot thrive, unless we can make meaning. We need to be able to make some sense out of things; we seek pattern, order, coherence, and relation in the disparate elements of our experience. If life is perceived as only fragmented and chaotic, we suffer confusion, distress, stagnation, and finally despair.[19]

This capacity and demand for meaning she calls faith. But it is apparent, I think, how closely this is connected to what we would normally think of as hope. As we mentioned in an earlier section, hope is not the same thing as optimism. It certainly is not the same thing as wishful thinking. Hope is what makes us endure in spite of our realism. It is what makes us continue even when we realize the difficulties and pain and struggle that something may require. It is the belief that growth is possible and the insight to see that such growth is more valuable than what one risks in the struggle. So, not only is hope very closely related to faith, it is also concentric with courage.

I know a high school math teacher who told me that her math students were handicapped in their problem-solving skills by what she called "a three-minute limit." She discovered that her students, who all thought of themselves as "math stupid," actually had far above average abilities in math aptitude. But somewhere along the route of their education they had all learned the habit of devoting not more than three minutes to working on any math problem. If they didn't solve it in that time, they gave up, saying, "I'm no good at math." Their failure was not a failure of mental ability, nor a failure in math knowledge, but a failure in problem-solving patience. Her problem was not figuring how to teach her students math but figuring how to get them past their "do it easy or not at all" attitude. That proved to be much harder to do than teaching new math concepts and methods, because it required a good deal of unlearning and because it required personal learning, a learning that changed the learner.

Three years ago I asked several faculty who taught freshman courses to append to their spring semester final exams the question, "What was the most important thing you learned in the past year?" A few of the answers focused on things they had learned in some class, from some teacher. But by far the majority of responses were things they had learned about themselves in the nonacademic dimensions of their college experiences: "I learned how to survive without my mom." "I learned from my roommate's lack of discipline how important self-discipline is." "I learned from my coach how hard I had to work to move up a notch in my performance." "I learned from the seniors what it means to be a team player." "I learned from my friend, Sarah, what an abusive relationship is. I learned that my boyfriend was not good for me. That was hard to learn but I'm glad I learned it." "I learned that a person may be gay and still be a genuine and good person. If someone had told me I was going to learn that here in the first week of school, I would have left. But I'm now a different person than I was then, and somehow I learned that." Did the students' academic learning have anything to do with such personal growth experiences? Most of the students would probably not have seen the connection; most faculty would probably not claim it. But somehow in the process of their learning these students learned how to have an idea, articulate it, examine it, defend it, expand it. All of that learning, as nonacademic as it may sound, requires a kind of confidence in one's ability to think, to inquire, to know what direction growth lies in, a confidence that one has made some progress from illusion toward truth in one's own development and not just change from one illusion to another.

We take hope seriously in the context of knowing when we are aware of these dimensions of learning. People are willing to take the risks of uncomfortable learning and the risks of criticism if they are confident that they will grow thereby. Where this growth is denied or ignored, learning will become shallow and excessively conservative precisely when it ought to be expansive and liberal. Sharon Daloz Parks once again:

> To become a young adult in faith is to discover in a critically aware, self-conscious manner the limits of inherited or otherwise socially received assumptions about how life works—what is ultimately true and trustworthy, and what counts—and to recompose meaning and faith on the other

side of that discovery. The quality of this recomposition and its adequacy to ground a worthy adulthood depends in significant measure on the hospitality, commitment, and courage of adult culture, as mediated through both individuals and institutions.[20]

A few years ago I wrote an essay titled, "On Becoming Learning Disabled."[21] It began: "Not all learning is enabling. Some kinds of learning are, in fact, very disabling. It follows, by an odd twist of language, that people can be learning-disabled in two senses: we may be disabled and thereby be kept *from learning*, but we may also be disabled *by learning* as well." I then went on to catalog with many examples ways in which such learning disablement occurs. I organized them under the following headings: (i) Learning that one is afraid to use. (ii) Learning that reinforces passivity and dependence. (iii) Learning that alienates us from our own experience. (iv) Learned cynicism and hopelessness. It is that fourth category that is particularly relevant here.

A student studying philosophy may learn seven theories and then come to see what is wrong with each one. He leaves the course believing not only that these theories are faulty but that all theorizing is faulty. A student studying political history learns many stories of political corruption and leaves believing that politics is evil, not something a decent person would ever be engaged in. A student of world religions discovers that many, if not all, people pursue their religions as it suits them, as buttresses for their life priorities, not as foundation stones. She abandons all religion on the grounds that "it's all hypocrisy." In each of these cases these students have learned something, perhaps even learned it well. They have come to embody the critical standards in their disciplines. But what they have not understood is the human necessity of using limited tools to accomplish good things. How silly it would be for a potter to lament, "My art is worthless because everything I make is made out of mere mud," or for a glass worker to lament, "My art is worthless because everything I make is breakable." Or imagine a poet complaining, "The problem of my work is that I am confined to the limits of language." What each of these workers says is correct, but it is only a fraction of the truth, a fraction that focuses only on the negative.

The discovery of imperfection can lead to cynicism, to an unwillingness to participate, to an unwillingness to try. But there is no necessity in that conclusion and there certainly is no wisdom in it. Perfection is always a false standard. The object of human work is not perfection, but modest accomplishment. Perfectionism and cynicism are closely related.

It is quite amazing to me to see students write, "This all sounds very good in theory, but you can't change society" (or "the system" or "the world"). There is a certain kind of wisdom in this, for the probability of effecting the kind of change we wish may indeed be very low. But it is also a kind of foolishness, for experience teaches us not just that change is not easy, but that it does happen. I think of the tremendous changes that have occurred in my own lifetime: the ways we think about race and what follows from it; the ways we think about sex, sexual identity, and sexual choices; changes regarding the rights and roles of women; tremendous changes in technology and its influence on lifestyles. It is certainly silly to say that everything will change, but it is just as silly to believe that nothing will, or to believe that we can predict it. No one had predicted the collapse of the Soviet Union, the end to apartheid in South Africa, the rise of Islamic fundamentalism, the change of fortune of the nuclear power industry, the AIDS epidemic, etc.

At the end of a class I taught on environmental issues one of the brightest students wrote in his final paper:

> I now know what the problems are. I see how my behavior has to change to make things better. But I can't change, I can't do what's necessary. I feel like a robot that's been programmed to understand its own problems and what it would take to change them. Still, I'm hard-wired to behave in ways I know are destructive. This class has made me wiser but also a lot sadder than I was before. I don't think I want to learn any more.

Like addicts who have come to the point of admitting their addiction yet feel quite powerless to do anything about it, this student has come to the point of seeing his behavior and lifestyle as a problem, yet feels incapable of doing anything about it. The awareness of the problem does not cause the problem, it only causes us to recognize it. But it is often very easy to confuse these two things. There's a joke that makes this point:

A: My uncle Fred heard on the radio that smoking cigarettes increases the probabilities of cancer and heart disease.
B: So, did that make him quit smoking?
A: No, it made him quit listening to the radio.

Perhaps you have felt this way about going to the doctor: "If I don't go I won't learn that there's something seriously wrong with me. Therefore I'll be OK." So, by some strange twist of illogic, you conclude that going to the doctor causes illness.

If learning can be pursued in a way that leads to cynicism and despair, it can also be pursued in a way that leads to hope and engagement. Rather than pretending that knowing is value neutral we should realize how it is connected to the doing, being, and becoming of the learner. Learning can disempower as well as empower; it can disable as well as enable. It seems naive to think about knowing without noting these things, and irresponsible not to take them into account in the design of learning/teaching occasions.

Avoiding a Mis-Conception

Some people whom I have told about my intentions to a explore a faith-related epistemology have supposed that this meant I was promoting the idea that because something is a religious belief it must therefore be true. They suppose this, I assume, because they have heard people make such inferences as "Because the Bible says X therefore X is scientifically or historically true." That is definitely not the idea I am advancing here. I would no more accept that argument about the Bible than I would if the source were the book of Mormon or any other sacred text. First, I do not think of the Bible or any other sacred text as primarily a source for scientific or historical claims. But, second, the inference wouldn't be valid even if they were.

The truth of a scientific claim must be examined by the best practices of the community of scientists. The truth of historical claims ought to be examined by the best practices of the community of historians. A faith-related epistemology is not the substitution of religious beliefs for scientific or historical work. That would be a parody of what we are arguing. A Lutheran epistemology comes into play, not as a substitute for the work of the disciplines but as an argument for what the best practices of those disciplines should include. We are not arguing that one should do Christian biology or Christian economics, but that one should do both biology and economics exceedingly well. That is not the same thing as arguing that we should pursue these inquiries by following their secular paradigms, because our argument is that following those paradigms has not resulted in pursuing those inquiries as well as they can be pursued. A Lutheran epistemology is concerned most of all with what "well" means when applied to all kinds of knowing. We have no interest in playing a religious "trump card" in arguments about the truth.

Some Concluding Thoughts

Most of us have a hard time seeing things like hope and service and freedom as connected to knowing. Many faculty might assume that if such topics should be addressed at all in a collegiate setting they should be done by the "nonacademic" departments of the institution, such as student services or the pastor's office. But I think this demonstrates what a poor and one-dimensional understanding of knowing we have often been working with. A particular (and I believe very wrong) notion of objectivity has divorced academic learning from the search for meaning, orientation, moral focus. To quote Sharon Daloz Parks once again:

Wherever a strict dichotomy between the objective and the subjective has been practiced, we have become vulnerable to exchanging wisdom for knowledge and moral commitment for method. Moreover, professors have been vulnerable to functioning as less-than-whole persons, the vocation of higher education has been impoverished, and young adults searching for a fitting orientation to ultimate reality—a faith to live by—have been abandoned by faculty and others in the academy who are distinctively positioned to serve the formation of a critical and worthy faith. Accordingly . . . professors are too often mere technicians of knowledge, higher education can offer no orienting vision or offer leadership toward a coherent unity, and discrete academic disciplines disclose only isolated (and thus distorted) aspects of truth. As a consequence, some of the most important questions of the contemporary world are difficult to address within the prevailing rubrics of the academy.[22]

Sometimes faith-related colleges have not had much more to offer. A colleague of mine showed me an e-mail letter from his daughter attending another ELCA institution, which I quote with the student's permission:

My professors are knowledgeable as long as one stays in their field of expertise. Some are even academically famous, for whatever that's worth. But as persons they are a great disappointment. When I have asked them questions that relate learning to larger issues, or when I have asked them how they relate their learning to issues of value and faith, I find them to be less mature than I am! I get the impression that they never ask themselves these questions at all, and consequently have never attempted to answer them.

If this is so, and not merely a student's misperception, it is a serious failure. It is such a failure because a Lutheran college ought to have a larger, more coherent, and more multidimensional understanding of knowing than these faculty seem to have.

Gift and Task – III

I believe that knowing shaped by such principles as I have described is a valuable gift. It is a gift to those engaged as knowers because it gives us a large, rich, open, humanly connected picture of knowing to work with. It is a gift to students because it allows for a learning of academic subjects and disciplines that may be directly connected to their own growth as persons. It is a gift to the culture and the society at large because it encourages a knowing that is open yet very critical; critical yet engaged and loving; loving, yet disciplined; disciplined, yet connected to praxis and service; connected, yet remarkably free.

My argument in this chapter has been to show that the Lutheran tradition has something very important to offer all of us, students and faculty alike, if only we would realize it. *Lutheran theology implies an enriched and critical epistemology.* Earlier in the text I referred to such an epistemology with the phrase, "answerable knowing." In pursuing such knowing we are answerable to:

— that which is known

— our gifts

— the givers and deliverers of gifts (our teachers, the tradition, the community of discourse)

— each other (faculty, students, fellows in the community of inquiry)

— the larger culture

— the deep needs of the world

— all who are victimized and marginalized by our ways and institutions of knowing

— future generations

— the earth we are called to steward

— God, whose reign all of this is and whose love sustains and empowers us

This epistemology is something our students need, our disciplines need, we as inquirers and teachers need, and, I believe, the world desperately needs. Developing an educational praxis that recognizes and enables human wholeness and engages us in answerable knowing is an essential part (do I dare say "the essential part"?) of our calling as Lutheran colleges and universities. I believe it is at the heart of our peculiar service as colleges and universities, and the establishment and maintenance of a community that practices such knowing constitutes a very large part of our vocation to the world.

VI.
Implications—Curriculum and Pedagogy

*Education can serve as the core of a lifelong journey towards
wholeness, rather than merely an accumulation of facts, figures,
or skills.*

—Steven Glazer, *The Heart of Learning*

So, what do these discussions imply about the shape of education in
Lutheran colleges and universities? What kind of education is shaped
by a Lutheran vision of human being? What kind of education is shaped
by a Lutheran approach to knowing? These things do have implications
and it is the purpose of this chapter to sketch out what some of them
are—for curriculum, for our approach to teaching and learning, for
building a faculty, and for scholarship. But before getting into detailed
discussions of these areas there are a couple of general comments that
should be made.

It is not the intention of this discussion to suggest that all Lutheran
colleges and universities should be the same. The cookie-cutter approach
to Lutheran higher education would be a serious mistake. These institutions have different locations, are of different sizes, serve different student
groups, in different competitive educational markets. And each is staffed
with wonderfully different persons who, daily in their own ways, shape the
identities of their respective colleges and universities. It is our hope that
our colleges and universities serve well the people and places they are given
to serve, and that they thrive in doing so. In that process they will incorpo-
rate different programs and grow in different ways. As a consequence, not
all the things that are talked about in this chapter will apply to all institutions, nor will all apply in the same way.

It is also not the intention of this discussion to suggest that all faculty
should be the same. The cookie-cutter approach does not work well here
either. It should have been clear from the discussion on epistemology that

the pursuit of knowledge requires a critical community of learners. One of the necessities of such a community is that it contain a diversity of courageous voices. So, a Lutheran college should embody diversity not in spite of being Lutheran, but because of being Lutheran.

Five Themes

It is my contention that education informed by the Lutheran tradition ought to be built around five general themes: Giftedness, Freedom, Faithful Criticism, Service/Vocation, and *Paideia*. The education provided at our colleges and universities ought to be known far and wide for the way we celebrate gifts, for the way we learn in freedom toward freedom, for the depth and engagement of our criticism, for connecting learning to doing that serves, and connecting learning to the self-becoming of the student. Most of these themes have been discussed in what precedes, so I will address each theme very briefly here.

1. The Celebration of Gifts

A Christian encounters all of life and all of creation as a gift. A Christian teacher, therefore, is a sharer and unwrapper of gifts: the gifts of the world or discipline or author to be studied, and the gifts each of us brings with us. There were teachers I had in college who opened the same gifts semester after semester, year after year, and took great delight in it. In some cases the gift was swamp ecology, in other cases the dialogues of Plato, cathedral architecture, the chorales of Bach, the poetry of Rilke. In each case the teachers were as excited as kids, not at finding what was in there (they had a pretty good idea about that already), but at our coming to discover what was in there.

There were also teachers (sometimes the same ones) who excelled in making students see the gifts that were inside them: the gifts of language, of music, of leadership, of scholarship, of teamwork, of art. Such teachers enabled, encouraged, cajoled, critiqued, and supported students in their process of self-becoming. Then there were also teachers (again sometimes the same ones) who led their students to see their own gifts (and sometimes their handicaps) as a vocation, i.e., as a gift to be shared in service to a needy world. And so that passing on of gifts continues and continues.

The classrooms and laboratories and studios of such teachers were a potlatch, a celebration of gifts—giving, opening, receiving, and sharing. A celebration of gifts and giftedness. Each campus should be an embodiment, at least in an intellectual and spiritual sense, of what Lewis Hyde refers to as "a gift economy."[1]

2. Freedom

Understanding freedom as a consequence of grace, as another of God's gifts, we are freed from the necessity to work out our own justification. As a consequence of this freedom there is no part of ourselves or of the human story we have to suppress in order to be pure or pious in some phony sense. This freedom should distinguish education in the Lutheran tradition from "religious education" commonly found in other traditions. Education in a Lutheran college or university should be surprisingly bold, open, multidimensional, challenging, experimental, diverse, and engaging; never frightened, closed, authoritarian, sanitized, and defensive. A religious view without freedom tends to reduce the world, to shrink it to one that confirms the opinion of the believer and does not open one to challenge. It is interesting how frequently secular education presents a reduced world as well.

Having graduated from Concordia College, I went off to pursue graduate studies at Yale University. One of my first days there I met two future classmates, one who had graduated from a religious college in Illinois, and one who had graduated from a large secular university in Michigan. In the process of our get-acquainted conversation (bragging about our accomplishments?), I mentioned writing an honors paper in philosophy as part of my senior-year program. They wanted to know what it was about. I explained that it was a comparison of Nietzsche's concept of eternal recurrence and Kierkegaard's concept, repetition. The graduate of the religious college admitted, "I don't think we even had books by Nietzsche in our library. Even if we did, we certainly weren't encouraged to read them. He was never talked about in any of our classes." The graduate of the secular university responded, "I was going to say the same thing about my school, but about Kierkegaard. Certainly no one there would have encouraged the reading of Kierkegaard. I think he would have been regarded with suspicion." I went away from the conversation feeling pretty good about myself and the Lutheran college I had been privileged to attend. It not only allowed me to pursue such studies but it challenged me to do so. It was open in a way the other two schools were not.

This freedom is also manifest in the fact that we do things other institutions don't seem able to manage. We teach religion, particularly Christianity, and we teach it appreciatively *and* critically. Secular institutions do not feel free to do the former, and many religious institutions are not free to do the latter. So this attitude of critical appreciation that seems so right and natural to many faculty in Lutheran institutions is very rare in the culture at large. The assumption is that if one is appreciative she is not critical, and if critical, not appreciative. This is but one more example of a

Lutheran approach that is founded on what, to many, appears to be the affirmation of a paradox.

This freedom also exhibits itself in the books read, the films viewed, the questions asked, the discussions launched, the new things tried on our campuses. It should exhibit itself in the way we treat each other, in the social ultimacies and stereotypes we challenge, in the way we regard our successes and, most particularly, in the way in which we respond to our failures. Darrell Jodock has summarized this freedom extremely well:

> The divine "yes" of the gospel sets people free to search for the truth, no matter how messy it may turn out to be. Because humans have no basis for any sort of claim on God, nothing needs to be protected. . . . No inherited ideas or practices are exempt from critique and evaluation. Religion itself can be critiqued because it is capable of getting in the way of the gospel. . . . The state can be critiqued. To the distress of presidents and deans, the college itself can be critiqued. Wherever loyalty to a learned profession gets in the way of education, it can be critiqued. Every area can be investigated. . . . The net effect is freedom of inquiry.[2]

There is a second dimension of freedom that has to be central to Lutheran education: educating students toward the realization of their own freedom. Thomas Merton wrote:

> Life consists in learning to live on one's own, spontaneous, freewheeling: to do this one must recognize what is one's own—be familiar and at home with oneself. This means basically learning who one is, and learning what one has to offer, . . . and then learning how to make that offering valid.
>
> The purpose of education is to show a person how to define himself authentically and spontaneously in relation to his world. . . . A superficial freedom to wander aimlessly here or there, to taste this or that, to make a choice of distractions . . . is simply a sham. It claims to be a freedom of "choice" when it has evaded the basic task of discovering who it is that chooses. The function of the university is, then, first of all to help the student discover himself: to recognize himself, and to identify who it is that chooses.[3]

Freedom is more than just not being prevented or limited, though that is how an eighteen-year-old just liberated from her parents is likely to think of it. It is also more than just "doing what I like." Even an addict may have that counterfeit of freedom yet be completely unfree. Freedom is choosing and acting consistently with who one really is. Until then we are dependent on what others tell us we are, and in this world we are surely puppets being manipulated by invisible strings. Freedom is not easy. It certainly is not as easy as moving away from home, or having the funds to support one's fantasies or habits. It requires some hard learning, a learning that finally reveals to us who we are and what we are called to do. About this sort of freedom Jodock also writes:

The goal of the liberal arts is not simply self-expression but a kind of transformation—indeed a transformation disquieting enough to be daunting for many students. Such an education endeavors to wean them (and their teachers) from their comfortable, uncritical allegiance to societal assumptions and to entice them into both an intense curiosity toward the worlds beyond their own experience and an intense desire to make their corner of the globe a better place to live. . . . Because the goal is genuine freedom (which goes well beyond political freedom) and because people are not in fact free, accomplishing or approximating the goal involves changing people—faculty and students alike. The objective is not merely to "meet the needs of students" or to "help them achieve their own goals"; the objective is to set them free—free "from" and free "for."[4]

For Lutherans freedom is intimately linked to grace and to vocation. These three rightly overlap each other. When freedom is pursued apart from identity or identity apart from vocation we get counterfeits of each concept. Since all three of these ideas are at the heart of the Lutheran vision, Lutheran colleges and universities have something quite distinctive to offer students: an education toward freedom that is also an education toward self-identity that is also an education toward vocation. No secular university, to my knowledge, makes such a claim. Nor would it occur to most faith-related colleges to do so either.

3. *Faithful Criticism*

Being critical is one of the manifestations of freedom. Christians are freed to serve the world by being critical and by challenging all human claims to ultimacy. We are called, in other words, to recognize idols when we see them. This is not an easy thing to do because most of us have been "captured" by some agenda our society has laid on us. We tend not to recognize the prisons we willingly live inside. Certainly materialism in all its modes is one such idol in our society. How often have we felt the temptation to believe that we are valuable for what we have, for those things we call "our possessions"? How frequently do all other concerns take a back seat to economic progress? How tempting is the idea that having more will bring us happiness and fulfillment? For how many of us is success defined by income and consumption? David Orr confronts this issue boldly in his book, *Earth in Mind*:

The plain fact is that the planet does not need more successful people. But it does desperately need more peacemakers, healers, restorers, storytellers, and lovers of every kind. It needs people who live well in their places. It needs people of moral courage. . . . And these qualities have little to do with success as our culture defines it.[5]

The question arises, where does the moral courage come from to challenge the pervasive god of success? Certainly secular education has no reason to do so.

So many students are convinced that education serves only to get a job, and that a job serves the end of copious and conspicuous consumption. Why is this so widely believed? For many it is believed because it is a story convincingly told daily in all the media. We are informed about what human excellence is mainly by people who are trying to sell us something. For many students this is their story because they have never heard any other story and because they have never heard anyone challenge it, much less embody an alternative. This is the work that Lutheran institutions of higher learning are freed (and thereby called) to do. We need to be asking, "What are those beliefs almost universally held in our culture? What are those assumptions that everybody seems so willing to make? What are those notions that demand our loyalty and obedience?" Then we also need to ask, "Where do these things come from? What do they depend upon? How well founded are they? Who benefits from our obedience? Who is harmed thereby? Why are we tempted to follow them? What do we fear will happen to us if we don't?" All these normally very frightening questions we are freed to ask because none of these things have ultimacy for us. And the diligent pursuit of these critical, yet faithful, questions is part of our service to a world in need.

4. Service/Vocation

Service is a common theme of higher education in the Lutheran tradition. It is an implication of each of the preceding themes. Having realized our own gifts we use them in service. Sometimes that service is helping others to realize their own gifts. Having been *freed from* bondage to the service of idols we are *freed to* serve the neighbor in need. Being critical of the claims to ultimacy our societies and their institutions make on us we are able to see human need in a new way and risk engagement that frees others.

Learning in a Lutheran setting should always have this practical piece, the place where theory is connected to practice, the place where classroom work is connected to the problems of real people in a real place. We need this because it brings its own critical agenda, asking, "Does it really work? Does it actually help those who most need it? What does it sound like communicated to real people in need?" We also need the service dimension because it provides an opportunity for those engaged in it to come to know themselves, their prejudices, their fears, their deepest dreams. That is why it is not uncommon to hear students comment, "I learned more in that service project than I learned in all my major courses combined."

The third reason for connecting service to learning is because it is a source of hope. Frequently, as we discussed earlier, college can be a route to a kind of learned despair, a situation of knowing the insurmountability of problems and the futility of one's feeble efforts. Paul Loeb writes about many of the obstacles to becoming engaged.

> Thirty-five years ago, the largest obstacle to social commitment among the young was a misplaced trust in received authorities. . . . Vietnam era movements challenged this blind trust. . . . America's current cynicism feeds on the assumption that these movements and their successors failed or betrayed noble ideals. It also grows out of the contrast between pious talk of democracy and realities. . . . Many [students] would like to be involved, but talk of infinitely deferring their involvement to some time when they will have more status, power, and standing. So do we for that matter. We need to teach them the meaning of, "If not now, when?" because justice deferred is justice denied, and involvement endlessly deferred is passivity.[6]

One of the best responses to this learned despair is to practice active engagement, even if in some small way, in confronting a problem. We will never solve the whole problem of poverty, but we can be kept from despair if we can help just a few kids overcome the handicaps that poverty would otherwise inflict on them. We cannot make the problems of racism and classism disappear, but we may show people in particular cases that someone cares enough about them to make an effort. A purely theoretical education produces optimists and pessimists. Service connected learning creates people who try. My friend Sig Royspern coined the phrase, "as useless as a convention of optimists." I would rather have two or three who are willing, in spite of the size of the problem, to make an effort that serves. That's where hope is connected to vocation.

5. The Paideia Paradigm

The word *paideia* comes from the Greek word for child, *pais*, and means roughly the same as nurture, intentional education. Werner Jaeger and several others have employed the term more generally to mean "the formative process of human personality and character."[7] Peter Hodgson more recently has used the term to mean a process of education (in the old Latin sense of *e-ducere*, to lead forth) toward wisdom and freedom.[8] And bell hooks has employed the term to talk about a concern to teach "that respects and cares for the souls of students."[9] I use the term here to talk about a kind of education that takes the connection between knowing, teaching, and human becoming seriously. In the introductory chapter of this book I talk about the way in which premiere secular institutions have separated those three tasks, giving elite professors the task of being pure knowers, giving grad students and lesser faculty the task of communicating such knowledge, and the student services office, if anyone, the job of being concerned with student processes of maturation and development. *Paideia* is the educational outcome of intentionally connecting these three functions.

A commitment to paedeutic education is a commitment to four things:

It is a commitment to recognizing the learner as a whole person. So much schooling regards students as mere registrants, mere numbers or names occupying a line in the teacher's grade book. Grades on quizzes are recorded along with assignments turned in and days missed, without any attempt to relate the learning to the person learning or other things happening in the student's life. In a place of knowing the student is often the thing most unknown. This unknowing of the student is frequently quite deliberate. It is too frequently the case that faculty have a kind of phobia of getting to know their students and their students' thoughts and concerns too well. Students, on the other hand, usually respond very positively to any attempt on their teachers' part to know them and take an interest in them as persons. Many students mention this as a major part of their motivation for greater efforts at learning. "Professor A thinks I'm a promising student and I worked hard on that assignment because I didn't want to let him down."

What are the parts of the whole-person view? We are all physical, mental, spiritual persons. We have hopes, fears, plans, uncertainties, difficulties, habits, loves, and we often find that the things we are learning for a particular class connect with, reinforce, or collide with things happening in other parts of our lives.

Several years ago I had a student come to see me after she had done poorly on an assignment in a philosophy of religion class. She said, "My mother is dying of cancer and I am having a hard time focusing on the material for this class. It's interesting, but most of it is so abstract and I'm having a hard time staying with it. I don't want to drop the class but I may need to." We talked for a while, about the class, about her mother's prognosis, about herself. By the end of the conversation we had come up with an alternative learning idea. She said she wanted to study what different religions and philosophies said about death, immortality, resurrection, the meaning of suffering, etc., since that was what she and her mother were talking about most of the time now. Her mother died very near the end of the semester, and four weeks later the student turned in a most remarkable paper titled, "Views of Death, Immortality, and My Mother's Suffering," in which she detailed in careful argument why she rejected all the views she considered except a version of reincarnation, because it was the only one that allowed her to see what her mother had endured positively, i.e., as a learning experience. It was not what either of us had planned for the course, but it was a way of creating a learning experience in a situation where other options had failed. I could easily have avoided that whole situation. I could have avoided the student, her pain, her mother's pain, and the extra work the whole thing turned out to be. But if I had done that I would have turned my back on learning—the student's learning, as well as my own.

The excuse we usually give for avoiding the personal in learning situations is, "I'm not trained as a professional counselor." I'm not suggesting that we should pretend that we are. Such things should be left to people who know what they are doing. But this "professionalization" of everything does not provide us with a reason not to be human. If I visit a student who is hospitalized I do not pretend to be a physician or a psychiatrist, but I can be a person concerned. Where the person's problems or hopes connect to what I teach, I think it makes sense to allow the student to make that connection. "But that's not my specialty," is an excuse we use too often. Many of us fear to come out from behind our "expert" mask. Many of us fear genuinely talking to each other or to students. We would much rather lecture.

It is a commitment to facilitating the human development of persons. Many people have written about human development as passing through stages. Recent work in these areas shows us that cognitive stages are related to stages of moral and spiritual growth, and growth toward wholeness as persons as well.[10] We, as teachers and shapers of curricula, should be aware of what is happening to students as they move through their studies. These lessons are not isolated but may well connect to issues of identity even the student is not aware of, yet the student ends up in a different place than where he began. I have found this to be true of adult learners (some in their fifties and sixties) as well as those in their late teens and twenties.

At Capital University where I teach, all students are required to take a senior-level course in ethics. Many people teach that course, and most of us are committed to not just teaching students "about ethics," but in having students progress as ethical thinkers and morally aware persons in the process. This influences the kind of assignments we give, the way we try to focus learning, and the ways we assess learning in the course. It would be a lot easier to make it a "learn about" course. But it would also then make it very questionable whether that is the sort of learning the university should want all its students to have. I don't think it is that important that all students know the difference between act- and rule-utilitarianism. But I do think it is essential that all have been required to do some serious ethical reflection about issues they will have to face in life.

Recall the earlier discussion that focused on Wendell Berry's claim that the "thing made" in education is a human being. We often are so focused on the "what" of teaching, on coverage, that we forget what kinds of persons we are creating in the process. David Orr comments:

> The goal of education is not mastery of subject matter but mastery of one's person. Subject matter is simply the tool. Much as one would use a hammer and chisel to carve a block of marble, one uses ideas and knowledge to forge one's own personhood. For the most part we labor under a confusion of ends and means, thinking that the goal of education is to stuff all kinds of facts, techniques, and information into students' minds regardless of how and with what effect it will be used.[11]

It is a commitment to exploring the larger, human-related dimensions of our knowing. We earlier considered Ursula Goodenough's story about the students' concern that there was no room for wonder in their learning about science. Here was something they were feeling deeply as a consequence of their learning in astrophysics, geology, and biology. How frustrating it is to not be able to talk about that with a teacher or with one's fellow students. How wonderful it is when the teacher recognizes such reactions and the students' attempts at making meaning out of what they have learned.

I once knew of a teacher of Shakespeare who graded his students completely on quizzes based only on the footnotes, historical and etymological, to the edition they were using. Students, of course, soon quit reading the plays and started reading only the footnotes. What a tragedy! The whole value of reading Shakespeare was lost, namely, what he has to teach us about the heights and depths of being human. It is not what we learn *about* Shakespeare that is important, but what we can learn *from* him. It is a miracle that any of that teacher's students survived with a love for literature. There ought to be a special level of Dante's *Inferno* for teachers like that.

It is a commitment to relating knowing to the larger issues of living in the world. At a university of my acquaintance they once had a general education requirement called Science and Life in the Modern World. Several particular courses met the general goals for this requirement, and such courses as The Threat and Promise of Nuclear Power, Gender and Science, The Chemicals You Eat, Genetic Manipulation: Who's Doing What to Whom? and Who Determines What's Normal? The Dilemmas of Mental Health Professions. These courses were challenging for the students who took them and the faculty who taught them. They all stretched beyond the bounds of the disciplines and practiced all who were there in thinking that was at once scientific, ethical, spiritual, political, and in some cases economic. Unfortunately over the years these courses were replaced by standard generic introductory courses in the sciences: Biology 111, Chemistry 120, etc. The reason that was given was that there weren't enough faculty to teach them and they required faculty to teach beyond their area of expertise. Now no courses at that university relate science to larger societal and moral concerns. It is possible to major in all the sciences, but it is not possible to do any thinking about the sciences that extends beyond the disciplinary boxes. A concern for keeping our studies safe, pure, and unworldly has kept us from becoming science-informed citizens and from becoming society-concerned scientists. Are scientists the high priests of some new religion, fearing pollution by contact with the world beyond the temple? If not, how else do we explain this? It certainly is not because the world does not need people who can make informed decisions about science. We need such people desperately. We need to educate people who are more than knowledgeable accountants who also are ethical. We need people who can reason back and forth across the boundaries between accounting and ethics. We need people who can reason across the boundaries of political science and economics, psychology and philosophy, the health sciences and sociology. The ability to relate disciplinary learning to larger human and world issues is part of the agenda for an education that is paedeutic.

Please be aware that none of this discussion implies that we should replace the learning of real content with something else. Those who would learn Greek still have to learn to conjugate verbs, those who study history still have to know the events that characterize the era, those who study physics still have to learn Boyle's law, those who study English still have to read Shakespeare's tragedies and Hardy's novels. Paedeutic education does not imply that education will be easy or undisciplined, or that the hard work of it be replaced by vague conversation and general "friendliness." All of those disciplines are worth learning and may be essential for certain studies. What paedeutic education affirms is that education is a larger process than the learning of any *what*. It is the simultaneous and connected becoming of a *who*. The *paideia* paradigm recognizes that and reminds us of it when we become solely preoccupied with the whats of the educational process.

Some Particulars – The Curriculum

Having in the preceding section said some things about the general themes of Lutheran higher education, I now want to assert some things of a more particular sort about curriculum. I do this knowing full well that my colleagues will argue with me here even if they haven't before. What I want to do is to provoke discussion. Failure will be signaled by silent indifference, success by the earnestness of debate.

1. *Every student should learn a discipline, i.e., should be practiced in a mode of inquiry.* That is not equivalent to saying that every student should have a major, because some things listed as majors in some institutions are not disciplines. A major might be a particular course of training preparing one to be licensed or certified for a particular employment. Majors in accounting or nursing or education probably fit that pattern. Other majors may be multidisciplinary, i.e., collections of one or two courses from a variety of disciplines. Religious studies may be such an example. In pursuing such a major a student will learn a bit of history, a bit of textual analysis, a bit of anthropology, perhaps some theology, etc. Please note that I am not arguing against students having majors nor against their having the majors I just used as examples. The question I want to ask about students who have any major is: Have they learned the disciplines of inquiry in a given area? Do they understand the epistemology and logic and rhetoric of a particular inquiry? Do they know what the phenomena are that the inquiry begins with? Do they know how to cast an hypothesis? Do they know how to verify or falsify it? Have they had practice in doing the inquiry, and learning in the process what success and failure are in that discipline? I think it is possible for a student to have taken a whole lot of courses in biology, for example, without ever doing the kind of inquiry biologists do. I can imagine the same thing happening in history. To use my own field, it is certainly possible to focus students' attention on *learning about* philosophy without ever encouraging or enabling their *doing* any philosophy. Sometimes we substitute textbook learning for genuine inquiry. A student might come out of such a curriculum thinking that what biologists do is memorize things from textbooks, or thinking that is the activity of doing history. Please understand, I am not condemning wholesale the use of textbooks as a tool of teaching. I use them myself and have authored two. What I am arguing is that there would be something essentially important missing if learning from textbooks is the only or even the main learning experience the student has. At some point in her collegiate studies the student also needs to learn how to inquire like a historian or a biologist by actually doing it.

Why is that important? It is important because every student needs to see where knowledge comes from (it doesn't come from textbooks), what knowledge claims depend upon (they are not all arguments from authority), what the epistemology and the logic of the inquiry is (what makes for good biology, responsible history, insightful philosophy), and how practicing a discipline makes one part of a critical community of discourse.

I will leave it up to practitioners in the disciplines to determine how many courses or what kind of work a student needs to have mastered before we would say they had learned a given discipline. Perhaps it takes a whole major, but I would hope that students begin to be practitioners in the discipline before their senior year. Departmental seminars ought to be places where students demonstrate their ability to *do* biology, history, literary criticism, etc., and where they are inducted into the community of discourse that any discipline of inquiry is.

Example: Capital University has an annual scholar day fairly late in the spring semester. The day begins with a convocation where scholarship awards are presented and where a noted scholar talks about her or his own scholarly work and what makes them excited about it. The rest of the day is devoted to concurrent sessions where students present their scholarly and creative work to the entire university community. The day ends with a reception in our campus art gallery. Last year the work of nearly three hundred students was heard or displayed. Four student papers that I heard that day still stick in my mind: one was on the mental health histories of persons who as children were placed in orphanages; one was on irony in Shakespeare's *King John*, a work I had never read; one was on whether a person could be a feminist and a Roman Catholic; and one was on self-knowledge, in particular on the problem of knowing (as opposed to assuming) one's sexual identity. As a consequence of this day of scholarship, the impression has been well communicated, at least in some departments, that this is what learning in the disciplines aims at—the student doing inquiry in the presence of a supportive but critical community.

2. Every student should have a broad and deep exposure to the human story. This exposure should include history, literature, philosophy, religion, and the arts, as well as the human sciences. It should include not only American and European exemplars but African, Asian, and indigenous American ones as well. Many programs already do this and do it well. But what many do not do is to tell the human story in all its dimensions, so it is a very selective story we end up telling, and a very selective story our students end up learning.

Let's consider a typical course in humanities as an example. It may focus on a given period, for example the Renaissance or the Enlightenment or the twentieth century. It will probably include exposure to "the greats" in art, literature, the sciences, the history of ideas, and it will demonstrate how in each of these areas there has been a kind of progress, with subsequent artists or thinkers solving problems posed for them by an earlier age.

I remember as a student taking a two-course sequence that sketched out—historically, philosophically, artistically—the human march toward liberty. We studied the Reformation, British political philosophy and history, the American and French Revolutions, the Communist Revolution, anti-colonialism, a whole host of important and interesting stuff. There were good guys and bad guys, and part of the fun of the course was watching how, just like in a good adventure movie, the good guys triumphed in the end.

What we did not learn was the underside of this history. We did not see how Protestants, once they had won the liberty to practice their religion as they wished, often set up equally closed and repressive regimes. We did not examine why the British, with such a noble history of promoting human rights, did not apply these principles to the peoples of their colonies. We did not study what happened in the French Revolution after the overthrow of the monarchy nor why "Liberté, Egalité, Fraternité" should occasion such a horrible bloodbath. We studied the documents of U.S. democracy but not why "All men are created equal" did not apply to well over half the humans in those states. Nor did we examine why a country liberated from a colonial power should, barely more than a century later, become one. Well, I could go on with this list. But the point of it is that when we teach, we should attempt, to the best of our abilities, to tell the whole truth, not just the bright side of it or the part of it that reinforces the story we want to tell. As Lutherans we have no reason to fear this aspect of human reality; in fact we confess it and have every reason to admit it. We have the freedom to look at the whole picture and recognize the potential horrors of our own ways before we realize them yet another time. No one should graduate from college who does not know about the great holocausts of human history and in the name of what ideology they were launched.

The unarticulated message of that humanities sequence I took was the same as that of many a movie I have seen: "Just about any violence is justified as long as you are one of the good guys, and they (your victims) are the bad guys." That may be permissible as the theme of a cheap Hollywood flick, but it is hardly justifiable as human history. It never occurred to me, nor I would guess to many of my classmates in that humanities sequence, to conclude that there is something tragically odd about a story where the good guys in one chapter end up being the bad ones in the next. Now there's something worth learning! Imagine the discussions that would follow such a lesson.

Examples: I have a colleague in political science who annually teaches a course on the Holocaust that examines its history, its ideological and religious roots, and how people have reacted to it. The course concludes with a trip to the Holocaust museum in Washington, DC. I have heard from many students what a shocking, and eye- and mind-opening course this is. I also have a colleague, a professor of modern languages, who frequently teaches a section of a required course called Global Awareness. In this course she focuses on colonialism and the postcolonial experience in North Africa. A student in that class who was one of my advisees said, "It's a real shock to discover that the view you have of history, and reality as a whole, has huge holes in it. I knew nothing about this horrible history, I knew nothing about the Belgian Congo or any of those countries until I took this course. That one alone was worth the entire semester's tuition."

What should be part of the human story every student learns? I'm sure that faculty could come up with fascinating lists that might be justifiably diverse. Besides the things talked about above, I think every student ought to have a substantial exposure to Hellenic tragedy and to the record of the Hebrews' dialogue with God that we call the Old Testament. I have my own favorites among artists and writers of the last century as well. What is simply inconceivable to me is (something that I know does happen) that students graduate from college without any exposure to the primary sources that represent the human predicament and the human story at its deepest and most profound. Can you imagine a college education that comes completely out of textbooks? I don't have to imagine it, for I have seen it happen.

3. Every student should learn to practice the critical arts. These are the studies by which we learn the skills and attitudes of critical thinking, come to recognize our own and others' presuppositions, and work out the implications of our thinking. Until one realizes the assumptions one is working with and recognizes alternatives, one cannot really be said to be acting freely. Sometimes we think we are critical thinkers but discover our critical processes do not cut very deeply. A student responded to an assigned essay in one of my classes by saying, "I really hate it when people push their ideas on me." I responded, "Then you must really get upset watching advertising on TV." Her response was, "Oh, no. They don't push that on me. Those are things I believe already."

The critical arts can, and should, be pursued in every major and every school of the university. But, as we have discussed earlier, there are some forms of criticism that ought to be given a prominent place in the curriculum of all students. They should include: a critique of the "gods" of the culture we live in, a critique of fractional truths, a critique of abstraction, a critique of the culture of mastery, a critique of the materialist ontology and the objectivist epistemology.

Just a brief review of college catalogues reveals that almost every institution claims that critical thinking is one of their primary learning goals. But a review of the rest of the catalogue shows that is just talk. Very few colleges, or majors, or courses, for that matter, require that students employ, develop, and demonstrate their skills in critical thinking. I am not promoting here the proliferation of courses in critical thinking. Many of those are just lessons in some particular technique. If we are serious about critical thinking as a primary learning goal we will require each faculty member to address in *every* syllabus the question, "How is critical thinking learned and assessed here?"

Examples: At a conference I attended I heard Sister Alice Lubin describe the course she teaches on the Victorian novel at St. Elizabeth's College. In the process of that class the students not only come to identify the roles and rules that apply to women and men in the world of the Victorian novel, but come to identify, by contrast, the roles and rules that apply to gendered life in our society as well. The outcome of the course is definitely a liberation, for the forces that daily pressure young women and men to specific roles and behavior can surface, be articulated, be seen in the light of day, and be considered with a new degree of freedom. A second example is a course (Communications? Media Studies?) one of my older children took at St. Olaf College. In this course students did an analysis of local and national news broadcasts, noticing the different ways stories were told, edited, and how all this was related to the sale of ad time for such programs. The students made field trips to Minneapolis where they got to interview producers and news anchors and meet with media critics and print-news representatives. The students came out of that course realizing that news is not just a "given," but that it is very intentionally scripted to convey particular messages and to avoid others. They came out much more critically aware than when they went in, and much less likely to gullibly consume the evening news in a passive way.

4. Every student should have experience in the "melioristic arts." The word meliorism was coined, I believe, by William James. His intention was to contrast it both to optimism—the belief that *the best* would occur, that all would come out well, and to pessimism—the belief that *the worst* would occur, that everything turns out badly. A contrast was needed, he claimed, because both optimism and pessimism support passivity. They are both completely consistent with doing nothing. To these he contrasted meliorism, the orientation to *the better* (*melior* being the Latin word for "better"). It was an attitude that tried to improve things, that worked actively with what was given to make things turn out better than they had been. It was an attitude that made sense of effort.

Examples: Though she never knew the word, one of the most thoroughgoing meliorists I have ever encountered was my mother. She was a creative cook. But she wasn't creative in the way some cooks are: seeing a recipe in *Gourmet*, going to the market to buy all the necessary ingredients, following the recipe to gustatorial paradise. She was creative in a different way. I remember her often, particularly late in the month, making what we came to call "end-of-the-month soup." She would go to the refrigerator, ponder what she saw there, and say, "Now what can we make out of this?" What she made was good, nutritious, and cleaned out the fridge. By the way, this image is so firm in my mind that when I think about God creating the universe I think of my mom, looking out on what is "without form and void," saying, "Now what can we make out of this?" This image shapes my understanding of redemption as well. God looks into the end-of-the-month refrigerator that is my life and ponders, "What can we make of this?"

Arts are melioristic that avoid the optimism/pessimism binges we are so fond of. The meliorist asks not, "How would I like things ideally to be?" but asks instead, "Can we make something good out of what we are given?" Such arts need to be learned by anyone who would be a parent, a teacher, a farmer, a spouse, a community case worker, a politician, or a dean. That leads me to my second example. I have been privileged to work under the direction of two deans who were both meliorists. Avoiding the despairing, and I'm sure very tempting, wish of wanting to create the college and its faculty from the ground up, these deans, each term, in their own way, asked and answered the questions: "What good thing can we make out of this?" and "Is there a way, next time, to do it a bit better?"

Where might such arts be learned and such an attitude be practiced? We learn such things best in concrete problem-solving situations, where wishing for some far-off ideal or wishing we could start over from scratch are not open options. I think these lessons are best taught by parents to their children. The lesson may be framed in terms of getting along with siblings, or cooking a meal, or mending a jacket, or repairing the car, or weeding the garden. But there are academic applications of these lessons as well. Meliorism is the art of making the best of the present semester rather than planning for the naively hopeful next one, a fantasy both students and faculty are expert at. Meliorism could be learned from a year's commitment to a communal living arrangement, particularly if there were an opportunity to be self-conscious and reflective about what one had learned from the experience. Not being able to trade these people in for a fresh batch, how do we learn to live together? What compromises do we have to make to make things work? As teachers we can design problem-solving modules where the problem must be solved with the materials at hand. Team projects require such thinking. I remember well the lesson a senior football player gave the rest of the team. "We came to play our best. We don't stop doing that just because we don't believe we're going to win." Meliorism can also be practiced well in service-learning situations: working with a community-based organization, or tutoring kids, or being a big sister to a kid whose family has mostly abandoned her. The learning that comes with such service opportunities can be connected to any part of the college or university as well as at any stage in a person's life. But the lesson is too important to be left to chance. It is one of those things we need to be intentional about.

5. All students should practice the arts of stewardship and sustainable living. Of all the things we have talked about students learning, this is probably one of the most important, but also the most difficult. It is difficult because almost none of us have a clue how to do it, to say nothing about how to teach it to others. This is a subject with reference to which we are all learners. But this should not prevent us from also being teachers (my definition for what a teacher is: a communicative learner).

The island of Crete was at one time covered by dense forests, habitat to monkeys, leopards, exotic birds of all kinds. When the trees were harvested without thought to replace them, the island lost its forest, the animals that made their home there, the rich and creative human culture that thrived there, and the soil that supported all of these. Anyone who has visited Crete can tell you that what is left is a rocky, barren island with some nice white sand beaches, barely enough soil for an occasional kitchen garden and olive tree, and an economy that survives on tourists who come to see the ruins of its former civilization.

This same pattern of unsustainable use has been repeated many times in human history. We have turned forests into deserts, farmland into wasteland, depleted animal and fish populations, and lost topsoil forever. In the past these disasters were not so serious because we could always pack our stuff and move to "greener pastures." This we have done over and over. But where will we move to when the whole earth is full of us? Where are the virginal farmlands, the old-growth forests, the unharvested wildlife and fisheries for our next frontier exploit? If moving on after wasting our homeland is no longer possible, we need to learn to live in a non-wasting way, a way that does not consume resources faster than it replaces them, a way that does not ruin the place for future generations—in short, a way that is sustainable.

At the end of my first year of teaching in Ohio I was invited by one of my graduating students to attend a "passing on the farm" ceremony. This young woman, Karin, was about to inherit the farm that had been in her family for four generations. She was the only one in her family interested in farming, and she had been "chosen" to become the next "steward of the farm." At the ceremony, Karin's great grandmother talked about what the farm had been like when she and her husband had started out. Her grandmother talked about how she and her husband had improved it, planted the orchard, built the present barn, etc. Then Karin's parents talked about their tenure in the place, how they had expanded the house, bought an accompanying forty acres from a neighbor, installed the new grain storage bins. At the end of this long story Karin was asked to make a pledge that everyone in the family to that point had kept; she was asked to promise to take care of the farm so that it could be passed on to the next generation in at least as good a condition as that in which she had received it. This she promised to do. I was mightily impressed by this ceremony, because it embodied in a formal way the whole important lesson about stewardship and sustainability. How many farmers can say that the soil of their farm is in as good a condition (or better) as when they received it? How many of us can say that about our own homes? How many college presidents can say that about the colleges they steward? Can we say this about our cities, our forests, our agricultural lands, our planet?

Now I admit that I am a poor one to teach this art to someone else, because I practice it so poorly myself. But I don't think that will do as an excuse. Simply because it was not a lesson we learned does not mean that it is a lesson we can afford not to teach to this (and future) generations. If persons of biblical faith do not initiate this process, who will? Those who view the goal of life as short-term material fulfillment certainly have no reason to do so.

Examples: Northland College, located in Ashland, Wisconsin, on the south shore of Lake Superior, has intentionally set out to make their own campus a study in sustainability. The buildings they build, the energy they use, the food they eat, the gardens and nearby forest they tend, all of these have become the focus of their self-study towards sustainability. It is an institution that has genuinely attempted to integrate its mode of living to the content of its teaching. They will be the first to admit that it hasn't been easy, but they are very eager to share what they have learned, both their successes and failures, and to go on learning more.

Oberlin College in northern Ohio is another good example. Their effort is more limited, but in some ways more dramatic. They researched, designed, built, and maintain a new building that houses their environmental studies program. And, *mirabile dictu*, all of this was done as part of the course work and studies of the Oberlin students. David Orr, the director of their program, says this building is 100% solar in terms of the heating, lighting, and other energy needs. They also recycle and clean all of their own waste water. The building itself is made from recycled, recyclable, and environmentally safe products. The building itself is visited by thousands of people annually who wish to study sustainable building practices. This building represents what Orr refers to as "architecture as pedagogy." Orr writes:

> It is paradoxical that buildings on college and university campuses, places of intellect, characteristically show so little thought, imagination, sense of place, ecological awareness, and relation to any larger pedagogical intent. . . . My point is that architecture is a kind of crystallized pedagogy and that buildings have their own hidden curriculum that teaches as effectively as any course taught in them. What lessons are taught by the way we design, build, and operate academic buildings?[12]

My guess is that most of us miss the chance to do many important and fascinating studies just because we do not see the relationship between what we teach and the place we teach it and the way we live in that place. The campus itself is a great place to study sociology, chemistry, biology, physics, engineering, psychology, political systems, economics, communications, ecology, law, health sciences, etc. It is a great place not only because it has faculty who pursue such disciplines but because it, as a complex ecology itself, embodies all of them.

6. Every student should have ample curricular occasions for meaning-making. The search for meaning is a process of sorting out the informing pattern in the things we perceive that is connected to our sorting out who we are and where we are heading. Meaning-making is an orientational inquiry, a seeking of direction, itinerary, a locating of home for ourselves. James Fowler goes so far as to identify this process with faith. He says, "I have chosen to use the term *faith* for the generic and inclusively human approach to meaning making."[13] He also goes on to see vocation as part of this process, a process of becoming personally and actively engaged by the meaning that faith makes apparent. Whether or not we wish to make the explicit identifications that Fowler does, almost all of us would admit that college and university years are a time for sorting things out and for attempting, at least, to find a "way" for ourselves and also finding ourselves in the process.

Examples: I'm not completely sure that this discussion of meaning-making belongs under the general heading "Curriculum" or under the heading "Pedagogy." It is the sort of learning that could take place almost anywhere, not just in specified courses. In fact, I would be slightly skeptical of any course that was so focused. The important thing is that we recognize this as a legitimate kind of learning and a legitimate student need and make room and time for it when it occurs. Two recent examples from my own teaching spring to my mind.

I was supervising an independent study with a senior philosophy student. The student I had known from previous classes as industrious, well-focused, eager to learn, an excellent writer. The focus of his study on this occasion was contemporary philosophers writing about the nature of religious language. About halfway through the term, his weekly reading responses started to wander in the direction of becoming dialogues, first with the authors he was reading, later with his girlfriend, and later still with some unidentified "other." The subject matter also changed, from being theoretical and analytic to personal and existential. I must have registered my upset with his work in some way (I don't think I said anything of that sort), because he said, "You're not very happy with what I'm doing, are you?" I said that he had left the track we had laid out for the study at the beginning of the term. He responded, "This is what I'm working through right now. I'm sorry I've been using you as my sounding board, but these are the issues I keep coming back to even when I try to keep the focus elsewhere." We worked out a compromise. He agreed to continue wrestling with the authors for the course, and I agreed to listen to what he called his "religious journal," with the proviso that he would not be graded on that part of his work. His work on the philosophers from then on was adequate, but not inspired. His work on his journal was inspired, one of the most honest and deep pieces by a twenty-two-year-old it has ever been my privilege to read.

Several years ago two very bright nursing students came and told me that they were going to be doing their nursing fieldwork semester in Ecuador. Unfortunately, they said, they also had to complete an ethics course required of all Capital students in the same semester. Would it be possible, they pleaded, to do the ethics class by correspondence while they were in Ecuador? My first thought was that by doing so they would miss my brilliant lectures. Finally, however, I agreed, and we worked out a plan. I wanted to have them keep a journal that they could e-mail to me bi-weekly that included their responses to some assigned readings and that would investigate the connection between these things and the nursing work they were doing in Ecuador. So I sent them off with my blessing, but all along believing they would not be getting the full value of that ethics class without the benefit of my lectures, class discussions, etc. How wrong I was!

The little journaling assignment provoked some of the deepest, most humanly meaningful student work I have ever read. Not only did the students get well into ethics, they got deeply into nursing, deeply into the connection between them, deeply into the people of Ecuador, and finally, deeply into themselves. With the students' permission, I shared their journals with some nursing faculty, and we decided to combine these two studies for nursing students whenever possible. Journaling, it turned out, left room for the students' own processes of meaning-making, for a creative dialogue between the subject being studied and the growing taking place in the learner. Too frequently we do not give that growing process its due, and focus only on the learning of content or technique.

7. *Every student should practice a self-expressive art.* Not every student needs to be a poet or painter or actor or great musician. We should certainly realize that not everyone is gifted in these particular ways. But one of the dimensions of human life is being able to express ourselves. There is something very sad about not having any way to express wonder, love, loyalty, etc. While not many of us are accomplished artists in the usual sense, many of us can be practiced in art forms that leave us able to participate self-expressively, even if not creatively or in some solo performance. Congregational singing is one such example; photography might be another one that many people could get into. Storytelling is a third I can think of. But the best example I can think of is dance.

Dance takes many forms: ballroom dancing, just jerking around in the pit at a rock concert, the bodily representation and expression of a moving story such as *Romeo and Juliet*, pow-wow dancing, ritual dancing of many forms, romping playfully on a hillside, slow dancing with one's love, energetic jazz dance, or just goofing off. All the arts are meant to move us, but I think dance more than any other form engages us as whole, embodied persons. Dance can express happiness, silliness, deep sadness, independence, community-connectedness, reverence, relatedness to nature, wonder. I am envious of my indigenous American friends and relatives for the role that dance plays in their communities and culture. I have watched young, agile fancy-dancers move aside to give privileged space to children and old folks with walkers dancing in the pow-wow. I have seen four-generational families dancing together on the South Dakota prairie as the larger than full moon climbed over the horizon to join the whole community in the dance. It was beautiful to see and even better to be invited to join in. We Lutherans, of all people, should have something like that—a tribal art that unites us in the celebration of the creation, the community, our own place in it. So what horrible twist of fate or history or bad theology has left us so poor in this way?

I attended a college that did not teach dancing. Not only that, they did not encourage it. But far worse than that, they forbade it on campus or in any college-related activities. So I had to learn the beauty and importance of dancing as an adult. From my children I am still learning it! Dancing has begun to penetrate my mind and my spirit, but having learned it late, it has never completely been learned by my body. Here I am, now in my sixties, dance-handicapped, and I'm still really p–ssed!

Some Particulars – Pedagogy

We make a very great impression on our students not only by what we teach, but by how we teach. So it should be no surprise that the Lutheran understanding of human being and human knowing will have implications for teaching. Looked at from the other direction, we would expect to find that every mode of teaching has its own implicit anthropology and epistemology as well. In this section I want to identify four attitudes or approaches that I think fit the Lutheran tradition particularly well, but I certainly don't think these are the only ones worth looking at.

1. *Teaching that leaves room for wonder.* The noted biologist, Ursula Goodenough, tells the story of teaching, with two science colleagues, a year-long science survey.[14] This class included astrophysics—the becoming of the cosmos from big bang to the formation of planetary systems, geophysics—the becoming of planet earth, and biochemistry—the becoming of life. Each of the instructors taught their own specialty and gave a comprehensive test at the end of their respective sections. Goodenough taught the last one. As the class was coming to an end, she engaged several of the students in conversation, asking them what they thought had gone well and what had gone badly. The student comments were overwhelmingly positive with a few complaints about how hard the exams had been. Goodenough said she was feeling really good about her own (and her colleagues') work when one of the students said, "The three processes you revealed to us are so awesome and so amazing, but you never gave us any chance in an assignment to process or assimilate that awe and amazement. The fact that you based grades only on exams said to us that our own reactions to what we were learning were not important. Is that what you meant to say?" Goodenough then went on to say that she and her colleagues had, because of that student comment, changed the way they taught that course. They now structure group discussions and personal response papers into the course. "The awe and wonder of science was certainly a large part of our motivation as scientists; why should we have all along been denying its importance to our students?"

I think the lesson Goodenough learned can be applied to all of us, not just to scientists. Anyone that teaches something that is deep, profound, awe-inspiring, provocative, challenging, invites a human response. That human response, thought out and articulated, is a very important part of learning. We should not only recognize it, but honor it by making room for it. Too often we, as faculty, run away from learning occasions that spill out of our academic boxes. "It's not my specialty," we argue. Sharon Daloz Parks laments:

> We have become vulnerable to exchanging wisdom for knowledge and moral commitment for method. Moreover, professors have been vulnerable to functioning as less-than-whole persons. . . . Accordingly, young adults are bereft of the mentors they need, professors are too often mere technicians of knowledge, higher education can articulate no orienting vision or offer leadership toward a coherent unity, and discrete academic disciplines disclose only isolated (and thus distorted) aspects of truth. As a consequence, some of the most important questions of the contemporary world are difficult to address within the prevailing rubrics of the academy.[15]

I think it frequently happens that we hide in our expertise because we are genuinely afraid of encountering ourselves and other selves in their full humanity.

2. Teaching that shows respect for language, for argument, for the tools of thinking and reasoning and investigating and creating. This is the learning of the disciplines of what used to be called "workmanship." I don't know of a better name. Every field and every discipline has something like this as part of it. My father left me a wooden trunk/tool chest that he made and the set of hand tools that fit in it. But along with, and more important than the tools themselves, he taught me how to use them and how to take care of them. I remember him showing me, then aged eight or nine, how to sharpen a plane blade and told me, "If you take good care of it, this blade should serve you your entire life." He showed me how to sweat a copper pipe joint and what it ought to look like when the job was well done. I still have that chest and those tools, many of them now over a hundred years old. Some of them are not now used much, some replaced by power tools, but all of them are still usable, and I'm proud to say, in good working order.

Cy Running, art professor at Concordia College, showed me how to stretch canvas, how to boil up a pot of rabbit-skin sizing and size the canvas. I learned from him how to make a cartoon and "ponce" it onto the wall or canvas the work would finally be on. He was also very particular about how we cleaned and stored brushes, and this was part of our learning as well. He would frequently say, "Learn to respect the materials."

I do not work with physical tools and materials in the teaching of philosophy, like my father and Cy did in their work, but there is a dimension of workmanship that needs to be learned here as well. Words are our material, concepts and arguments our tools. It is important in philosophy that they be kept both clean and sharp, otherwise all kinds of intellectual messes can be made. I know a story, told about the American poet E. E. Cummings, but I have not been able to find the source for it in print. A young man came to see the poet at his house and begged him to give lessons in the writing of poetry. Cummings said he was not able to give such lessons but that he knew a book the young man might find helpful. Cummings told him that if he came back the following day he would give him a copy. The young man returned, full of enthusiasm, expecting a book of instructions. Cummings handed him a dictionary and then closed the door.

Part, perhaps a large part, of learning any art or discipline is learning to respect, even to love, the tools and the medium. For poets and for philosophers the medium is language, for chemists and biologists it is the apparati of their laboratories, for painters the canvas and paints, etc. Learning to be stewards of and with these tools is an important dimension of learning.

Sometimes students are surprised that their essay grades reflect points deducted for lack of care in grammar, construction, as well as argument. They whine, "But this isn't an English composition class." What this shows me is that not everyone in the university they submit written work to is holding them to a high standard. Learning to write, and proof, and rewrite is part of the workmanship of the academy, and it should be expected of all work students do.

3. Teaching that is an induction into a community of discourse. College education can be viewed as the training and induction of persons into a community of discourse. When students become part of that community they have to learn what is expected of them. Both for their own good and the good of the community created the expectations should be very high. When my own kids went off to begin college they were anxious about what would be expected of them, but very eager to find this out and to meet the challenge. One of my daughters remembers going to a recital the first week of her freshman year, where the senior students in music were asked to perform for the first-year students. She remembers being so impressed by the seniors' preparation, their presence, their professionalism. She came away thinking to herself, "Now I know what's expected of me. Now I know what I have to strive for." And she was excited by it, not put off by it. I think we should do something like that for all our incoming students, demonstrating for them what a really good performance, or piece of lab work, or essay looks like, and what the critical standards are that it embodies. We would be saying to them, "Here's what studying X requires of you. Here are the critical standards we expect you to meet. We are training you to be full participants in a community that respects these standards and performs to this level." In the Lutheran tradition this attitude toward workmanship is connected to the idea of stewardship, which is, in turn, connected to vocation and a respect for the creation.

4. Teaching that encourages student creativity. Creativity is the natural partner of critical thinking. We will not be very creative if we always assume that there is one right answer or one right way to do things, particularly if we also assume that we know what the right answer and right way is. This is part of the reason we see children as creative; they are not yet burdened with knowing the right way, and so are able to think of others. As a consequence a good part of learning towards creativity needs to be de-constructive, an unlearning of things we have supposed have a kind of necessity about them.

I frequently teach a course on philosophy of religion and I like to begin this course by examining our assumptions about what religion is. I like to show some slides of Hellenic vases that picture nude males running, wrestling, throwing spears, a discus, etc. I ask students, "What's being pictured here?" The most common answer is "athletes training." But I can count on someone saying, "But why are they naked?" Someone else will then suggest this isn't athletics at all, but sexual goofing off. Then the question is usually raised about why such things would be preserved in a work of art? Some even suggest there's a kind of homosexual eroticism at work here. I usually ask, "Any other ideas?" There seldom are any. A long silence ensues. I then ask, "How about something religious? Is something religious taking place here?" They almost always dismiss the idea. What could possibly be religious about naked young men racing or wrestling? For most, such activities are the very antithesis of religiousness. The suggestion is shocking, to some even disgusting. I then show some slides I took at Delphi, Olympia, and Epidaurus, pointing out that all these important religious centers in the Hellenic world had running tracks and a stadium in which people could watch athletic contests, and that the pan-Hellenic games, precursor of the Olympics, always were also a religious celebration and a festival. Those old Hellenes had blended together things we normally keep very separate: religion, drama, the arts, athletics, and even a bit of "sexual goofing off." I then show some pictures of Sumo wrestlers, of Native American games and contests, and read the passage in Samuel that describes David dancing naked before the ark of the covenant.

The point of all this is not to shock students. That's easy enough to do. The point of it is to loosen up the gridlock that our categories often have on our thinking that keeps us from seeing, understanding, and imagining alternatives. I need that exercise as much as the students do. What happens in this dialogue is that we all come away with less rigid ways of thinking about the religious, but also less rigid ways of thinking about athletics, about the human body, about spirituality, and about the way we, like those ancient Hellenes, celebrate human struggle, the *agon*, in our sports, the stories we tell in fiction, the movies and TV, and the arts. A deconstruction of those categories allows us not only to see and understand many things about Hellenic culture, but also to see and understand many things about our own. A serious study of the religious dimensions of sports activities is thus made possible, and the running back pointing toward the heavens after scoring a touchdown takes on a different dimension of meaning. The creativity here is not in an artwork produced or a new theory devised but in a more flexible and more self-aware way of thinking about the world. After such a deconstruction I often ask myself, what other part of my way of thinking about the world actually limits my perception of it? Where else has a hardening of the categories taken place? Where else would we all benefit from a rethinking or perhaps an un-thinking of things?

Creativity is seldom enabled simply by a blank sheet of paper and the demand, "be creative." Herbert Kohl relates his experience getting young children to write poetry. He says that the blank sheet and the demand to write a poem will get nothing but a blank stare in response. What is required is a prompt that challenges with its peculiar mixture of particularity and openness. So he suggests it is better to start by saying, "Try a four line poem, not more than six words per line, and each line should have a color word in it." Or from a visual arts teacher I heard, "It doesn't do any good to say, 'Draw an interesting shape.' But it's much more productive to say, 'See what interesting shapes get generated by the overlapping of thick capital letters.'" The latter gives the student less creative space to play in, but is a much better enabler of creativity.

Are there some areas of learning where creativity is inappropriate? I suppose there might be, if what one is supposed to learn is some established way of doing things, sorting things, naming things. There may be an importance in learning this way. Some people do have to pass standardized tests that demonstrate their mastery of such things. But it seems that after such things have been learned there is still the possibility of posing the questions, "Is there another way to do this? Is there another way to name this? Is there another vocabulary with which to think this through?" Posing such questions loosens the grip that categories have on our minds and may move us toward a better way of doing things.

When I taught at Concordia College a friend of mine bought property in the hills just east of the Red River Valley and built a house there. One weekend I was helping him with some finishing work on it. While I was there many folks who lived in the area drove over to see what this "new place" looked like. I remember overhearing their comments: "Look at the way these big windows look out on the woods on one side and the rolling hills on the other. What does our big window look out on? Our driveway. Why didn't we think of that?" The husband replied, "The picture window is always on the same side of the house as the front door. Everybody knows that." Of course the husband is right; 99% of houses have their biggest windows on their front-door side. But what his wife had been able to do was see the lack of necessity in this and the inappropriateness of it if the house was situated in the country, not on a street in town, and situated where there were beautiful views to be seen from the house in other directions. Knowing that "this is the way it's always done" may be an advantage in some circumstances, but it may also be a terrible handicap in others.

Whether one is a student in art or music, psychology or physics, communications or philosophy, I believe there is occasion for creativity in all learning. It honors reality, honors the spirit of the learner, and makes teaching a whole lot more interesting. Alfred North Whitehead wrote:

> The justification for a university is that it provides the connection between knowledge and the zest for life by uniting the young and the old in the imaginative consideration of learning. The tragedy of the world is that those who are imaginative have but slight experience, and those who are experienced have feeble imaginations. . . . The task of a university is to weld together imagination and experience.[16]

The assumption of Whitehead's approach is that the old will provide the experience and the young will provide the imagination. But my experience is that the young are just as likely to lack imagination, to be thoroughly confirmed in the world's account of how things are, as old folks are. And sometimes the old are not particularly experienced either, or have learned little from the experiences they have had. It requires a particular attitude in both the old and the young, an attitude of openness that needs to be continually exercised, to make creativity possible. Yet this is what makes the academic life particularly attractive, that it is an adventure and all of us who are still learners are embarked on it. I really cannot imagine teaching the same things, year in and year out, without the promise of learning something radically new. Curricular space and a community that honors creativity—both of these are as important to faculty as they are to students.

Gift and Task – IV

There are many gifts realized in a discussion of educational praxis, curriculum and pedagogy. Some of those we have already talked about: a rich, suggestive tradition; freedom to explore and try new things; ways of knowing that are open, non-reductionistic, and answerable; a paedeutic approach to the educational task. But the translation of all this into a working curriculum and pedagogy still requires three more gifts. The first is *a group of faculty who care*, faculty who are willing to reargue curricular and pedagogical concerns again and again, and rewrite their syllabi again and again, and reeducate themselves again and again. My experience is that our Lutheran colleges and universities have such faculty, and they are a fantastic gift. The second gift is *a kind of particularist creativity*, a willingness to solve the curricular and pedagogical problems not in general but for the particular students in the particular place and time we find ourselves called to serve. The third is the topic of the next chapter, namely *a vital, critical, inclusive learning community.*

VII.
A Community of Learners

When the Stranger says: "What is the
meaning of this city?
Do you huddle close together because
you love each other?"
What will you answer? "We all
dwell together
To make money from each other"? or
"This is a community"?

—T. S. Eliot, "Choruses from 'The Rock'"

All of the things we have thus far talked about—a lively theological tradition; a realistic conception of whole humanness; a dynamic, multidimensional, and answerable epistemology; a curriculum and pedagogy—all of these require a functioning community in order to occur. None of these are activities that happen in a vacuum; none are realities without humans gathered who make them work. Yet this essential thing is very easy to take for granted. I have many times seen how easy it is to focus only on the what and how and why of education and completely forget about the essential *who*. Yet when community dissolves and falls apart all of these other things become counterfeits.

The importance of community was made extremely clear to me in a conversation I had with students at Gustavus Adolphus College. They talked about significant learning experiences they had had, and so many of them, unprompted by me, mentioned a sense of community in their learning that allowed them to appropriate learning, grow from it, and be motivated toward it. I have often heard from faculty about how learning, teaching, and scholarship all go sour when the basic relations between persons become hostile, antagonistic, and untrusting. Community is not really another thing besides the others we have talked about. Rather, it is the way these other things are realized, the way they are worked out in concrete relationships. Yet it is a topic about which much misunderstanding is possible.

Senses of "Community"

"Community" is a term that gets used in a variety of contexts, so it is probably a good idea to explain the differences in some of its senses and designate the ones that will be of importance to us here.

(1) The loosest sense of the term is a geographical use. I live in a community called Berwick. It has fairly well defined geographical boundaries and these pretty well define the meaning of the term. I *live in* this community. That is the only sense in which I can really be said to be part of the community. I know only a few of the other people who live in it; most of them do not know me. Community membership, in this case, is geographically accidental. I really don't have anything else in common with these people other than the fact that we all live on the same side of Livingston Avenue. Even being neighbors is not a criterion, since the people who live across the street from me live in a different community. In some ways "collectivity" is a better word for this than "community" is. We are collected more or less by accident; there is little that is intentional about the whole process and certainly no kind of commitment is required.

(2) The second sense of community is what I would call chauvinistic community, that is, the sense that I have something in common with some other people whom we all think of as being "us" but only because we are not "them." We may have little or nothing else in common than that we have a common enemy or an "other" that we define ourselves over against. I remember an older gentleman at a church in North Dakota saying to me, "You know, when I grew up in Iowa we used to know what it meant to be a Lutheran." I bit at the bait and asked him, "Yes, what did it mean?" He responded, "It meant we weren't one of those damn Catholics. Now that there are all these ecumaniacs (his exact word) running around we don't know who we are anymore." The man had explained very clearly this chauvinist understanding of community. The identity of the group (and the identity of its individual members) lay in the clear sense of *what they were not*. Lots of leaders understand that unity of this kind can be produced by providing otherwise divided people with a common enemy. When the common "other" disappears, however, everyone is at each others' throats once again.

(3) A third sense of community is established by gathering persons who do have a common focus, a common heritage or belief or purpose. It is the positive version of which chauvinistic community is the negative type. In that sense, there may be a community of Republicans, or a community

of Methodists, or a community of Irish immigrants, or a community of pacifists, a community of Freudians, etc. They are a community by virtue of what they all have in common.

Do any of these senses of community fit the group that is gathered to do the work of a college or university? The first might apply, since we all happen to be gathered in this one institution. The second might as well. All folks at Ohio State know clearly that the "other" is the University of Michigan. The folks at Yale know this about Harvard, etc. But many schools, sad to say, do not have a single "other" or a single "them" to compare themselves to, so this negative commonality does not work very well for them.

My guess is that when the idea of community is mentioned in the context of a college or university it is the third sense that people have in mind. Isn't this what presidents desire? Isn't this identification of the members with the institution what alumni coordinators want to accomplish? I'm sure it is, and that is why this third sense is such a temptation for us. It is, after all, the sort of community one would expect in a church (commonality of belief), so why not also in a church college? Yet, I would argue, in spite of its tempting qualities, this is not the model of community we want to pursue, at least not without looking further into the ways communities may have a common focus.

Gregg Muilenburg in his essay, "Welcome Strangers," talks about how often the expectation is expressed that new faculty coming to an institution (particularly if they are non-Lutheran) will be expected to achieve "institutional fit." He states:

> The real question is whether or not this "fitting" relation is sufficient for the task. I believe it is not. Here the verb choice makes a difference. If the goal of a Lutheran institution is to preserve an identity somewhat like the preserving of a pickle, then looking for institutional fits is fine. That will not, however, readily sustain an identity in a rapidly changing culture. Nor will it serve to encourage the development of a vibrant new Lutheran identity from the roots of a valued tradition. . . . An identity must be sustained and developed and the notion of institutional fit is ill fitted to that task.[1]

In place of asking new people to fit in, Muilenburg suggests we genuinely welcome new faculty by making them know that they, as they are, are a valued part of the debate. That is, rather than suggesting to them that we would really prefer them to be other than they are, we make it clear to them that we want them, being who they are, to "participate in a significant but non-hypocritical way in the religious identity and mission of the college." Muilenburg, borrowing imagery from Nikos Kazantzakis, sees such participation as an ongoing struggle, a struggle engaging faith and reason and moving toward a larger and more inclusive sense of truth.

First, Second, Third Order Focal Communities[2]

Communities with a common focus may differ greatly from each other depending on the level at which they hold something in common. To designate these different levels I will use the language of first-order contrasted to second (or higher) orders of commonality. Let me explain further.

A first-order focal community is identified by some belief, ideal, purpose, or tradition shared by its members as their focal center. This is the sense we employ in talking about the Jewish community, the Buddhist community, the Freudian community, or any community of first-order like-mindedness. It is the notion of "first-order" that needs explaining, and can best be elucidated by establishing a contrast with what second-order like-mindedness might be. Two persons might agree that the big bang is the best theory available to account for the beginnings of the universe as we know it. We and all others (whether physicists or not) who agree with us in this belief could be considered a community—the community of big-bang believers. Such a community exhibits first-order like-mindedness insofar as its members welcome in all who agree in the belief without any particular concern about the reasons why they hold it. You may hold it because you have conducted a disciplined inquiry that leads you to this conclusion. I might believe it because I read in *Scientific American* that most physicists hold such a view. My mother-in-law might hold it because "Big Bang" was spelled out once on her Ouija board. In a first-order focal community agreement in reasons is not important, but agreement in focal belief is.

Imagine, by contrast, two astrophysicists, well-trained and respected within the community of physicists, who disagree about this theory. One thinks big bang is the best theory; the other thinks it is flawed and is busy working out an alternative theory. In spite of their first-order disagreement about this issue, there is still an agreement present, the agreement that makes them both part of the scientific community, namely, a basic agreement about what kinds of reasons and inferences are considerable in the discipline of physics. There is an agreement (and a community) at a theoretical or procedural level. Both respect each other as physicists, while disagreeing about a particular first-order conclusion derived by the discipline which both practice. It is this second-level agreement that makes their first-level arguments a possibility. *A second-order focal community is a community based on a second-order commonness that overrides or survives first-order differences.*

It should be obvious that we can also meaningfully talk about third- and fourth-order agreements. Two people might, for example, disagree about the adequacy of the scientific methods employed in physics yet still share with each other a fundamental respect for reasonableness and experimental evidence, i.e., both are corrigible and support claims with reasons, etc.

The distinction between first-order and meta-order communities is, I believe, an important one. It explains, for example, the possibility of presenting reasons to people we disagree with. Martin Luther King Jr.'s "Letter from a Birmingham Jail"[3] is addressed to a group of religious leaders who obviously do not agree with what King and his colleagues are doing. But rather than assuming, therefore, a complete discontinuity between them ("White folks just can't understand black folks"), King assumes a fundamental community among them all by explaining his actions with reasons and examples that they would be likely to understand and deem considerable. King appeals to a second- and third-order community including himself and his critics that overreaches their first-order disagreements.

Most religious communities understand themselves as first-order positive communities, sharing in focal beliefs, practices, and traditions. Historically they have proven to be quite intolerant of persons within or without who question first-order commonalities even in the name of second-order principles. Martin Luther's attack on traditions within the church, for example, earned him an excommunication even though his challenge was founded on a second-order commonality, namely the assumption of the authority of Scripture itself. He assumed that his appeal to that higher-order commonality would, in his case, override the first-order challenge his reforming activities presented. It turned out he was wrong, and the church condemned him.

Mohandas Gandhi seemed to have a third- or fourth-level focal community in mind when he defined God not as the particular deity of a particular religion but as the highest-order universal, truth. "*Sat* (Truth) or *Satya* (Being, Reality) is the only correct and fully significant name for God," he wrote.[4] Consequently Gandhi was quite consistent in saying in the midst of violence between Hindus and Muslims, "I cannot be a Hindu without being a Muslim." The fanatics of first-order Hindu community purity assassinated Gandhi because of his unwillingness to understand what seemed so obvious to them: that being a Hindu meant one was not Muslim, in fact that one was anti-Muslim. They, of course, could not see what was so obvious to him, a commonness that made all people, as he said, "children of the same God."

The kind of community that we need to pursue in our Lutheran colleges and universities is definitely not first-order focal community. Such a community will have a very hard time tolerating, to say nothing of welcoming, first-order "outsiders" into their midst. Having a heritage of being excluded for noncompliance with first-order orthodoxies, Lutherans should be particularly sensitive to this problem. But we have often forgotten our own story and its implications and have formed our own too exclusive Lutheran communities. I believe that higher-order focal community is what we wish to pursue.

Failure

We shouldn't pursue the idea of community without realizing that it is possible for the attempt to go wrong. We certainly know that happens. A very good object lesson comes out of the Enlightenment. After centuries of persecution, inquisition, and religious war, the Enlightenment thinkers held open a new promise of universal human community based on reason. Here, finally, it was hoped, humans could learn to see past their first-order religious and sectarian differences to see the basic unity of all persons as rational beings and potential users of the scientific method. Here, it was argued, was something that could unite men across religious, ethnic, and national boundaries. There is no such thing as Christian science or Muslim science, German science or British science. Enlightenment thinkers from many nations welcomed the possibility that old divisive "certitudes" of religion, philosophy, and ethnic identity could finally be replaced by the uniting certitudes of science and rationality. The framers of the Constitution of the new America appealed to religious toleration founded on the discovery of personal rights of conscience. These rights, in turn, were to be respected on the ground that each person was an embodiment of a rational principle. Religious differences could be tolerated if they were seen as incidental to the identity of someone as a person.[5] The Enlightenment ideal of reason was to replace the divisive identity of creed or ideology with a new unity of method.

Who, then, would have guessed that this Enlightenment agenda, focused on the possibility of a universal human community of reason, would itself turn out to be an instrument of judgment, exclusion, and oppression? Only an eighteenth-century Nietzsche, if there were such, or perhaps someone who already suffered from the new Enlightenment tyranny: women, who to Enlightenment eyes did not seem quite as rational as men; or aboriginal peoples whose deviance from the Enlightenment norm earned them the category "savages"; or colonized people everywhere who were treated like children at school by their European tutors; or stubborn religious faithful who fought the demotion of their religious views to "superstition," "pre-science," or "psychological projections." What was discovered, in other words, is that beneath the rhetoric of the universal community of reason lay a new agenda of power: male, Eurocentric, and technological.

Visions and Imaginings

But in spite of such failures (and there are many of them) I believe in the possibility of a community that has the capacity to be inclusive at the same time that it does not create a new exclusivism or a new form of violence done in the name of the new inclusivism. Such a statement of belief is bound to raise two serious questions: What could be the focal principles of such a community? And, what does it mean to believe in such a thing? Let us consider each in turn.

The focal principles of such community cannot be first-order commonalities. They must, however, be meta-principles that allow the widest latitude of first-order instantiation. The meta-principles must be stated in such a way that it is remembered that the first-order instantiations are only that; they are not themselves the defining conditions of community. Can we, for example, find a way to remember that as Christians we are welcomed to God's table, not God to ours? The difference is crucial. There must be something about the statement of such meta-principles that continually reminds us of this difference. (Would calling the meal Eucharist [Thanksgiving] or the *Lord's* Supper help us?) In spite of this, of course, it is still humanly possible to forget it.

Here is my offering of such meta-principles. I state them not as proper names nor as universals but as statements of intention. They seem to me clearest that way.

1. An understanding of reality consistent with our affirmation of divine creation: "I do not possess it and you do not possess it, but all of us belong to it." That is, understanding ourselves as comprehended by something we cannot completely comprehend.

2. A critical and self-critical understanding of rationality: "I am corrigible, that is, I am willing to learn of and from my own mistakes as well as the mistakes of others." That is, I begin by understanding that my own methods need themselves to be tested, rather than assuming that they define rationality.

3. A critical and self-critical understanding of knowing and inquiry: "I got it wrong last time when I was sure I was absolutely right and you were wrong. Consequently, I have come to trust your colleagueship and our partnership more than my absolute rightness. Can we please work together?" (Imagine how different Descartes' thinking would have been if he had started with such a principle.)

4. A compassionate understanding of truth: "Compassion shapes my

knowing," Gautama Siddhartha said. "Any supposed truth that cannot be spoken in love is not truth." Or, as Gandhi put it, "There is no
violent road to the truth."

5. A critical and self-critical understanding of ethics: "There is one
thing worse than doing wrong. That is not seeing the evil we do and
calling it morality." Or as Jesus put it, "Let the one who is without sin
cast the first stone," and "Why do you see the speck in your brother's
eye when you do not see the beam in your own?"

6. A suspicious understanding of myself as knower: "I know this about
myself, that I am tempted by power in all its disguises, including defi-
nitions of reality, rationality, knowing, truth, the good, myself, others,
community, the sacred or the divine. And I probably always will be."

7. An understanding of our relation to all who are other: "You are my
eye, my ears, my lungs, my hands. Thus we are all part of one body
and we need each other to survive and flourish" (see Romans 12:4–5).

8. An understanding of community as commitment to and solidarity
with each other in spite of (and because of) our differences.

9. An understanding of God's presence: "Inasmuch as you have done
it to the least of these," Jesus said, "you have done it to me" (Matthew
25:40). Or as Martin Buber so clearly put it, "We expect a theophany of
which we know nothing but the place, and the place is called community."[6]

Now we must return to the second question voiced about such community: What can it mean to believe in such a thing? A very natural reaction to this picture of community would be to say, "It's a fine ideal, but
how does it translate into a way of living and acting in the imperfect world
in which we live?" An adequate response to this challenge would require a
great deal more practical experience with community building than I have.
What I will attempt to do here is to respond in a way that takes the question and the difficulties seriously without pretending to have finished the
task.

Perhaps the model I have sketched is an unrealistic ideal. Let us begin
by supposing so. It is important to remember that sometimes unrealistic
ideals can be very practical. Newton's first law of motion described natural
motion in a way that never actually occurs: "A body in motion will remain
in motion in a straight line unless perturbed by some outside force." In one
sense this is a very unrealistic description. There is no body in the entire
universe that behaves that way. Why? Because they are all perturbed by
some outside forces. But in spite of its lack of strict exemplifications it is a
very useful description simply because it tells us what needs to be looked
for (perturbations), and it tells us what does not need to be explained. We
need to explain, for example, why the moon does not fly off into space, why

instead it circles the earth. The answer is, of course, a perturbing force that comes to be called gravitation. So the power of this description of ideal motion lies in its leading us to ask other creative and critical questions. The ideal description is vindicated not by its descriptive accuracy but by its fecundity.

So, will this model of community provoke us to ask such suggestive questions? Perhaps it will, for example, get us to seriously ask the question, "Why not?" Perhaps it won't. What I can foresee is that it might set a critical standard for our thinking about community and its possibilities. But this may turn out to have consequences that are both good and bad. It would be beneficial if it made us see that things we may have been satisfied with in the past will no longer do at all. The advancement of a new critical standard has many times in human history allowed us to see the previously acceptable as unacceptable. The ideal of inalienable rights helped us see the unacceptability of government without representation, of persons without full rights, of the injustices of slavery, sexism, and racism. Perhaps a model of community, though it is nowhere a fully actualized ideal, may serve as a critical standard for a reevaluation of what is acceptable. At the very least we may reevaluate what is acceptable rhetoric.

Such a critical ideal would be maleficent if it turned us away from actual imperfect communities in disgust or despair. Some people find it hard to tolerate imperfect actualities. Most of us have felt this way on some occasion. Some neo-Marxists, despairing of turning society toward the ideal, cheered its movement away from the ideal, toward what they believed was the ultimate downfall of the actual. Critical ideals can also work this way in practice.

I was willing, above, to suppose the ideal unrealizable, but we shouldn't become too easily convinced of the unrealizability of such a community, at least not without an argument. Several actual communities have and do approximate it. Gandhi established ashrams both in South Africa and in India to provide a dimension of reality to his practical politics. In his political action he practiced provocative civil disobedience as a means to justice. In the ashram he lived out the ideal that his politics aimed at, a community where different kinds of people could live together in equality and loving concern for each other. The practical action aimed at long-term results. The ashram tried to embody those results in the present. The two practices together informed each other. If anything, Gandhi learned more about politics from the practical necessities of living in the ashram than vice versa.

Practical experimental communities like this, striving toward radical inclusivity and justice, are worth much more than theorizing. The eros of community is not usually found first in the purity of its ideal but the other way around. The ideal is more frequently brought to life by the concreteness of realized relationships. We move toward real community one actual relationship at a time. I think this is what Jesus intended to convey by saying, "A new commandment I give to you, that you love one another even as I have loved you. By this people will know you are my disciples, that you love one another" (John 13:34–35).

So we return to the question, is such a community a possibility? Honestly and realistically the answer is, "Yes and no." Yes, because we have the witness of those who have turned their lives this way. No, because such efforts have failed so often. Yes and no, because, as Martin Buber wrote, "True unity cannot be found, it can only be done." Yes, again, because all these other things we value are essentially connected to it.

On Selecting Faculty

Nietzsche cynically remarked, "What a thing is called is more important than what it is." Unfortunately often, Nietzsche is right. We do often pay more attention to what a person is willing to call him/herself more than to what qualities the person has. It is easier, and easier to keep track of, but it is still a bad way to operate.

If I were a dean or provost interviewing potential new faculty, I would encourage departments to look for good Lutheran candidates. But it is important to state that this focus on being Lutheran not become a kind of nominalism. So what I would do is look not so much for nominal Lutherans as for people who embody what Lutheranism implies. I would look for people: (1) who are wonder-awake, (2) who demonstrate the double love necessary for a good teacher—a love of their subject and a love of sharing it with students, (3) who are continuing learners—open, multidimensional, critical, and creative in the ways we have sketched here, (4) who will participate in and advance the kind of conversation we're having here, (5) who have a sense of calling in what they do and a sense of responsibility to their disciplines, their students, to the truth, to the world that their learning ultimately serves. I would say, "If you've got that, then you've got what it takes." Our Lutheran colleges ought to be places where we nurture and enable such people. They ought to be places where we begin to grow them for the next generation. These characteristics don't always coincide with the application of the word Lutheran, for I know many people like this who are not Lutheran and many Lutherans who are not like this.

Nurturing a Learning Community

Somewhere along the way I have learned to love Italian food and to enjoy cooking it as well. As a consequence I have come to use many pounds of garlic and a couple of bushels of sweet basil every year in cooking. Garlic is usually quite easy to find at the market, but fresh basil is harder to come by. I have only a small garden in our urban backyard and now a full half of it is annually reserved to be planted in basil. Sometimes it's necessary to grow what is precious but hard to find.

It is important, of course, that faculty be involved in college and university governance and that they make essential decisions about curriculum and policies affecting the whole institution. That is a good thing. But it is also a dangerous thing. It is dangerous not because they might make bad decisions, but because faculty might become exhausted in the process. I have seen this happen more than once. It is also dangerous to become too involved in governance because faculty business meetings may become the only occasion when faculty gather as a whole community. If that is so, faculty get in the habit of supposing that faculty-meeting discourse is the model of academic discourse. It is a very poor model.

Faculty need to gather regularly to converse with each other about what excites them, what puzzles them, what amazes them, what is difficult for them. Faculty, therefore, need to have regular conversations, probably in smaller groups, about issues of scholarship, learning, epistemology, as well as curriculum and pedagogy. Faculty are, or at least ought to be, communicative learners. The opportunity for learning must be part of academic life. This doesn't just mean that the dean will support sabbaticals and travel to conferences, though these are very important. Faculty must also have the opportunity to learn from each other and learn together. That is why regular retreats and seminars and Friday informal discussions need to be part of the faculty development picture. Faculty development efforts of this kind should be one of the college or university's highest priorities.

At a Lutheran college it is important that faculty get to talk, in deep and continuing conversations, about the kinds of things addressed here. And among those things should be discussions of a theological sort. Joseph Sittler, several years ago, began by addressing the theological education of students:

> How can one's college years be spent in such a way that they are not a period of diminishment from religious understanding or a laming of true piety? . . . During such a period, what the student's intellectual maturation demands is an expanding doctrine of God. . . .
>
> The way to do that is to ask the faculty to come together to talk about theological enrichment and growth in theological discourse. . . .
> I meet many faculty people who, despite the enormously sophisticated research they do, are living with an adolescent or childhood notion of God,

which is seemingly unable to open any discourse with their learned discipline. Therefore they simply create a compartment. On Sunday they may be pious Christians. During the rest of the week they are physicists, chemists, biologists or what not, and there is no intersection or crossover among the categories in which they live.

Sittler concludes with the following:

> Thus the church related college and its faculty must make conscious efforts to incorporate high-level theological study into the institution's general curriculum. For, indeed, the Christian faith is entirely capable of the ever more capacious interpretation that can parallel a student's expanding needs and understandings.[7]

I completely agree, but such high-level theological study must begin and continue with the faculty, not just with students. By what logic do we insist that students should be theologically literate but the faculty who teach them should not?

Our fearful reactions to such an idea (and I'm sure there will be plenty of them) are mostly based on the assumption that such study is an effort to convert the faculty, to make us all Lutheran. But why don't we then suppose the same about our students? Are faculty more vulnerable, more incapable of critical yet appreciative learning than students are? I am afraid the answer may in many cases be yes. But this yes has its roots in the condition that Sittler describes so well and we have addressed earlier in the book, namely that faculty, for all their brilliance and expertise, may not all be well educated, and may not all be continuing learners, particularly where matters of faith and personal development are concerned. We may be children or adolescents, spiritually considered. The steel-trap mind may be strong and it may be sharp, but it has little chance at learning if it is already sprung shut and rusted beyond reopening. Yet this reopening is what we must, in a critical and respectful way, ever and again attempt to do. If, on the other hand, we cannot discourse about such matters in a critical and respectful way, then we should forget the whole thing. But as cautious as we may have become from prior wounding, I think we should try to speak with each other once again. If we cannot critically and respectfully converse about those things that matter most to us, then our efforts at educating others will surely be counterfeit.

Gift and Task – V

Sometimes we respond to the call to come together for conversation with the response, "Oh no, this again!" Having been frustrated in our efforts toward significant conversation in the past we feel like Charlie Brown being invited by Lucy one more time to kick the football. But if what we have said about community here is true, the value of such conversation may go well beyond our ability to reach consensus, to have everybody agree. In the process of our very disagreement a strong sense of community may be found, a way of honoring and valuing our differences. Community is a very valuable thing, where it already exists, and a thing worth working hard to achieve where it does not. In many colleges and universities it is the most valuable thing they have, more valuable than endowment, famous faculty, and new buildings.

People bring different gifts to a conversation. Some bring breadth and the ability to see connections, some bring depth and new ways of seeing a problem, some bring a concrete example that explains more than many paragraphs of abstractions, some bring a long memory, some bring a willingness to start over again, some bring a homely story, some bring great humor, some bring a sense for where the heart of an issue lies, and the ability to return to it.[8]

VIII.
Questions and Responses

No question is a bad question if it's a question
you genuinely have.

—Sig Royspern

The following are questions raised by people who read or heard me talk about the issues raised in this book. In some cases their critiques were so profound that they made me rewrite or add on to sections I had already written. In some cases the same question was raised by different people in different places, in which case I have tried to state it in a way recognizable by all who formulated it. But in all these instances I am grateful for the care and engagement these questions demonstrate. I know that the questions have made this a better book than it would have been otherwise. So to all of you who voiced them, thank you.

Q1: You refer to the Bible as a source of Luther's and Lutheran thinking about a good many things. But certainly you are aware that not everyone has read that biblical material the same way. Much in your reading (for example in your section on creation) is shaped by a very modern or postmodern consciousness. Doesn't that concern you?

R: What you say is true. The text has been (and is being) read in some very different ways. It is important for all of us to realize that everyone who comes to the text interprets it. There is no uninterpreted or pre-interpreted reading of that or of any text. But one of the advantages of postmodern readings is that they are aware of this and make a point of it. We can ask, and begin to answer, the questions: "Within what worldview and with what assumptions were these texts likely to have been written?" "What human concerns were they expressing?" We can see, for example, how completely unlikely it was that the Genesis narrative was written as a scientific account of cosmic beginnings because science, as we know it, was not then a viable category of thought.

Though I do recognize there are a variety of interpretations, I do not think that all readings of the text are equally plausible nor equally responsible. I have heard people read the book of Revelation, for example, as though it were about contemporary world affairs. But the consequence of reading it thus is that those who wrote it and those who were intended as its primary, contemporary audience could not possibly have understood it. So, though we always will bring our contemporary way of looking at things to bear on reading the texts, we ought at least to try to correct that reading with an historical awareness of the world of its contemporaries. Reading thus can be a kind of dialogue between the contemporary world and a world that is culturally quite distant from us. Yet these two worlds are alike enough for that old text to speak to us in our contemporary situation. Thus it is possible for me to say that my faith is informed by that very old creation hymn in Genesis. And that faith is strengthened by the fact that I know what I do about ancient history, about other creation myths, about why people tell them and live lives informed by them. These do not make the text less important to me, but more so.

Q2: You talk about the usefulness of knowledge, that we ought to ask about how knowing serves human purposes, the neighbor's need, etc. I know you don't mean crass, materialistic usefulness, but more about service and vocation. But shouldn't we sometimes respect the purposelessness of some knowing, the pursuit of some knowing just for the fun of it, learning something, as they said about climbing Mt. Everest, "just because it's there"?

R: I think you make an important point, and interestingly it's a point that Luther also made. Sometimes learning and knowing are pursued just for the pleasure of it. I'm sure there are many important discoveries that have been made by people who were inquiring for the joy of it, just in the hope of understanding something they hadn't understood before. You're quite right; more should be made of that.

What I was trying to say is that very often disinterested knowing actually ends up serving two masters: (1) the powers that be, the status quo, those that pay the bills; (2) and it ends up serving to further our disinterestedness, to remove knowing from any kind of service to those who may need it most. If our research ends up serving only those who can afford it, then we have done the former; if it ends up serving to persuade us that we needn't care about anything that "isn't our field," then we have done the latter. It's those two things that I think the Lutheran concept of vocation gives us critical insight about, and makes our learning connected and important.

Q3: You bring up the issue a few times, but never explicitly answer the question: "Is there such a thing as Christian physics or Christian biology or Christian economics?"

R: Maybe I've avoided answering the question directly because I think that both yes and no are inadequate answers. If we answer yes, then we set out to try to build science on a foundation of Christian beliefs. The result is usually a travesty of Christian beliefs *and* a travesty of science. It would be as if we argued to add "soul-substance," or "angel-substance" to the periodic table because the Bible talks about both things. If we say no, then we leave the disciplines just as they are on the assumption that they are paradigms of responsible knowing. Faith then becomes completely irrelevant to inquiry and to teaching and learning. I think both of those alternatives are inadequate.

I think the best alternative is a middle way, where we honor the kinds of knowing that have been developed in the disciplines and learn how to do it well, but also bring insight and criticism to bear on it, informed by our faith. In the case of a discipline like economics, for example, I think this can make a huge difference. E. F. Schumacher, you may remember, wrote a book a while back subtitled, *Economics as if People Mattered.*[1] It makes a great difference whether economic productivity is considered the measure of personal worth or whether a rich concept of the person is a measure of the usefulness or harmfulness of economics. I would like to see an open and ongoing dialogue of economics with Christian concern about creation, giftedness, stewardship, vocation, etc. In cases like economics I can imagine a very interesting and fruitful dialogue. In cases like chemistry I can't imagine it, but that doesn't mean it couldn't happen.

Q4: You put a good deal of stress on being critical and self-critical inquirers. Are you suggesting that in addition to teaching a discipline we should also teach students to be critical of it?

R: Yes, precisely. And the best thing would be if the same person can teach both. It's sad for a student to have to leave a department in order to hear a good critique of its approach to knowing.

Over the years I have taught logic many times. The longer I do this the more important I think it is to show students what logic can do, and also to show what it tempts us to do and what it cannot do. Logic is the perfect example of an intellectual tool. It's extremely useful if used properly, but dangerous if misused.

Every discipline carries with it the temptation of reductionism, the temptation to say something is a real problem only if it's formulatable in my calculus, or something is real only if it's a variable in my equations. We should point this temptation out to students. Someone said, and I wish I remembered who, "the disciplines make wonderful servants, but they make horrible masters." Students should know that.

Q5: You speak about suspiciousness approvingly. But I'm not at all sure I want to teach my students to be suspicious. You also speak disparagingly of optimism, and it seems to me we want our students to be optimistic. I'm not sure I like the sound of the sort of education you're advocating here; it sounds very negative to me.

R: I was worried about saying both of those things because I knew that both might be misunderstood. In the text I critique optimism because I want to recommend realistic hope. We, Americans, like to be optimistic; it's a psychologically positive state. We like to believe we are on the side of good and that things are getting better. But, I believe, we are able to maintain such a view only with a good deal of denial. It's also possible to go on optimism/pessimism binges, moving from one extreme reaction to the other while doing nothing much to make the situation better in any respect. I think that realistic hope is a better practice; I think it's more practicable and more consonant with a Lutheran view and much less easily disillusioned.

It's important to realize that the suspicion I'm advocating is not a suspicion of others. I'm not suggesting paranoia, or going around accusing others of the worst motives, etc. I'm suggesting that we be suspicious of our own motives. The lack of suspiciousness, in the sense I wish to convey, is blind arrogance. If we cannot question ourselves and our own motives we become the worst kind of ideologue, a "true believer" in pursuit of ends that can harm uncountable others and harm the world.

My younger son, when he was an eighth grader, was assigned the reading of *Oedipus the King*. I asked him why he thought it was important to read such a thing. His response was, "To teach us not to be so sure of ourselves that we can't recognize our own blindness." That's what I mean by suspiciousness, and I think it's a thing we all need to learn. But I'd be very happy if someone could come up with a less misleading term.

Q6: Would a college operating with a realistic view of the human and a complex understanding of human knowing attract students? Would it attract alumni support? Do people really want reality and critical awareness?

R: I really do not know the answer to that question. I've often wondered about how colleges get "sold" to prospective students and how they make decisions to go where they do. It's pretty much a puzzle to me. But, to tell you the truth, I really don't worry very much about that as I go about the tasks of being a learner and teacher and community member at my university. I teach the way I do and devote energy to the tasks I do because I think that's what the issue or topic deserves and because I believe that's what the student (and ultimately the world) really needs. Whether my activities are consistent with the marketing that brought those students to my class or office door is a question that really does not cross my mind. Maybe it should.

A student told me at the conclusion of his studies at Capital University, "You know, I came here to get a degree. But now I realize that what I received was an education." In his case he was pleased by the change. Not all students will be, I suppose. Does that mean we should stop trying to educate? I don't intend to. If my teaching gets reduced to the facilitating of degrees I hope I will have the honesty to quit like John Gatto did, after he had received teacher of the year awards for the state of New York three different times. He said he quit because he came to realize, "I teach how to fit into a world I don't want to live in."[2]

It's my belief that we are doing a service to our students and to the world by pursuing knowing in the complex, critical way I outline here, and that we are doing a service to our students and the world by connecting this knowing to the development of whole humans and by working at being a genuine community. If I'm right about this, then it can be our vocation. For a Christian, that's enough of a reason.

Q7: You are a philosopher yet your discussion of epistemology doesn't look like most of the essays on epistemology I have seen. Are you sure you're really writing about epistemology and not instead writing about pedagogy?

R: Many years ago Joseph Knutson, then president at Concordia College, told me I couldn't be much of a philosopher because he understood what I was saying. I admit that this discussion doesn't look a lot like discussions of epistemology one finds in philosophical journals. Those discussions are focused on a rather narrow set of issues, e.g., the refutation of skepticism, how knowledge is different from true belief, what an epistemological warrant is, etc. What I am interested in here is a larger, more fundamental question, a question like the one Descartes was posing—about what knowing is, how our conception of knowing shapes the ways we pursue the disciplines, structures the academy, structures learning and teaching. Epistemology, in that larger sense, is connected to everything, to how we conceive reality, how we understand ourselves, how we relate to others, etc. Perhaps a more inclusive word would have been better than "epistemology." But the only such one I know, *Wissenschaftslehre*, would not be as well understood.

Q8: What difference does it make that this book was written by a philosopher? What difference would it have made if it had been written by a Luther scholar, or a theologian, or a historian?

R: If it had been written by a Luther scholar all the parts about Luther would have been written better and with more authority. If it had been written by a theologian the explanations of the focal theological themes would be more trustworthy and more aware of what the different issues are that needed to be clarified. If it had been written by an historian the huge gap between Luther and contemporary interpretations of his work would have been filled in. That is, if it had been written by one of these it probably would have been a lot better in many ways than it now is. Besides, there is a good book written by a theologian that covers some of this same ground, namely Ernest Simmons's *Lutheran Higher Education: An Introduction*,[3] and two very different books written by historians, Richard Solberg's *Lutheran Higher Education in North America*[4] and Mark Schwehn's *Exiles from Eden*,[5] that I would strongly recommend.

So the question is, what gifts, if any, are brought to the writing of this book because I am a philosopher? I'm probably not a good one to be answering this question, but I'll give it a shot anyway. (1) I tend not to see the issue of Lutheran identity as a relation between institutions, i.e., between church and university, but I tend to see it as a question about how the task of the university (or college) is understood and practiced. That is, I see the Lutheran-ness of a university/college not as an external relation, but as the way it pursues and practices its essential educational tasks. (2) I tend to see the activity of Lutheran higher education as an activity performed by all learners and teachers in the institution, not just the activity of those who are given the task of being keepers and interpreters of the theological tradition. That is, if, as I claim, the heart of Lutheran higher education lies in the view of the human we work from, with, and toward, and the understanding of knowing we practice in these communities, then it is the task of every professor in every discipline. The role of theologian will be important at such a place, but probably no more important than the role of physicist, or economist, or professor of nursing or business or law. An implication of this is that non-Lutherans (and non-Christians) of all sorts can play an essential role in advancing the mission of the institution. Most accounts of faith-related higher education have a hard time being more than tolerant of such "outsiders." From my point of view there is no reason to regard them as outsiders at all. (3) My training in philosophy and the history of ideas probably contributed a good deal to my seeing how important epistemology is, how foundational it is, to all of our thinking. The modern era was primarily a revolution in epistemology that sparked revolutions in everything else, politics, technology, economics, society, and religion included. The critique of that epistemology now has the power to change things profoundly again. We would be foolish and irresponsible not to be aware of it. Of course there is no way to tell how much of this comes with being a philosopher, and how much comes from being the peculiar person I am. I can't distinguish such things anymore.

Q9: I think California Lutheran was the last Lutheran university to be founded. Why aren't we starting any more of them? If we were going to found more Lutheran universities what ought to be their focus?

R: I think that's a very provocative question. If Lutheran universities are, as I've suggested, not just a leftover from a previous sociocultural milieu, but an answer to a real present need, then I think we ought to be founding new ones. But probably a higher priority would be to see that the ones we have take their own task and gift seriously. That's why I'm writing this book.

I recently read about some other religious groups, for example Soka Gakai, starting a new university in downtown Los Angeles. This interested me because I wanted to know how (and whether) they were going to make their own religious orientation work in a university setting. I still don't know the answer to that question. But if Soka Gakai can do that, why can't Lutherans? I think it's very interesting to think through the question: "If we could start such an institution 'from scratch,' what should it look like, and what should be its priorities?" Such a thought project would be relevant, I think, to working out developmental plans for our existing colleges and universities.

I think it would be interesting to start an urban university, for example, whose express purpose is to rescue and revitalize people who have been "left behind" by the systems of schooling we now have. For too long, perhaps, we have desired to make it into the ranks of elite liberal-arts colleges. As a consequence we have created some institutions that look "semi-elite." Maybe it's time to stop and ask ourselves whether that's our real vocation.

I think that one of our Lutheran institutions ought to intentionally become a laboratory for sustainable living and then share that knowledge with the rest of us. Maybe an existing institution can do that, but maybe it takes a new initiative, jointly sponsored by churches and existing institutions, to make that happen. Anyway, I think we ought to be thinking about such possibilities and not just going down the same track we've run for so long.

Q10: You are no doubt aware that your interpretation of Lutheran themes relies heavily on sources that are not Lutheran. Does that bother you? Should it?

R: Yes, I am aware of this. And I'm a bit puzzled myself as to what to make of it. I just recently wrote an essay titled, "Is There a Lutheran Aesthetic?" In that essay I argue that there definitely is such a thing and then go on to illustrate the aesthetic with several examples. Curiously, most of the examples are works of artists who are not Lutheran, for example, Pieter Breughel, Georges Braque, John Updike, William Carlos Williams, etc. Your question forces me to think about this.

My use of non-Lutheran exemplars of Lutheran themes is quite consistent with what I said earlier (response to Q7), namely, that non-Lutherans can be important carriers of the gift and performers of the tasks of Lutheran higher education.

Christians have, from their first-century beginnings, been great borrowers. Many of the metaphors in Paul's letters are things he borrowed from predecessors and contemporaries outside the Christian fold. That fact has never seemed to bother Christians very much, and I'm not sure it should. Mary Solberg's provocative book, *Compelling Knowledge*,[6] reads Luther in terms of contemporary feminist thinkers and reads those thinkers, in turn, in terms of Luther. She sets up a dialogue between the two that illumines important things about both sources. Douglas John Hall, in *Lighten Our Darkness*,[7] does much the same, but there the dialogue is between Luther and contemporary economic, political, and social history in North America. So, if you see me doing that, I guess I'm in good company. We all, of course, should make it clear that this is what we are doing and not make it sound as if Luther is a contemporary. I guess the claim all of us are making is that Luther is relevant to the contemporary world, and then trying to show what that relevance is.

Q11: Doesn't every college student learn a discipline? Does it even need to be said that this is something all should learn?

R: I only wish that were so. It's important to pay attention to what I say a discipline is. A discipline is a mode of inquiry. Learning a discipline is not just *learning about* a field of study, it is being practiced in *doing* it. We may provide students with plenty of occasions to do the former, but my perception is that there are many fewer opportunities for students to do the latter. Some learning *about* is necessary. But if that's all a student gets in college they have every right to ask, "Where's the beef?" I am sad to report that there are things a student can major in that never require that the student engage in a genuine inquiry.

Q12: I find your discussion of community quite interesting, particularly your comments on the Muilenburg essay. But hasn't a first-order community of Lutheran (or at least Christian) believers always been what our colleges and universities have striven to be? Wouldn't many institutions really like to be a Lutheran version of Calvin College?

R: At some time in our past some Lutheran institutions might have been like that. They might, for example, have had more than 90% of their faculty Lutheran up to the end of the Second World War. When they got a large influx of veterans after the war, many colleges had to find faculty from other sources and the faculties began to be "secularized" by necessity. So what you say may be historically accurate. But I don't think we would want to go back to that even if we could. We've found the diversity of voices and views on our campuses to be extremely valuable. They have added to our ability to hear and speak the truth. That's why I think that we do not want a community that's merely tolerant of difference. We want a community where people are valued for their difference. Difference makes a bigger difference in a community aimed at learning than it does in any other kind of community. So it's very important not to confuse the university with a seminary or with the church. There, first-order commonality of belief makes some sense (though still not as much as some would have us believe). In a university or college, on the other hand, it's a counterfeit of what we really want and need.

Q13: Regarding the epistemology you present here, on the one hand you seem to be opening up the range of things we count as knowing, and on the other hand you seem to be espousing a knowing that is open to criticism. Are you advancing both a more inclusive version of knowing and a more skeptical account of what knowing is?

R: Yes, that's very perceptive. I probably should have made that more explicit in the text, because that's exactly the direction I want to go. It was Descartes' search for certainty that lead him to define knowing in the exclusive way he did. What I'm arguing is, in an important sense, the very reverse of Descartes' approach. I think certainty (indubitability) is a fruitless quest with disastrous consequences. The knowing I want to advance is embodied, social, culturally and historically located, fallible, engaged, and answerable.

Q14: I understand why, practically speaking, it might be hard for Lutherans to reproduce a Lutheran version of Calvin College, but, honestly now, wouldn't that be the ideal? Just imagine a whole community of Lutherans engaged in the project of rethinking the ends and means of higher education on Lutheran premises. That's what you are doing here, so why wouldn't you want to generalize that and make it the model for Lutherans to follow whenever possible?

R: You've posed the question in a very tempting way, and I'm sure there are many Lutheran thinkers who would affirm what you are saying. But I have a problem with this "ideal," on what I think are Lutheran grounds. If we were an all Lutheran educational community we'd have to convince only ourselves that we were doing the right thing. Some would consider that a great advantage, not having to explain to relative "outsiders" over and over again what we are doing.

But the problem here is the temptation of all ideologies, namely that we become answerable only to those who are already true believers. I'm suggesting that, given Luther's proposition that the saint and the sinner are one, not two distinct groups, that we be suspicious of ourselves and work toward becoming intentionally open communities *because we are Lutheran*. Now, I know that sounds paradoxical but, being Lutheran, that doesn't scare me away, it just makes me keep my eyes wide open.

Q15: You've critiqued the idea of "critical mass," but surely there is a point where any college would begin to be concerned about numbers of people in the institution who know and care about and can interpret the tradition?

R: Well, I critiqued the idea that critical mass implies a quota. But I do think there need to be enough people in the right places to keep the pile "cooking." But there are other ways to do that than setting faculty or administrative quotas. Some institutions, Roanoke and Gustavus Adolphus colleges for example, have established chairs to be filled by people whose task is to interpret the tradition and engage the faculty in dialogue about it. Other places have institutionalized the dialogue with annual seminars for faculty, thereby keeping the conversation alive.

That's where the concern ought to be focused, on keeping the conversation alive. And there are many creative ways to do that, not just one. I know so many cases of extremely valuable non-Lutheran faculty voices who, by their persistent concern and questioning, keep the conversation going. It would have been a tragedy if, at some point, they had not been hired just because there was some kind of Lutheran quota to meet.

Q16: In chapter one you contrast questions about the quantity of Lutherans on a faculty with the issue of the quality of participants in the Lutheran conversation, suggesting that it's the latter and not the former that matters. But doesn't quantity ever affect quality?

R: Yes, it does. That's the argument of those who support affirmative action, and I think it's very persuasive. If a minority becomes too small their voice is diminished no matter what the quality of those participants might be. I think that's true whether we're talking about black or Hispanic students or about faculty representation. If a minority gets too small it becomes token. I think the same could be argued for Lutherans on the faculty.

But the assumption behind the argument is that people need to feel supported in order to find and have a voice. I think that's true. But support can be found in more than one way. It may be a function of numbers, but it may also be a question of *who* it is that supports. Having the right people is important, but having them in the right positions is also important. Even if a quarter of the faculty in a university were Lutheran, but no deans or provosts or vice presidents or presidents were, it might still be hard to feel well supported.

So, I certainly don't want to be heard as saying that numbers of Lutherans are not important. At some crucial points in an institution's history numbers may be very important. If no Lutheran faculty have been hired in the last twelve years then it's probably time that an aggressive search for some be undertaken. But what I'm worried about is the situation where, having plenty of Lutherans, we suppose that the problem is now solved. The thing to look at is the liveliness, the depth and breadth of the conversation. Is there even an informing conversation going on? Concern for that will sometimes mean aggressively looking for Lutheran faculty. But sometimes it will mean aggressively looking for a strong and engaged non-Lutheran voice. It has more than once been the case that the addition of such a person is the kick in the pants that gets the conversation going again and improves its quality immensely.

Q17: Many faculty might agree that it's appropriate to let our faith shape our agenda for knowing, i.e., what questions we pursue, what research priorities we might have, but that it is not appropriate to let faith influence the *criteria* for knowing. That ought to be regulated by the secular rules of the discipline. I'm interested in how you would respond to that, because you seem to be saying that faith ought to be involved in doing both.

R: I certainly agree with you if you mean that we can't simply say, "X is true because I (we) believe it." People keep trying to pull that inference and it's not just religious communities that are guilty of it. Ideologues of all sorts make the same inference. It doesn't become a legitimate move just because my group does it, if it isn't legitimate when others do it.

On the other hand, our basic beliefs do, and often should, influence our most serious thinking. Descartes' philosophy was strongly influenced by the belief that things that could be sharply distinguished in thought were completely separate in reality, for example, body and mind. That ended up being a big mistake. But we can't conclude on the basis of it that beliefs should never influence our thinking. Instead we should look for a better, more adequate set of basic beliefs, for example the belief that humans are thoroughly embodied creatures and that whatever we mean by "mind" and "soul" has to keep that embodiedness out front where we don't forget it. If Descartes had had such a belief he might have thought twice before inferring from distinctness to separateness.

Economics (or a good bit of it anyway) seems to operate with the basic belief that what people want is a very good measure of what people need; that what is desirable is measured by what people actually desire. Is that a good belief to work from or are there some reasons to doubt it? I would say that it's a good principle to follow within certain parameters, but as a universal rule it's disastrous. How am I able to say that? On the basis of experience shaped in turn by some other basic beliefs, e.g., that often we want things that are not what we need, and that we desire things that turn out not to be worthy of desire. There is certainly more of a market for pornography than there is for philosophy. If wants and needs were the same, perhaps I should be publishing child porn rather than publishing things that try to get people to be critical and reflective.

Sometimes we suppose that beliefs are connected like strings in a series with the first string being connected to the real world in some obvious way. It seems to me they are more like strands in a rope, no one of which runs more than a few feet, but because they are twisted so tightly together the whole thing can carry a good deal of weight. In the first case the whole string is no stronger than its weakest part. In the latter case the whole is much stronger than its weakest part. We test our beliefs, therefore, not in some simple way by comparing them to the facts, but by seeing how they fit together, and by what, fitting together as they do, we are able to lift with them.

Q18: Does this account of knowing really result in a different way of practicing inquiry in a discipline? Don't we just end up doing things as we've always done them?

R: No, I don't believe so. And I think there are some good examples to consider. Economics, for example, looks different if you decide that we have to account for all the costs, including damage to the environment and consequences for future generations, i.e., if you take the idea of ultimate stewardship seriously. Would anyone have ever argued that nuclear energy was cheap if they had counted the cost of the Yucca Mountain nuclear waste storage site into the equations? What will be the costs of global warming? Who will pay them? On whose spreadsheet are they now appearing as a debit? What will be the costs of soil depletion in our nation's grain belt? Who's entering that as a debit in their accounting? Who will be left with that bill?

How would we teach literature if we took the *paideia* principle seriously? What role does literature (or film or the other arts) play in the becoming of whole persons? How would that idea shape our understanding of health care and the education of health care professionals, doctors, nurses, hospital and clinic administrators, etc.? Does chemistry really aim at serving the end of better living as the old Dupont ad claimed it did? How would the activity of a chemist change if she thought that was so?

Q19: Alasdair MacIntyre argues that one of the things that characterizes Catholic higher education is a belief in the unity of all knowledge. It was this unity that made their institutions "universities," and gave their students confidence that anything at all could be learned because eventually we would see that it all fits in somewhere. It may be that we haven't historically pursued such a unification, but why wouldn't we?

R: I don't have a good answer to that question. That is, I don't have an answer that totally convinces me, but I'll offer it anyhow and let you judge. I begin by asking the suspicious question, "Why would we want (or need) a comprehensive, unified theory? What need are we fulfilling by having such a thing? Are such theories always superior to working with several, more limited accounts?"

My guess is that we're talking about a kind of power agenda here. A single comprehensive view allows us to say, "Your ideas don't fit, so sit down and shut up." I'm not convinced it would be truer, or more creative, or more insightful. But I might be shown otherwise.

Q20: Is it possible to be too critical? Can't too much criticism and self-criticism handicap us? If you doubted the truth of every sentence you wrote how would you ever be able to move on to another one?

R: You're certainly right. That's why the critical dimension of knowing must be tempered by care, connectedness, faithfulness, and social engagement. That's why I combine it to talk about "critical faithfulness," "engaged suspiciousness," etc. But still we haven't reached the level of being too critical. There ought to be a phrase, "as critical as a Lutheran," to indicate just how culture-critical we ought to be. That's a large part, I think, of our service to the world. It's part of our vocation.

Q21: Many of the comments in your book reflect a de-absolutized picture of faith—a faith that is tolerant, conversational and, to a certain extent at least, relativized. Is this a faith fierce enough to inspire real life commitments? Is this a faith one can imagine someone becoming a martyr for?

R: Let me respond with a little story: A few summers ago I was teaching a philosophy of religion class. Toward its end an older student posed a very similar question, though she put it a bit differently. She said, "You have such a critical view of theology. Don't you believe in the absoluteness of God?" I responded, "I do believe in the absoluteness of God, but that's why I also believe in the non-absoluteness of theology and any human expression of the sacred. The absoluteness of God does not imply the absoluteness of theology." I still would say that and I think it's a very Lutheran stance to take.

As to whether such a view is "fierce enough" to inspire martyrdom—I'm not sure. I suppose none of us know that until we are faced with it. But this I can say, and say happily—I don't think it's fierce enough to inspire religious wars, persecutions, or burning heretics at the stake. We have to be careful what we wish for when we want to see more "true believers" in that old crusader and inquisitor sense of the word.

Q22: If you were going to go back to writing marketing copy for Lutheran higher education what would you say? How would you summarize what you've said here for the prospective student reader?

R: I'm completely out of practice for this—but I guess I would emphasize the general outline of this work. The gift and task of Lutheran higher education is:

A vital and challenging theological tradition, which enables –

An honest and multi-dimensional view of what it means to be human, which informs –

An open and answerable approach to human knowing that connects to the self-discovery of the student,

All supported by a lively and critical community – a community of learners.

With some work, we ought to be able to make that understandable to the entering students and their parents.

Q23: Is it really necessary to be so hard on Descartes and the Enlightenment? Don't we owe both a good deal?

R: You're surely right about our debt to Enlightenment thinkers. I don't mean to paint them as making no positive contribution. That would be wrong; a gross oversimplification. But I do think that we were turned in the wrong direction by Descartes and those loyal to his agenda. We would have been better off had someone like Montaigne, also a skeptic and his predecessor, been seen as the father of modern philosophy. I am serious when I comment that the modern age will be seen as the greatest philosophical mistake in human history, and I do think that we are, to a very large degree, still living out the consequences of that mistake, particularly in the shape that higher education has taken in the West.

Q24: I imagine there are lots of Lutherans who do not agree with one or another part of what you present here. Assuming that is so, in what sense can you be the definitive Lutheran voice on issues of higher education?

R: Whoa! If my colleagues from Capital University were here now they would laugh, because they don't think of me as the definitive voice on anything. I laugh, too.

You're perfectly right to remind us that North Americans and Europeans cannot speak for all Lutherans. So there are a lot of Lutherans out there, particularly in Africa, who would not understand why we are so concerned with Descartes or the post-Enlightenment world. That's not been part of their history, and that may be an advantage they have over us that allows for a new kind of Lutheran freedom and creativity in addressing issues of higher education. We should hear what they have to say about these issues and learn from them. There are also Lutherans in Asia and Central and South America and we shouldn't expect that their views will be the same either. No one, in this day and age, should try to speak for all Lutherans. I hope I did not give the impression that I wanted to do that.

My views are certainly socially and historically conditioned. Perhaps they're also conditioned by my gender, my race, my age, and my poor agrarian background, etc. That's why I can make no claims to speak for everyone nor be the definitive voice on any topic. Who can?

My purpose in writing, as I said in the introduction, has been to provoke and enable discussion. I certainly never imagined that I was saying the last word on anything. As I said, the very suggestion would make my colleagues laugh as well as my whole family.

Gift and Task – VI

These questions, and of course the persons who posed them, demonstrate many of the gifts talked about in this book: the gift of critical faithfulness, of engaged suspiciousness, of loving criticism, of knowledge of and care for the informing tradition, of insight and creativity, of community that enables such conversation. For all of these gifts we should be grateful and custodial.

NOTES

Introduction

1. The quote is from Luther's *Large Catechism*, the explanation of the first article of the Creed., where Luther writes:

> A "god" is the term for that to which we look for all good and in which we find refuge in all need. Therefore to have a god is nothing else than to trust and believe in that one with your whole heart. As I have often said, it is the trust and faith of the heart that makes both God and idol. If your faith and trust are right, then your God is the true one. Conversely, where your trust is false and wrong, there you do not have the true God. For these two belong together, faith and God. Anything on which your heart relies and depends, I say, that is really your God. (Quoted in *The Book of Concord*, ed. Robert Kolb and Timothy Wengert [Minneapolis: Augsburg Fortress, 2000], 386.)

2. This is Martin Buber's translation of the answer given to Moses' encounter with God at the burning bush (Exod 3:14) when he asks, "But who shall I say has sent me?" (Martin Buber, *I and Thou*, trans. Walter Kaufmann [New York: Charles Scribners & Sons, 1970], 160).

I. How Is a College or University Lutheran?

1. Of course some have argued that the relation should be purely external and should not inform what takes place within the institution. An argument of this sort can be found in Mark Edwards's unpublished essay, "Lutheran Heritage at Lutheran Colleges." Edwards bases his argument on Luther's distinction of the "two kingdoms," and argues that, since the college belongs to the "kingdom of the left hand," theological concepts and reasoning are not relevant to it. Edwards states: "Situated within this realm [the earthly, left-hand kingdom], we in higher education are called to pursue truth with all the intellectual rigor at our command." Thus far I agree completely with Edwards. But he continues, "In this respect a college of the church should differ in no significant respect from a secular college or university" (p. 6). Here I disagree with Edwards insofar as he assumes that secular institutions are the paradigm of intellectual rigor. I'm not convinced they are.

I agree with Robert Benne's critique of the use (by Edwards and others) of the two-kingdoms argument. Benne says, "Were this version of Lutheran theology taken to its logical conclusion it would deprive the gospel of any intellectual content. . . . The biblical narrative and theological reflection would not be given any epistemological status to engage secular learning" (*Quality with Soul* [Grand Rapids, MI: Eerdmans, 2000], 133). In a recently published response, Benne writes:

"While I agree that there is no such thing as a Lutheran biology or a Lutheran economics, the Christian faith (Lutheranly construed) certainly ought to have insights and claims that can enter the conversation at the biological and economic tables. There is a Christian intellectual tradition that makes claims about human nature and action. Those claims ought to be given voice in a church-related college" ("Response to Bishop Olson and President Tipson," *Intersections* 16 [Winter 2003]: 34).

2. More than one writer has made the worship life of the college or university community an essential "mark" of its being a vital Lutheran college or university. Two examples spring immediately to my mind: the first is Robert Benne in *Quality with Soul*; the second is DeAne Lagerquist, "What Does This Mean?: Lutheran Higher Education," *Lutheran Education* 135 (March/April 2000).

3. Baird Tipson, "Review Essay: Paul Dovre's *The Future of Religious Colleges*," *Intersections* 15 (Winter 2002): 34–40.

4. It is interesting to note that Robert Benne discusses "critical mass" in language that is both qualitative and quantitative in *Quality with Soul*, 185–187. He talks about separating faculty into concentric circles of influence and then discusses the importance of the Lutheran presence and voice in that most influential circle. Benne also allows that the Lutheran point of view might be represented by persons who are not Lutheran, although he seems more skeptical of that possibility than I am. The Lutheran voice I am interested to encourage may very often be expressed in the form of hard and persistent questions as well as by professions of faith.

5. Rachel Naomi Remen, "Educating for Mission, Meaning and Compassion," in *The Heart of Learning: Spirituality in Education*, ed. Steven Glazer (New York: Tarcher/Putnam, 1999), 40–41.

6. Alasdair MacIntyre, "Catholic Universities: Dangers, Hopes, Choices," in *Higher Learning and Catholic Traditions*, ed. Robert E. Sullivan (Notre Dame, IN: University of Notre Dame, 2001), 9.

7. Wendell Berry, "The Loss of the University," in *Home Economics* (San Francisco: North Point, 1987), 78.

8. Ibid., 81.

9. Ibid., 82.

10. Walter Moberly, quoted in Page Smith, *Killing the Spirit: Higher Education in America* (New York: Viking, 1990), 295–296.

11. Berry, "Loss of the University," 96–97.

12. Mark Schwehn, "Lutheran Higher Education in the Twenty-first Century," in *The Future of Religious Colleges: The Proceedings of the Future of Religious Colleges Conference, October 6–7, 2000*, ed. Paul Dovre (Grand Rapids: Eerdmans, 2002), 211.

13. I am aware of the typology offered by the now dated Danforth Report (*Eight Hundred Colleges Face the Future: A Preliminary Report of the Danforth Commis-*

sion on Church Colleges and Universities [St. Louis, MO: Danforth Foundation, 1965], 65–70). Another typology is offered in Benne's *Quality with Soul*, 49, where he lists types of church-related colleges. These typologies are not, strictly speaking, comparable, because each seems addressed to slightly different questions and concerns.

14. Tom Christenson, "Learning and Teaching as an Exercise in Christian Freedom," *Intersections* 16 (Winter 1999): 4.

15. Joseph Sittler, "Church Colleges and the Truth," in *Faith, Learning, and the Church College*, ed. Connie Gengenbach (Northfield, MN: St. Olaf College, 1989), 27.

II. Luther, Lutheran Theology, and Eight Focal Theological Themes

1. Some of the sources on Luther most helpful to me have been: Roland H. Bainton, *Here I Stand: A Life of Martin Luther* (New York: Abingdon, 1950); Erik Erikson, *Young Man Luther: A Study in Psychoanalysis and History* (New York: W. W. Norton, 1958); Bernhard Lohse, *Martin Luther: An Introduction to His Life and Work*, trans. Robert Schultz (Philadelphia: Fortress, 1986); Arthur McGiffert, *Luther, the Man and His Work* (New York and London: AMS, 1911); Richard Marius, *Martin Luther: The Christian between God and Death* (Cambridge, MA: Harvard University Press, 1999).

2. McGiffert, *Luther*, 87.

3. Philip Jenkins, "The Next Christianity," *Atlantic Monthly*, October 2002, 54–55.

4. Joseph Sittler, *The Doctrine of the Word in the Structure of Lutheran Theology* (Philadelphia: Muhlenberg, 1948), 3–4.

5. Martin Luther, in *What Luther Says: An Anthology*, comp. Ewald M. Plass (St. Louis, MO: Concordia, 1959), 919, 920.

6. Martin Luther, "Against the Robbing and Murdering Hordes of Peasants," in *Luther's Works*, 55 vols., ed. Jaroslav Pelikan and Helmut Lehmann (Philadelphia and St. Louis: Fortress and Concordia, 1955–1986), 46:45–55 (hereafter *LW*).

7. Martin Luther, "On the Jews and Their Lies," in *LW* 47:121–306.

8. Benne, *Quality with Soul*, 88–89.

9. Some people have asked whether there ought not to be discussions of other themes added. The two most often mentioned have been "church" and "the two kingdoms." These are certainly important themes and extremely deserving of commentary, so some explanation is probably necessary about why they are not included.

My approach to the study of Lutheran higher education is not primarily focused on the relation between two institutions, church and college, but on the way a faith tradition might shape our understanding of the educational task. I am not arguing against approaching Lutheran higher education in that institution-relational way; I am just saying that is not the way I have approached it. That is why I have not explicitly addressed that relationship, although several others have—e.g., Darrell Jodock, "The ELCA College and the Church: Strengthening the Partnership," unpublished address, and Stanley Olsen, "The Marks of an ELCA College: One Bishop's Reflections," *Intersections* 15 (Winter 2002).

I have chosen not to include Luther's "two kingdoms" distinction as one of the themes for three reasons: (1) I, quite frankly, do not understand it. My attempts to understand it have made it less clear, not more clear for me. (2) Though I have heard many talk about the concept and employ it in argument, there seems to be very little unanimity about what it means and how the distinction should be used. I'm not even sure that Luther employs it consistently. It is often used as a stop-gap explanation, attempting to repair a leak in a bucket with chewing gum rather than with a proper repair. (3) I have heard the distinction so badly employed so often by Lutherans that I have made a vow to declare a personal moratorium on its use until I understand it clearly. It is an idea that can (and has) done a lot of damage. That is why I would rather explain what I have to say without employing it.

10. Bertrand Russell, "The Free Man's Worship," in *Russell on Religion: Selections from the Writings of Bertrand Russell*, ed. Louis Greenspan and Stefan Andersson (New York: Routledge, 1999), 32.

11. Annie Dillard, *Pilgrim at Tinker Creek: A Mystical Excursion into the Natural World* (New York: Bantam, 1975), 144.

12. Douglas John Hall, *Lighten Our Darkness: Towards an Indigenous Theology of the Cross*, rev. ed. (Lima, OH: Academic Renewal, 2001), 77.

13. Alexander Solzhenitsyn, from his "Nobel Prize Lecture" (1970), quoted in Fred E. Katz, *Ordinary People and Extraordinary Evil* (New York: New York State University Press, 1993), vii.

14. Martin Buber, *Between Man and Man*, trans. Ronald G. Smith (New York: Macmillan, 1965), 18.

15. Martin Luther, "The Small Catechism," in *The Book of Concord*, ed. Theodore G. Tappert (Philadelphia: Muhlenberg, 1959), 345.

16. Martin Luther, Letter to Charles, Duke of Savoy, in Plass, *What Luther Says*, 860.

17. Martin Luther, "The Freedom of a Christian," in *LW* 31:327–377.

18. Harold Kushner, *How Good Do We Have to Be? A New Understanding of Guilt and Forgiveness* (Boston: Little, Brown, 1996), 169–170, 180.

19. Darrell Jodock, "Vocational Discernment: A Comprehensive College Program," *Intersections* 14 (Summer 2002): 3.

20. Sallie McFague, *Super-Natural Christians: How We Should Love Nature* (Minneapolis: Fortress, 1997), 172.

21. Martin Luther, "Heidelberg Disputation," in *LW* 31:50–53.

22. Hall, *Lighten Our Darkness*, 117.

23. Curtis Thompson, "Do You Teach in a Different Manner at a Lutheran College? Unraveling the Lutheran Knot and Highlighting the Glory in the Theology of the Cross," *Intersections* 16 (Winter 2003): 5.

24. Martin Luther in *LW* 35:370–371.

III. Whole Humans—Toward a Lutheran Anthropology

1. Jean Antoine, Marquis de Condorcet, *Sketch for a Historical Picture of the Progress of the Human Mind*, trans. June Barraclough (Westport, CT: Hyperion, 1979).

2. Alexander Pope, "An Essay on Man," in *Invisible Light: Poems about God*, ed. Diana Cuthbertson (New York: Columbia University Press, 2000).

3. Henri, comte de Saint-Simon, *Selected Writings*, trans. F. M. H. Markham (New York: Macmillan, 1952).

4. François Furet, *Le passe d'un illusion* (Paris: Colmann-Levy, 1995).

5. Robert Heilbroner, *An Inquiry into the Human Prospect* (New York: Norton, 1974).

6. Alain Finkielkraut, *In the Name of Humanity: Reflections on the Twentieth Century*, trans. Judith Friedlander (New York: Columbia University Press, 1999).

7. William Ospina, *Too Late for Man*, trans. Nathan Budoff (Cambridge, MA: Brookline, 1995).

8. Milan Kundera, *The Book of Laughter and Forgetting*, trans. M. H. Heim (New York: Penguin, 1982).

9. T. S. Eliot, "Choruses from 'The Rock,'" in *Collected Poems, 1909–1962* (New York: Harcourt, Brace, and World, 1963).

10. Wislawa Szymborska, "The Century's Decline," in *View with a Grain of Sand*, trans. Stanislaw Baranczak and Clare Cavanaugh (London: Harcourt Brace & Co., 1995).

11. R. G. Collingwood, *An Autobiography*, quoted in Glazer, *Heart of Learning*, ix.

12. Neil Postman, *Amusing Ourselves to Death: Public Discourse in the Age of Show Business* (New York: Viking, 1985), 106.

13. Paul Tillich, *Theology of Culture* (New York: Oxford University Press, 1964), 43–46.

14. Ibid., 46.

15. Carlos Fuentes, *Myself with Others: Selected Essays* (New York: Farrar, Strauss & Giroux, 1988), 16.

16. Hall, *Lighten Our Darkness*, 158, 159, 175.

17. Ibid., 165.

18. Ibid., 199.

19. Jean Bethke Elshtain, *Who Are We? Critical Reflections and Hopeful Possibilities* (Grand Rapids, MI: Eerdmans, 2000).

20. Ibid., 137.

21. Ibid., 132–133.

22. Ibid., 154.

23. Ibid.

24. Ibid.

25. Emmanuel Levinas, *Difficult Freedom: Essays on Judaism* (Baltimore: Johns Hopkins University Press, 1990), 201.

26. Hall, *Lighten Our Darkness*, 77.

27. Ibid., 152.

28. Robert Conquest, *Reflections on a Ravaged Century* (New York: Norton, 2000), 3.

29. Ibid., 8.

30. Jacob Bronowski, *The Ascent of Man* (Boston: Little, Brown, 1974), 373, 374.

31. Norman Cousins, "Is Modern Man Obsolete?" *Saturday Review*, November 1945.

32. William D. Ruckelshaus, "Toward a Sustainable World," in *Managing Planet Earth: Readings from Scientific American* (New York: W. H. Freeman & Co., 1990), 126.

IV. Toward a Lutheran Epistemology: Sources and Models

1. Parker Palmer, *To Know as We Are Known: Education as a Spiritual Journey* (San Francisco: HarperSanFrancisco, 1993), 21.

2. An excellent recent examination of the connection between knowing and doing is to be found in Warren G. Frisina, *The Unity of Knowledge and Action: Toward a Nonrepresentational Theory of Knowledge* (Albany: State University of New York Press, 2002). There he attempts to show how the work of a variety of thinkers can be read as pointing toward the reunification of knowledge and action. He includes discussions of Dewey and Whitehead, from the first half of the twentieth century, and Charles Taylor, Donald Davidson, Richard Rorty, Daniel Dennet, Richard Bernstein, and Wang Yang-ming from the last half. I would argue for adding William James and Hannah Arendt to that list.

3. Stephen Toulmin, *Cosmopolis: The Hidden Agenda of Modernity* (New York: Free Press, 1990), 34.

4. Douglas Sloan, *Faith and Knowledge: Mainline Protestantism and American Higher Education* (Louisville, KY: Westminster John Knox, 1994), viii.

5. Ibid., 227–228.

6. Ibid., 232.

7. Ibid., 230.

8. Douglas Sloan, *Insight-Imagination: The Emancipation of Thought and the Modern World* (Westport, CT: Greenwood, 1983), 159.

9. Ibid., 165.

10. For those interested in reading more about Polanyi and his epistemology, I recommend two very readable books: Marjorie Grene, *The Knower and the Known* (London: Faber & Faber, 1966), and Drusilla Scott, *Everyman Revived: The Common Sense of Michael Polanyi* (Grand Rapids, MI: Eerdmans, 1985).

11. Michael Polanyi, "Science and Man," *Proceedings of the Royal Society of Medicine* 58 (1965): 976.

12. Michael Polanyi, *Personal Knowledge: Toward a Post-Critical Philosophy* (New York: Harper & Row, 1964), 134.

13. Michael Polanyi, *The Tacit Dimension* (London: Routledge & Kegan Paul, 1966).

14. Nicholas Wolterstorff, *Reason within the Bounds of Religion* (Grand Rapids, MI: Eerdmans, 1976), 66ff.

15. Nicholas Wolterstorff, *Art in Action: Toward a Christian Aesthetic* (Grand Rapids, MI: Eerdmans, 1980).

16. Ibid., 22.

17. See my review essay on Wolterstorff's *Art in Action*, "High Art, Tribal Art, Popular Art & Christianity," published in *The Cresset* 49/5 (March 1981).

18. Alvin Plantinga, "Reason and Belief in God," in *Faith and Rationality*, ed. Alvin Plantinga and Nicholas Wolterstorff (Notre Dame, IN: University of Notre Dame, 1983). Plantinga's argument has generated quite a large body of work in response. I will list only two sources here for readers who may wish to pursue the issue further: Lewis Pojman, "Critique of Plantinga's Reformed Epistemology," in *Philosophy of Religion* (Mountain View, CA: Mayfield, 2001), and Anthony Kenny, *Faith and Reason* (New York: Columbia University Press, 1983).

19. Schwehn, "Lutheran Higher Education," 221–222.

20. Palmer, *To Know as We Are Known*, 6, 7.

21. Ibid., 7–8, 9.

22. Ibid., 26–27.

23. Ibid., 34–37.

24. Ibid., 51.

25. Iris Murdoch, *The Sovereignty of Good* (London: Routledge & Kegan Paul, 1985), 91.

26. Marilyn Frye, *Politics and Reality: Essays in Feminist Theory* (New York: Crossing, 1985), 75, 76.

27. Don Sheehan, quoted in Bruce A. Heggen, "Working Toward the Night Complete: Teaching and Working at the Public, Secular Institution," *Intersections* 16 (Winter 2003): 28.

28. Polanyi, *Personal Knowledge*, 15, 135ff.

29. Agnes Arber, *The Mind and the Eye* (Cambridge: Cambridge University Press, 1954), 20.

30. Mary Solberg, *Compelling Knowledge: A Feminist Proposal for an Epistemology of the Cross* (Albany: State University of New York Press, 1997), 17.

31. Ibid., 90.

32. Ibid., 118.

33. Ibid., 125.

34. Ibid., 111.

35. These examples come from three sources besides my own imagination. About a quarter of them are examples offered by Michael Polanyi, particularly from his book *The Tacit Dimension*. About a quarter are suggested by reading Ludwig Wittgenstein's *Philosophical Investigations*, and at least a quarter of them were suggested by students at Capital University in an epistemology seminar I taught a little over a year ago.

V. Toward a Lutheran Epistemology: Framing a Rich and Fallible Account of Knowing

1. See Nietzsche's *The Genealogy of Morals*. A good source for reading about Nietzsche's suspiciousness is Merold Westphal's *Suspicion and Faith: The Religious Uses of Modern Atheism* (Grand Rapids, MI: Eerdmans, 1993).

2. Jean-Claude Guillebaud, *Re-Founding the World: A Western Testament*, trans. Donald Wilson (New York: Algora, 2002), 143, 147.

3. E. F. Schumacher, *Small Is Beautiful: Economics as if People Mattered* (New York: Harper & Row, 1973), 97.

4. Frederick Franck, *Zen Seeing, Zen Drawing* (New York: Bantam Collins, 1993), 133.

5. Sam Keen, *Apology for Wonder* (New York: Oxford University Press, 1969), 30–31.

6. Wendell Berry, *Sex, Economy, Freedom and Community* (New York: Pantheon, 1993), 103.

7. Iris Murdoch, "Against Dryness: A Polemical Sketch," *Encounter* 16 (January 1961): 16–20.

8. David Orr, *Earth in Mind: On Education, Environment and the Human Prospect* (Washington, DC: Island, 1994), 23.

9. Joseph Sittler, "Ecological Commitment and Theological Responsibility," in *Evocations of Grace*, ed. S. Bouma-Prediger and Peter Bakken (Grand Rapids, MI: Eerdmans, 2000), 174.

10. John Updike, *Self-Consciousness: Memoirs* (New York: Knopf, 1989), 230–231.

11. The most thoroughgoing critic of our culture and its tendency to create self-serving institutions is Ivan Illich. I recommend three of his works in particular: *De-Schooling Society* (New York: Harper & Row, 1971); *Disabling Professions* (New York: M. Boyars, 1978); and *Medical Nemesis: The Expropriation of Health* (London: Calder & Boyars, 1975).

12. Wendell Berry, *Life Is a Miracle: An Essay against Modern Superstition* (Washington, DC: Counterpoint, 2001), 10, 11–12.

13. This meaning of suspicion is well explained and illustrated by Merold Westphal, *Suspicion and Faith*. There he argues that suspicion, rather than being inimical to faith, may actually be an important element in its dynamic.

14. Palmer, *To Know as We Are Known*, 25.

15. Smith, *Killing the Spirit*, 7.

16. John Henry Newman, *A Newman Reader: An Anthology of the Writings of John Henry Cardinal Newman*, ed. Francis X. Connolly (Garden City, NY: Doubleday, 1984), 221, 222.

17. Derek Bok, *Universities and the Future of America* (Durham, NC: Duke University Press, 1990), 105.

18. Robert Coles, *The Call of Stories: Teaching and the Moral Imagination* (Boston: Houghton Mifflin, 1984), 17, 21.

19. Sharon Daloz Parks, *Big Questions, Worthy Dreams: Mentoring Young Adults in Their Search for Meaning, Purpose, and Faith* (San Francisco: Jossey Bass, 2000), 7.

20. Ibid., 7–8.

21. Tom Christenson, "On Becoming Learning Disabled" (unpublished manuscript read at Lilly Conference on College Teaching, Dayton, OH, 2000).

22. Parks, *Big Questions*, 162–163.

VI. Implications—Curriculum and Pedagogy

1. Lewis Hyde, in the opening chapters of *The Gift: Imagination and the Erotic Life of Property* (New York: Vintage, 1983), presents several myths and historical examples of what he calls a gift economy, a community organized around the sharing and realizing of gifts. The Native American potlatch ceremony is a good example of this. I once was privileged to be at such a ceremony where a young man, just recently released from prison, was celebrating his return to the tribal community. Though he only had wages from about two weeks work, he had purchased gifts for everyone in attendance, including me, just because I had picked up himself, his mother, and his niece who were hitchhiking in rural South Dakota. I barely knew the man, yet he included me in his gift circle, and I was profoundly touched by his costly generosity.

2. Darrell Jodock, "The Lutheran Tradition and the Liberal Arts College," in *Called to Serve: St. Olaf College and the Vocation of a Church College*, ed. Pamela Schwandt (Northfield, MN: St. Olaf College, 1999), 23.

3. Thomas Merton, *Love and Living* (New York: Bantam, 1979), 3, 4.

4. Jodock, "The Lutheran Tradition," 25.

5. Orr, *Earth in Mind*, 12.

6. Paul Loeb, "Against Apathy: Role Models for Engagement," *Academe* (July/August 1959): 4, 7.

7. Werner Jaeger, *Early Christianity and Greek Paideia* (Cambridge, MA: Harvard University Press, 1961), 86.

8. Peter C. Hodgson, *God's Wisdom: Toward a Theology of Education* (Louisville, KY: Westminster John Knox, 1999). Let me especially recommend Hodgson's book for a more detailed examination of *paideia* and its relation to *sophia,* wisdom, and to the Hebrew understanding of *Torah* translated as "instruction for living." Hodgson argues for *paideia* as "the Lord's way of teaching," i.e., as a way of leading out what is potentially in the creature through empowering its own creativity.

9. bell hooks, *Teaching to Transgress: Education as the Practice of Freedom* (New York: Routledge, 1994), 13.

10. There are a great number of works related to human development and developmental theory, far too large a bibliography for me to include here. But I will mention just four authors that continue to interest me: Erik Erikson and his focus on lifelong personality development: *Childhood and Society* (New York: Norton, 1963); Lawrence Kohlberg on moral development stage theory: *Essays on Moral Development* (San Francisco: Harper & Row, 1981); James Fowler on faith development stages: *Stages of Faith: The Psychology of Human Development and the Quest for Meaning* (San Francisco: Harper & Row, 1981); and Mary Field Belenky and her colleagues on patterns of intellectual development in women: *Women's Ways of Knowing: The Development of Self, Voice, and Mind* (New York: Basic, 1986).

11. Orr, *Earth in Mind*, 13.

12. Ibid., 111, 112.

13. James Fowler, *Weaving the New Creation: Stages of Faith and the Public Church* (San Francisco: Harper, 1991), 118.

14. Goodenough shared this story at an American Association of Colleges and Universities conference in San Francisco in November 2002. Her concerns about integrating wonder into science learning are also illustrated by her book *The Sacred Depths of Nature* (New York: Oxford University Press, 1998).

15. Parks, *Big Questions*, 161–162.

16. Alfred North Whitehead, *The Aims of Education and Other Essays* (New York: Free Press, 1959), 93.

VII. A Community of Learners

1. Gregg Muilenberg, "Welcome Strangers," *Intersections* 15 (Winter 2002): 11–16.

2. A large part of this section is adapted from an earlier essay of mine, "The Possibility of Community: Dream, Nightmare or Moral Possibility," *Dianoia: A Liberal Arts Interdisciplinary Journal* (Augustana University College, Spring 1994).

3. Martin Luther King Jr., "Letter from a Birmingham Jail," in *Why We Can't Wait* (New York: Harper, 1964).

4. Mohandas Gandhi, *Satyagraha, Non-Violence and Resistance* (New York: Schocken, 1991), 17.

5. This, in substance, is the argument of Kant's *Religion within the Bounds of Reason*, first published in the 1790s.

6. Buber, *Between Man and Man*, 6.

7. Joseph Sittler, quoted in Heggen, "Working toward the Night Complete," 12–13.

8. I hope that when I die I have sufficient funds left in my estate to will an endowment to my university, with enough income to buy several cases of good wine to be drunk by the community on occasions of genuine conversation about issues that really matter. In that way I hope to provoke and enable conversation (and community) in spirit even if I'm no longer there to enjoy it or add my two cents worth. Then, when I am not able to bring any of the gifts I have just listed, I can still bring the wine!

VIII. Questions and Responses

1. E. F. Schumacher, *Small Is Beautiful: Economics as if People Mattered* (New York: Harper & Row, 1973).

2. Quoted in Glazer, *The Heart of Learning*, 151.

3. Ernest L. Simmons, *Lutheran Higher Education: An Introduction for Faculty* (Minneapolis: Augsburg Fortress, 1993).

4. Richard W. Solberg, *Lutheran Higher Education in North America* (Minneapolis: Augsburg, 1985).

5. Mark Schwehn, *Exiles from Eden: Religion and Academic Vocation in America* (New York: Oxford University Press, 1993).

6. Mary Solberg, *Compelling Knowledge: A Feminist Proposal for an Epistemology of the Cross* (Albany: State University of New York Press, 1997).

7. Douglas John Hall, *Lighten Our Darkness: Towards an Indigenous Theology of the Cross*, rev. ed. (Lima, OH: Academic Renewal, 2001).

DATE DUE